THE BRITISH JOURNAL OF POLITICS & INTERNATIONAL RELATIONS

Volume 11   *Number 4*   *November 2009*

ARTICLES

doi: 10.1111/j.1467-856X.2009.00387.x   *BJPIR: 2009 VOL 11, 557–573*

Intractable Policy Failure: The Case of Bovine TB and Badgers

Wyn Grant

The failure to eliminate bovine TB from the English and Welsh cattle herd represents a long-term intractable policy failure. Cattle-to-cattle transmission of the disease has been underemphasised in the debate compared with transmission from badgers despite a contested evidence base. Archival evidence shows that mythical constructions of the badger have shaped the policy debate. Relevant evidence was incomplete and contested; alternative framings of the policy problem were polarised and difficult to reconcile; and this rendered normal techniques of stakeholder management through co-option and mediation of little assistance.

Keywords: government failure; stakeholder management; symbolism; politicisation

This article examines an intractable, long-term policy failure: the inability to eradicate bovine tuberculosis from the English and Welsh cattle herd as is required by the European Union (EU). If success is defined, as it has been by the Department of Environment, Food and Rural Affairs (Defra), in terms of slowing down and preventing the spread of the disease to areas free of it and achieving a sustained reduction of the disease in high-incidence areas, 'then it is uncontroversial to claim that successive badger control policies have failed' (Macdonald et al. 2006, 131). Part of the problem arises from a lack of agreement on the relevant evidence and gaps in that evidence, leading to uncertainty about the appropriate course of action to deal with the problem, in particular whether culling of badgers should occur.

This article does not focus primarily on the evidential problem (for a discussion, see Wilkinson 2007). Rather it suggests that the absence of an expert consensus creates a challenge for evidence-based policy-making given that a situation in which the evidence is contradictory is worse than one in which there is no evidence. The resultant policy vacuum allows greater play to arguments that are not evidence-based but often rely on emotional appeals based on particular values or images. The emotional sensitivity of the policy area is often referred to by civil servants in government papers.

'Intractable policy controversies exist and are fundamental to the policy-making process ... Frame analysis helps us to account for their origin and stubborn survival' (Schön and Rein 1994, 56–57). This article considers the ways in which the disputes about bovine TB policy have been framed and how this affects their resolution. In summary, the argument advanced is this: relevant evidence was incomplete and contested; alternative framings of the policy problem were polarised and difficult to reconcile; and this rendered normal techniques of stakeholder management through co-option and mediation of little assistance.

Depoliticisation narratives would suggest that issues of this kind can be more expediently handled by transferring them away from ministers and policy civil servants to agencies that can be the first line of defence against criticism, the Chemicals Regulation Directorate and pesticides offering a good example within Defra. However, this has not proved possible in the case of bovine TB. While Defra has effectively ended its involvement in other endemic cattle diseases such as Johne's disease and the bovine diarrhoea virus, both of which have substantial effects on productivity and animal health, it has had to maintain a substantial team of civil servants to deal with bovine TB. The expertise that government has sought to utilise to find solutions to the policy problem has itself become politicised.

Archival evidence from the National Archives extending up to the early 1990s is used to show that particular constructions of the badger have had a shaping influence on the debate. The relaxation in practice of the 30-year rule meant that it was possible to view files up to 1992. The files are extensive and appear to be a complete sequence. It is never possible to tell whether and how files have been weeded, but there is material in the files that would be embarrassing from a government perspective.

The discussion provides a contribution to the debate on government and policy failure. Some of the existing literature on government failure does not fit particularly well with cases that involve animals. Conventionally, that involves a calculation of whether a policy outcome is Pareto inefficient in the sense that Pareto efficiency provides society with a utility possibility frontier where an individual cannot be made better off without another being made worse off. Human individuals are able to make assessments about whether they or others are better or worse off, but in relation to animals this founders on the question of whether animals as 'sentient beings' can be counted as individuals or as members of society. 'The recognition that animals are sentient is held to mean that we have direct moral obligations towards them, and not their owners or those seeking to represent their interests' (Garner 2008, 111). However, the argument presented here has a more general applicability beyond this special set of cases and the debate about the legal status of animals. The literature is replete with examples of where rent-seeking behaviour by particular interests has produced distorted and suboptimal policy outcomes. However, another important case is where the politicisation of an issue by strongly opposed interests of relatively equal weight leads to policy paralysis. Government resorted to a number of familiar devices to unblock the policy impasse, such as reviews by advisory committees, and even constituted a special body which lasted for over 30 years in an attempt to reconcile the opposed interests. Although policy modifications resulted from these efforts, the underlying problem remains unresolved.

Government Failure and Policy Failure

Timothy Besley (2007, 45) notes that 'Government failure is a term that is often used but rarely defined'. In this discussion, policy failure is treated as a subset of government failure. Typical government failures such as the suboptimal provision of public goods necessarily lead to policy failure. However, one needs to be cautious about how far an approach based on a model derived from welfare economics, which predominates in the government failure literature, can help us to understand the politics of policy failure. As Besley (2007, 25) has pointed out, 'it has tended to say little about the process of policy choice and implementation. To that extent it gives a highly technocratic perspective'. The argument made here is that intractable policy failure in the form of policy paralysis needs to take account of the way in which the debate about the policy problem is constructed and even the pictorial depiction of symbols which is a highly effective way of appealing to deeply held values. The approach taken in this article is influenced by Abigail Woods (2004) in her history of foot and mouth disease (FMD) in Britain. Her argument is that FMD was transformed from an inconsequential ailment to a terrible animal plague by a range of social, economic, scientific and, above all, political forces. Understandings of FMD were manufactured and it became 'an ideological affair that was closely bound up with the role and status of science in society, the accountability of government bodies and Britain's international standing' (Woods 2004, 101).

Patrick Dunleavy (1995, 52) suggested that Britain was 'a state unusually prone to make large-scale, avoidable policy mistakes. The most generally used label for this category is "policy disasters", generally construed to mean significant and substantially costly failures of commission or omission by government'. Michael Moran (2001) seeks to relate the problem of policy catastrophe to the phenomenon of the regulatory state. He poses the question: 'Why is the age of the regulatory state also the age of policy catastrophe?' and one answer he provides is that 'Catastrophes are due to the incomplete penetration of the regulatory state' (Moran 2001, 415). He distinguishes between five types of catastrophe, one of which is 'symbiotic politics' which he illustrates with the case of BSE, drawing attention to the tightly knit policy community that developed in agricultural policy with its inbuilt production-ist priorities which led to the husbandry practice that produced BSE.

The case of bovine TB was somewhat different in so far as the reluctance of the National Farmers' Union (NFU) to get involved in the issue was complained about by officials and the NFU's influence was counterbalanced by organisations purporting to represent the badger. Moran concludes (2001, 426) that 'Symbiotic politics holds the most imponderables for the regulatory state. The case of the Ministry of Agriculture, Fisheries and Food (MAFF) and BSE shows the extraordinarily destructive consequences of fusing public institutions and private interests'. In the case of bovine TB, policy-makers sought to involve a much wider range of interests than those of farmers. However, the result was not the dogged pursuit of perverse and counterproductive policies, as in the case of much of what emerged from the traditional agricultural policy community, but no effective or consistent policy at all.

It could be argued that there are some policy solutions that are intractable in the sense that no solution is available. The term 'failure' might be seen to imply that policy solutions are available that policy-makers have failed to identify and implement. Current government policy places reliance on the development of a vaccine for bovine TB. A vaccine administered by injection will be available soon, but that poses the problem of catching badgers to administer it, which is difficult. An oral vaccine that could be administered with bait is still some way away. It is suggested later in the article that there is an interim policy strategy which, although carrying some political costs, would reduce the extent of failure compared with current policy.

The Development of Policy

A brief chronology of the development of policy is set out in Table 1) to inform the subsequent discussion. The original driver for government involvement in the eradication of bovine TB was a public health concern, although high levels of infection of cattle were also a factor with as many as 30 per cent of cattle in Britain dying from the disease in the early 20th century. In the 1930s some 2,000 deaths a year were attributed to bovine tuberculosis derived from cows' milk. This particular route of infection was overcome by pasteurisation (except where raw milk was consumed), although transmission could occur through an aerosol effect to someone in contact with infected animals. Bovine TB is therefore no longer a major zoonosis, but this has not diminished political interest in the subject.

By 1960 it was widely believed that bovine TB had been brought under control in the British cattle herd. Complete eradication may not be achievable but 'between 1960 when the whole country became an attested area and the end of 1964, the incidence of reactors had fallen from 19 in 10,000–6 in 10,000' (Ministry of Agriculture, Fisheries and Food 1965, 227). Subsequently, the badger population increased while the end of the Attested Herds Scheme removed a constraint on the movement of cattle from infected herds to those that were uninfected.

Table 1: Key Dates in the Development of Bovine TB Policy

1923—Government encourages voluntary eradication on dairy farms
1935—40 per cent of cows infected. National programme of attesting herds as TB free begins
1950—Compulsory campaign of eradication
1960—Reactors decline to negligible proportions
1971—Bovine TB discovered in badger in Gloucestershire
1973—Badgers Act
1976—Badger Panel starts work
1980—Zuckerman Report
1986—Dunnet Report
1992—Protection of Badgers Act
1997—Krebs Report, leads to field trials of culling
2003—Badger Panel abolished
2007—Report of Independent Scientists Group, King review
2008—Hilary Benn decides not to allow culling

Bovine TB was discovered in a badger for the first time in 1971 and badger culling began in 1975. 'In 1975 MAFF was presented with the unenviable task of controlling badger-transmitted TB in cattle in the almost total absence of any relevant research on the biology and control of badgers. Badger control tactics have changed in response to public relations needs ... but the strategic principles on which the tactics are based have hardly changed since their inception' (NA PRO: MAF 459/19 1986, 12). It is arguable that initial responses relied too heavily on a perception of the badger as the problem and hence the focus of any solution. The submission to the minister made in May 1974 referred to 'the disquieting circumstances in which badgers were linked with the upsurge of bovine tuberculosis in the South West' (NA PRO: MAF 459/37 1985a, 3). MAFF documents referred to 'The most intractable animal disease problem' as 'badger-borne tuberculosis' (NA PRO: MAF 459/12 1983). It is only since the mid-2000s that faced 'with scientific evidence which confirms the importance of cattle-to-cattle transmission, the NFU, the British Veterinary Association (BVA) and other farming organisations have been forced to accept the necessity of cattle based control measures' (Wilkinson 2007, 13).

In 1979, the incoming Minister of Agriculture, Peter Walker, established a review of policy chaired by Lord Zuckerman which endorsed existing policy (Zuckerman 1980). There was always provision for a follow-up review to Zuckerman, generally referred to by civil servants as 'son of Zuckerman', and this appeared as the Dunnet Report in 1986 (Dunnet 1986). This recommended a scaling down of culling, the so-called 'interim strategy'. This remained in place for 10 years, despite criticism from both farmers and conservationists, in part because attention switched to the problem of BSE, which constrained the resources available for dealing with bovine TB.

In 1996 the government commissioned a new independent review of policy chaired by Professor John Krebs. This report recommended a programme of experimentation to determine whether badgers were responsible for the spread of bovine TB in cattle and whether culling strategies would reduce its incidence. The Independent Scientific Group on Cattle TB was set up by the government in 1998 to conduct the Randomised Badger Culling Trial (RBCT) in order to establish the effects of badger culling on the incidence in herds of bovine TB. This led to the contradictory reports and the Defra secretary, Hilary Benn, decided not to proceed with a cull. While a cull might work, 'it might also not work' and would be too risky. One factor he took into account was that public opposition would render a cull more difficult (Stocks 2008, 6).

Thus, nearly 40 years after the first tuberculosis-diseased badger carcass was found, there is still no settled policy to tackle the problem. This is partly a question of the lack of a scientific consensus which allowed mythologies to develop, as in the case of the 'old rogue badger' discussed below. It was not surprising that civil servants meeting in the Badger Steering Group discussed options such as 'let's do as little operational work as possible while we continue to try to discover more clearly what we should be doing' (NA PRO: MAF 459/12 1982, 2). In practice, badger control was 'influenced by practical and political expediency, field experience, research, public relations considerations, the perplexities and imponderable nature of TB badger/cattle relationships and much discussion among interested parties, especially the views of veterinarians whose primary concern, rightly, is the health and welfare of cattle' (NA PRO: MAF 459/19 1986, 12).

The Problem of Evidence

This section sets out the costs that arise from attempts to manage bovine TB. It shows that there has been a lack of scientific evidence, or agreement on the interpretation of the scientific evidence, which makes it difficult for policy-makers to arrive at decisions on how the disease should be tackled.

The persistence of bovine TB at a time when there is increased concern about the security of food supplies is undermining the livestock industry when it is also beleaguered by rising fuel and feed costs. Exports can suffer when cattle are sent to countries that are free of the disease. Dutch farmers imposed a ban on live cattle exports from Britain after calves imported in 2008 tested positive for bovine TB and Belgian farmers also refused to take British calves and cattle. Culling animals involves emotional and financial costs to farmers, particularly where pedigree herds built up over many years are involved. The public expenditure costs of dealing with bovine TB are substantial and have been increasing. Forty per cent of the Animal Health Agency's resources are devoted to dealing with TB, currently around £100 million a year. Government estimates suggest that the total annual expenditure on TB could increase to over £300 million a year by 2012–13. 'This would mean that the total expenditure on cattle TB between [2008] and 2013 would be approximately £1 billion' (House of Commons 2008, 12). At a time when public expenditure has to be cut in response to the recession, Treasury pressure for the reduction of expenditure that does not secure desired outcomes is bound to increase.

'Critical gaps in the knowledge about cattle TB and the way it spreads remain' (House of Commons 2008, 4). There is substantial evidence that badgers contribute significantly to the disease in cattle, but 'The evidence is ... mainly of a circumstantial nature, proving that infected badgers *can* cause infection of cattle, that infected badgers *can* shed significant amounts of infectious material, that cattle *may* interact with badgers in real situations' (House of Commons 1998, 14, emphases in original). However, 'what is still not known is the precise method of transmission from badger to cattle, i.e. it is still not known whether direct contact is necessary for the transmission of the disease' (House of Commons 2008, 10). In addition, 'The role and extent that cattle-to-cattle transmission plays in the maintenance and spread of TB is unknown'. Moreover, 'Current tests for bovine TB in cattle are not completely reliable. Tests for TB in badgers and other wildlife are less reliable' (Welsh Assembly 2008, 2).

Could badgers be catching TB from the cattle? This issue is certainly raised in the scientific literature. There is discussion about whether badgers are acting as 'spillover' hosts (i.e. badgers become infected from cattle but do not disseminate it) or 'reservoir' hosts (i.e. badgers become infected and maintain the infection and can pass it back to cattle at some point in the future). What is still unclear is whether badgers are 'maintenance' hosts, i.e. whether TB can remain in the badger population indefinitely without continual exposure to infection from cattle.

The lack of any consensus among scientific experts is shown by two contrasting reports commissioned by the government. The final report of the Independent Scientific Group (ISG) (2007, 14) stated: 'we conclude that badger culling cannot meaningfully contribute to the future control of cattle TB in Britain'. The government then commissioned a review of the ISG's report by the then government Chief Scientific Adviser, Sir David King, assisted by a group of five experts. The King Group concluded that 'In our view a programme for the removal of badgers could make a significant contribution to the control of cattle TB in those areas of England where there is a high and persistent incidence of TB in cattle, provided removal takes place alongside an effective programme of cattle controls' (King 2007, para. 5).

Apart from this contradictory advice, a further complication for policy-makers is that there is evidence of a perturbation effect when badgers are culled. Put at its simplest, this means that the disrupted social groups disperse and relocate. Moreover, 'perturbation increases incidence of bTB in badgers' and 'can cause the spatial distribution of bTB in badgers to change from one in which it is contained within spatially discrete patterns of high prevalence to one where it is more widely, or thinly spread' (Macdonald et al. 2006, 286). Thus, 'to have any prospect of contributing significantly to controlling bTB in cattle, a badger cull would have to be undertaken over a very large area' (Macdonald et al. 2006, 268). Given the level of emotional attachment to the badger, such a large-scale cull would be highly politically unpopular.

Constructing the Badger: The Myth of the Old Rogue Badger

The badger is an omnivorous mammal which is the largest surviving land carnivore in the British Isles, following the extinction of the wolf and the bear. It has lived in the islands for at least a quarter of a million years. Around a quarter of the population is estimated to be concentrated in the south-west of England and only 10 per cent in Scotland. It is a largely nocturnal animal with poor eyesight. It is estimated that there are some 300,000 badgers in Britain and it is not an endangered species, although it receives strong legal protection. Cultural constructions of the badger in literature and elsewhere treat it as a cherished species endowed with elements of magic and mystery.

Perhaps it was the very mysteriousness of the badger, and the lack of real (as distinct from self-proclaimed) experts on the badger that led to the development of the myth of 'the old rogue badger' which had a significant and continuing influence on public policy. The concept of the 'rogue badger' is still present in frames of reference as it was referred to in a discussion between the author and the Defra bovine TB team in May 2009. The myth of the rogue badger permitted the construction of an image of a bad, deviant or antisocial badger, a 'senile and virtually toothless' creature (NA PRO: HO 285/39 1965), whose actions could be presented as a basis for intervention against a cherished animal. This was only possible by asserting that there were very few rogue badgers. The categorisation could not be extended to the much larger number of badgers afflicted with TB.

© 2009 The Author. Journal compilation © 2009 Political Studies Association
BJPIR, 2009, 11(4)

Prior to the discovery of bovine TB in a badger carcass in 1971, the Ministry of Agriculture had generally taken a benevolent view of the badger: 'On the whole, the badger is generally regarded as a friend of the farmer since it has some beneficial effect in its destruction of many harmful insects and other pests'. However, no quarter was to be shown to an old rogue badger that had been demonstrated to have been responsible for damage: 'we recommend that it should be shot by an expert marksman when emerging from its sett at dusk' (NA PRO: MAF 131/170a 1965). Such a drastic measure was necessary because it was believed that it could not be easily trapped. 'The so-called "rogue" badger is less afraid of such things [traps] than other members of his species and, if his accusers are to be believed, will push through the small pop-hole entrance to a hen-house' (NA PRO: HO 285/40a 1966). This was somewhat at odds with the characterisation quoted earlier of the rogue badger as a senile animal, but it was the orthodoxy rather than its internal consistency that seemed to be important. Anyone deviating from the departmental line was likely to draw a sharp rebuke from Animal Health Division. Commenting on a draft ministerial reply, a civil servant in the division stated: 'because of the activities of "rogue" badgers, we could not say that badgers are not harmful' (NA PRO: HO 285/40b 1966).

One of the difficulties was that these issues were being dealt with by generalist civil servants and even when they sought the advice of specialists such as the Infestation Control Laboratory at Worplesdon, they were advised that 'Very few scientific investigations have been made of the life and habits of the badger and all but one or two of these have been uncritical and superficial. The literature abounds with conflicting theories' (NA PRO: MAF 131/170b 1960). Nevertheless, within the Nature Conservancy, which was then the official advisory body on flora and fauna, officials shared among themselves their doubts that the 'rogue badger' really existed: 'Between ourselves, I find the reference to "rogue" badgers puzzling. Do we know that such a creature exists or is it merely that badgers (along with other species) are likely to become opportunists when the occasion arises?' (NA PRO: FT 1/59 1965). However, the Nature Conservancy Council was more of an external advocate than an internal adviser in the policy process and did not see fit to challenge the established orthodoxy. Indeed, it was characterised as 'unhelpful' in one policy review document (NA PRO: MAF 459/37 1985a, 7).

Symbolism and Discourse

As Donald Schön and Martin Rein note (1994, 34), 'In order to reflect on the conflicting frames that underlie policy controversies, we must become aware of our frames, which is to say we must construct them'. Quite apart from the problems created by fictional creations like the rogue badger becoming embedded in the understandings of policy-makers, the politics around badgers invokes a highly charged discourse which takes visual as well as written forms. Such symbolic representations can be an important element in political discourse. 'Every symbol stands for something other than itself, and it also evokes an attitude, a set of impressions, or a pattern of events ... associated through imagination with the symbol'. The symbols discussed here are 'Condensation symbols [which] evoke the emotions associated with the situation' (Edelman 1964, 6). They may contribute to 'an injustice frame, a way of viewing a situation or condition that expresses indignation or outrage over a perceived injustice, as well as finding some human agency to blame for that transgression' (Jasper 1998, 414).

A picture in *Farmers Weekly* showed the badger, red in tooth and claw, devouring its prey, a strong contrast to the images used by animal welfare groups found in the National Archives. The Dartmoor Badger Protection League ('formed to prevent the unjustified slaughter of badgers') shows two badgers gambolling happily in a sylvan setting. An organisation called Brock has a more soulful picture, with a rather anthropomorphic badger looking out wistfully from behind the bars of a cage. The National Federation of Badger Groups has two badgers in a supplicant stance below the organisation's name.

These pictorial descriptions were matched by the language used in the debate by stakeholder organisations and interested individuals. The badger is depicted in highly positive terms as an innocent victim, while public policy is portrayed in highly negative terms. Terms such as 'cruel', 'slaughter' and 'extermination' are frequently deployed to describe government policy. Civil servants were aware that this was an area of great public controversy which entailed the involvement of Mrs Thatcher as prime minister. They emphasised 'that we in the Ministry of Agriculture dislike having to take action against the badger. It gives us as much revulsion as it gives our critics' (NA PRO: MAF 459/20 1984). What this represents is an instance of parties to a policy controversy seeing 'issues, policies and policy situations in different and conflicting ways that embody different systems of belief and related prescriptions for action' (Schön and Rein 1994, xviii).

Stakeholder Groups and the Policy Context

Relations with stakeholder groups in the area were very difficult in spite of the prevalent British policy style of seeking to consult and work with a range of interests. In some quarters of MAFF, particularly among those with scientific backgrounds, there was deep suspicion of conservationist groups because of their lack of scientific understanding and their perceived lack of openness to argument: 'I would suggest that very few local naturalists and conservationists will have much to contribute on badger social groups' (NA PRO: MAF 459/14 1985). There was a concern that badger organisations might be 'wholly comprised of "cranks" ' (NA PRO: MAF 459/26 1984). Nevertheless, they were perceived as potentially formidable adversaries who had an 'anticipated reactions' effect on policy over a long period of time An advisory leaflet on keeping badgers and cattle apart had a restricted distribution because 'It might ... attract criticism from the conservation lobby who might accuse us of overstating the role of the badger' (NA PRO: MAF 459/52 1991). There was concern that 'Conservation interests could renew their attack at any time' (NA PRO: MAF 1983b). There was what a major review document characterised as the 'mounting pressure from pseudo environmental pressure groups (EPEGs)' (NA PRO: MAF 459/37 1985a, 1). The Ministry faced 'a steady increase in pressure via MPs through a variety of *ad hoc* bodies such as "Brock" whose pronouncements have been hostile and downright misleading':

> There is now a minority of persons prepared to intervene physically
> in badger control organisations ... It is difficult to foresee this pressure

diminishing. Given the increased militancy of animal rights' organisations it may increase ... It is possible that any major confrontation would stimulate a whole series of such confrontations for a longer or shorter period. This factor can no longer be dismissed as irrelevant for practical purposes (NA PRO: MAF 459/37 1985a, 7–8).

Apart from a constant concern that any action to protect badgers might provoke the field sports societies, the Ministry also considered that they were undermined by a lack of support from their most important interest partner, the National Farmers' Union:

> Over the years [the NFU] have adopted a very low profile and have not attempted to defend the policy. Following the publication of the Dunnet Report they did not even issue a press statement ... It is not going to be easy for MAFF to adopt a high profile if the NFU adopts a very low one. It was only by a squeak that the Minister was not undermined by the NFU on hormones policy because of a similar divergence in PR effort (NA PRO: MAF 459/37 1985b, 3).

Following the publication of the Dunnet Report, MAFF pointed out to the NFU that 'for a considerable period MAFF has borne criticism for its badger control policy—action aimed at supporting the livelihood of NFU members who are livestock producers'. Disappointment and ministerial criticism were expressed to the NFU but the hope that the NFU 'will, however belatedly, now take up its cudgels on behalf of a policy which benefits its members' produced no response (NA PRO: MAF 459/39 1986). This continued to be a problem in the early 1990s, a memorandum noting that NFU representation on the Badger Panel 'has been weak' (NA PRO: MAF 459/66 1992a).

A further challenge was media criticism of government policy. 'Badger control has never had a good press since it was first mooted'. The Ministry was particularly aggrieved by what it considered to be 'provocative television broadcasts by Mr Phil Drabble' (NA PRO: MAF 459/37 1985b, 1). Lord Arran expressed on television the view that 'My only wish is that if the Minister proves to be wrong then he'll be eaten by badgers as Bishop Hatto was eaten by rats' (BBC 1975). The print press was also highly critical. A not untypical report was one that appeared in the *Sunday Times* with the strapline 'Farmer's wife Phyllis Crook weeps as ministry men pump cyanide gas into a badger sett in Lyneham, Wilts' accompanied by an appealing picture of a badger. The article opened: 'Badgers are being wiped out in south-west England because of an official report [the Zuckerman Report] which is now being widely attacked as scientifically spurious, biased and factually misleading' (Grice and Gillie 1980). In 1982 a strategy of actively defending the policy was initiated by the then minister, Peter Walker, but 'Although considerable resources went into the exercise there was no discernible effect on the volume of hostile criticism' (NA PRO: MAF 459/37 1985b, 2).

Defusing the Issue: The Advisory Committees

Given the intractability of the issue, ministers resorted to a number of devices to seek advice and to try and reconcile opposing interests. External advisory committees were one such device, in this case committees headed by Lord Zuckerman and Professor Dunnet. The prevailing atmosphere made appointments to head the various advisory committees and panels set up in the policy area particularly challenging, requiring special qualities of those appointed. 'It may not be easy to find someone with the appropriate qualities who is prepared to take on a task which is likely to make him a new target for extreme critics of our badger control policy' (NA PRO: MAF 459/16 1987a, 2). In relation to what became the Dunnet review, the prime minister, Mrs Thatcher, was advised, 'the individual concerned could well become the target of personal abuse as Lord Zuckerman was ... All members should be able to tolerate some criticism given that the subject is one raising considerable emotion in some quarters' (NA PRO: MAF 459/22 1984, 2). Dunnet was, however, more successful than the combative Lord Zuckerman in developing a policy stance that defused the issue for a decade.

The Zuckerman committee, which reported in 1980, was set up by Peter Walker shortly after he became minister in response to criticism of departmental policy on badgers and TB. Lord Zuckerman was a distinguished individual who proved to be broadly supportive of existing policy, arguing that 'Half-measures or measures taken without an understanding that the situation we are facing is a TB epidemic of serious proportions in badgers, are not going to succeed' (Zuckerman 1980, 42). He did, however, stir up controversy with his robust criticisms of badger organisations.

The 1986 Dunnet Report reaffirmed the badger/cattle link in bovine TB, but recommended restricting badger control to the farm where the disease outbreak occurred. This had the advantage of killing few badgers and also reduced the demands on public expenditure. This was becoming increasingly important with 'pressure for financial savings on ADAS expenditure and a need for numerical savings on posts' (NA PRO: MAF 459/37 1985b, 1). The Dunnet Report 'was, in the absence of adequate scientific information, obliged to be pragmatic and to compromise in its conclusions and recommendations' (NA/PRO: MAF 459/40 1986). It sought to pursue a middle course between the conflicting interests and in that sense it was a greater political success than Zuckerman, although whether it represented effective policy is another matter. The archival evidence shows that in some respects civil servants were uncomfortable with what eventually emerged. Despite their reservations, it served its purpose in ensuring a basis for policy for the next 10 years that evoked less controversy than the preceding policy.

Defusing the Issue: The Badger Panel

Creating spaces where the views of opposing stakeholders can be exposed to expert evidence, mediated and hopefully reconciled is one technique available to government for dealing with an intractable policy problem. The Badger Panel was set up in 1976 'for the express purpose of providing a forum for the views and advice of leading experts and interested organisations on the problems posed by bovine tuberculosis in badgers. The membership ... includes a wide range of scientific, veterinary and conservation interests and individuals' (NA PRO: MAF 458/26 1984, 1). As an advisory body, it is evident that its effect on policy was limited, in part because 'Given the wide spectrum of opinion represented on the Badger Panel it has frequently not been easy to achieve a unified view' (NA PRO: MAF 459/37 1986b). When an independent chairman was appointed, it was noted that the 'main need in guiding Panel's operations will be to try and achieve compromise so can offer unified advice to Government' (NA PRO: MAF 459/16 1987c). In reply to an inquiry about whether the Ministry ever took a more liberal or cautious line than an advisory committee recommended, it was stated:

> The [Badgers Panel] periodically churns out recommendations to the Minister. Adoption is by no means certain but they also get a polite hearing. Given the political flavour of conservationist views it is hard to know in which direction liberal lies. Farmers think we are too liberal and conservationists too draconian. Can't win really. A classic piece of Ministry fence sitting at the moment (NA PRO: MAF 459/66 1991).

MAFF was well aware that the panel performed a very valuable function in terms of explaining its own policies and legitimising policy:

> At present the Panel's support for the Ministry's policy in this emotionally sensitive area is most valuable as a means of putting our views to organisations that might be critical or hostile. Secondly, its existence enables the Minister to say that his policy is continuously monitored by all of the organisations who have a legitimate interest in the issues arising and thereby constitutes a powerful political weapon (NA PRO: MAF 458/26 1984, 2).

The Panel 'plays a major role in allowing us to demonstrate that all shades of opinion on badgers have been taken into account before we kill them' (NA PRO: MAF 459/66 1992b). The seriousness with which the political cover it provided was taken is illustrated by the presence of a number of senior MAFF officials at meetings and the effort that went into briefing the chairman before meetings. There was also a wish to secure as encompassing a membership as possible. Officials did consider at one point whether the panel was too large but 'all the organisations represented at present have a legitimate interest and there would likely be a strong reaction from any excluded organisation which would outweigh the possible benefits of a smaller Panel' (NA PRO: MAF 459/17 1986a). The most difficult decision MAFF faced about membership was when the National Federation of Badger Groups was formed in 1986 and asked to be represented on the Badger Panel, leading to a meeting with officials:

> Their representatives proved to be well informed and more moderate in their views than might have been expected and the NFBG could be expected to play a reasonably constructive role on the Panel. There would, of course, also be a political advantage in such an appointment. On the negative side, the NFBG is a very new organisation whose durability must be in some doubt. However, the NFBG are the only body who can claim to represent the 'badger lobby' and, on balance, officials believe they should be invited to put forward a nominee for appointment (NA PRO: MAF 459/17 1986b, 4).

The first representative of the NFBG on the Panel proved to be somewhat outspoken, but his successor caused even more qualms. The chairman of the Panel 'recognised that Mr Hancock [*sic*] was likely to be a difficult member, given his previous views' (NA PRO: MAF 459/65 1990). Mr Hancox resigned in 1992 complaining that discussion in the Panel was 'an insult to the intelligence and political integrity of those taking part', that 'he was not willing to be a political pawn' and 'has had little support from Badger Groups' (NA PRO: MAF 459/66 1992c). MAFF also had difficulties with the British Veterinary Association, which had been a stalwart supporter of its policies, but where an internal dispute broke out about whether they should be represented by a scientist or a practising vet. The BVA telephoned to see whether MAFF might give a steer in favour of a large animal practice vet, but were told: 'I thought this unlikely as I did not think MAFF would want to influence organisations to such an extent' (NA PRO: MAF 459/65 1989, 2).

The Badger Panel ceased to meet after the establishment of the Krebs review in 1996 and was disbanded in 2003. The ostensible reason given was that it was no longer necessary as an expert group would supervise culling (Defra 2003). However, it also reflected an attempt by Defra to construct a more evidence-based approach to policy on bovine TB. The strategy of creating encompassing groups which attempted to reconcile differences between highly divergent positions was seen not to have worked and reliance was placed on much smaller, more exclusive groups. In 2006 Defra created a small TB Advisory Group which was set up to 'consist of those with experience of working with the disease rather than a representative selection of interested organisations. The group is not intended to provide another forum for the usual debates over badger culling to be rehearsed by farming and wildlife organisations' (Wilkinson 2007, 11). The inbuilt preference for veterinary expertise in this new arrangement was not necessarily a way of generating a workable solution as large animal vets tended to be sympathetic to their farmer clients and were inclined to see the problem in terms of the badger rather than cattle-to-cattle transmission. 'The use of veterinary advice is likely to cause further controversy ... as their approach to disease control is frequently at odds with other forms of scientific expertise' (Wilkinson 2007, 11). In November 2008 Defra created a small bovine TB eradication group which, apart from Defra officials, was composed just of farmers and veterinarians and was charged with developing a strategy to reduce the incidence of bovine TB. It has been meeting once a fortnight.

Conclusions

Given that there is no 'obvious workable policy option' (Wilkinson 2007, 15) it could be argued that having no settled or effective policy is the least bad outcome. However, this has to be balanced against a continuing deterioration in the incidence of the disease. There were 2,639 new herd TB incidents in the first six months of 2008 in Great Britain, as against 2,275 for the whole of 2007, and 18,793 reactors slaughtered as against 12,795 in 2007. Current policy is not even containing the disease. The Conservative party has announced that if it achieves office it will embark on a strategy of culling badgers.

There is a more radical policy option which would not be popular with the farming industry. Even in countries like Australia that do not have a wildlife reservoir, eradication of the disease was very expensive. It has to be accepted that the cost of eradicating TB would be far greater than either the government or the industry, or both of them together, would be willing to pay. Indeed, it is doubtful if any animal diseases would have been eradicated historically if one had to mount a business case as current Defra policy-making procedures require. One therefore could think in terms of a feasible containment strategy. This would involve accepting that some areas of the country are lost to TB. In practice, farmers in those areas already have to live with the disease, as interviews with farmers in Gloucestershire in February 2009 confirmed. Resources would then be concentrated round the edge of infected areas to stop the spread of the disease to clean areas.

What are the main general lessons to be derived from this case study about policy failure? First, there are limits to the extent to which the transformation of the state in Britain affected this particular political arena. The replacement of MAFF by Defra produced a new approach to the problem which attempted to rely on evidence rather than political bargaining processes, but 'the results have been highly contentious and many alternative truth claims have been made' (Wilkinson 2007, 15). More generally, it shows the constraints operating on efforts at depoliticisation in policy areas where evidence-based discourses do not predominate and hence it points to some of the limits of the depoliticisation narrative which has been so predominant in recent explanations of British politics. Indeed, rather than experts depoliticising the issue, what can be seen is a 'politicisation of expertise' (Wilkinson 2007, 15). Moreover, the issue has now become one of controversy between the two main political parties.

Yet this politicisation fails to take account of how different forms of expertise may 'frame' the problem in different ways, in this case the differences between the perspectives of vets and epidemiologists. In policy areas in which mythology, as in the case of old rogue badgers, and values and images permeate the policy process, mechanisms such as external inquiries do little to resolve the underlying conflicts. MAFF resorted to traditional devices such as advisory committees and stakeholder fora to manage the problem, although their efforts were undermined by the unwillingness of one of the key stakeholders, the NFU, to support their policy in private but not in public. The Badger Panel provided useful political cover for MAFF, but produced little common ground between the opposed interests. The lesson that Defra learned was that such broadly based fora were not going to reconcile strongly opposed interests, nor were they going to produce workable solutions. Hence, Defra has pursued a stakeholder strategy that engages with a more limited range of key interests. This could be interpreted as a process of policy learning, although there is recognition within Defra of the tension between working more effectively with a limited group of core stakeholders and being open to charges of exclusion.

One implication is that some account has to be taken of the role of emotion in the policy process, the specification of blame and the generation of villains and the extent to which notions of injustice come into play (Jasper 1998). Models derived from welfare economics with its technocratic perspective are unlikely to capture such factors. What one needs is an understanding of how the policy problem is constructed, often from different assumptions which lead to divergent conclusions.

About the Author

Wyn Grant, Department of Politics and International Studies, University of Warwick, Coventry CV4 7AL, UK, email: *w.p.grant@warwick.ac.uk*

Note

The author acknowledges the support of the UK Research Councils through the Rural Economy and Land Use Programme (RELU).

Bibliography

BBC (1975) 'Extract from *Nationwide*, BBC TV, 24 September 1975'.

Besley, T. (2007) *Principled Agents? The Political Economy of Good Government* (Oxford: Oxford University Press).

Defra (2003) *Animal Health and Welfare: The Government's Response to the Krebs Report*. Available online at: http://www.defra.gov.uk/animalh/tb/publications/krebsresponse.htm (accessed 2 October 2008).

Dunleavy, P. (1995) 'Policy disasters: Explaining the UK's record', *Public Policy and Administration*, 10:2, 52–70.

Dunnet, G. (1986) *Badgers and Bovine Tuberculosis* (London: Her Majesty's Stationery Office).

Edelman, M. (1964) *The Symbolic Uses of Politics* (Urbana, IL: University of Illinois Press).

Garner, R. (2008) 'The politics of animal rights', *British Politics*, 3:1, 110–119.

Grice, E. and Gillie, O. (1980) 'Badgers may be innocent, ok?', *Sunday Times*, 28 December.

House of Commons (1998) *Research Paper 98/63, Bovine Tuberculosis* (London: House of Commons).

House of Commons (2008) Environment, Food and Rural Affairs Committee, Fourth Report of 2007/08, *Badgers and Cattle TB: The Final Report of the Independent Scientific Group on Cattle TB* (London: Stationery Office Limited).

Independent Scientific Group (2007) *Bovine TB: The Scientific Evidence* (London: Defra).

Jasper, J. M. (1998) 'The emotions of protest: Affective and reactive emotions in and around social movements', *Sociological Forum*, 13:3, 397–424.

King, Sir D. (2007) *Tuberculosis in Cattle and Badgers: A Report by the Chief Scientific Adviser* (London: Defra).

Macdonald, D. W., Riordan, P. and Mathews, F. (2006) 'Biological hurdles to the control of TB in cattle: A test of two hypotheses concerning wildlife to explain the failure of control', *Biological Conservation*, 131, 268–286.

Ministry of Agriculture, Fisheries and Food (1965) *Animal Health: A Centenary 1865–1965* (London: Her Majesty's Stationery Office).

Moran, M. (2001) 'Not steering but drowning: Policy catastrophes and the regulatory state', *Political Quarterly*, 72:4, 414–427.

NA PRO: MAF 459/39 (1986) 'Badgers and bovine tuberculosis: Professor Dunnet's Review Team; draft reporting and printing arrangements', The Dunnet Report. Draft note for Mr Smith's use when telephoning BVA and NFU, undated.

NA PRO: MAF 459/40 (1986) 'Consultative Panel on Badgers and Tuberculosis: Preparation and issue of papers', Memorandum from RSNC on the Dunnet Report (1986), Badgers and Bovine Tuberculosis.

NA PRO: MAF 459/65 (1989) 'Consultative Panel on Badgers and Tuberculosis: Membership', Membership of the Panel—representative of the BVA. Memorandum by Miss B. J. Bolze, 12 December.

NA PRO: MAF 459/66 (1991) 'Consultative Panel on Badgers and Tuberculosis: Membership', Advice from Advisory Committees. Handwritten note on memorandum, signature indecipherable, 11 June.

NA PRO: MAF 459/66 (1992a) 'Consultative Panel on Badgers and Tuberculosis: Membership', Submission to the Parliamentary Secretary (Mr Soames) by Miss C. J. Harrold, 18 June.

NA PRO: MAF 459/66 (1992b) 'Appointments in confidence', Membership of the Badger Panel.

NA PRO: MAF 459/66 (1992c) 'Consultative Panel on Badgers and Tuberculosis: Membership', Letter of resignation from Martin Hancox, 23 June.

NA PRO: FT 1/59 (1965) 'Badgers: Mammalian predator working party minutes', letter from Michael Blackmore to G. Christian, 5 February.

NA PRO: HO 285/39 (1965) Badgers: Consultation with Ministry of Agriculture Fisheries and Food on control and protection. 'Badgers in Forestry Commission areas'.

NA PRO: HO 285/40a (1966) 'Badgers: Proposed private members bill presented by Donald Chapman MP', Note on letter from Mrs R. Murray to Chairman of League against Cruel Sports.

NA PRO: HO 285/40b (1966) 'Badgers: Proposed private members bill presented by Donald Chapman MP', Letter from V. H. Bath to P. E. Baker, Home Office, 5 December.

NA PRO: MAF 131/170a (1965) 'Badgers: Proposals for control', letter from E. A. Ricot to H.J. Montgomery, 5 November.

NA PRO: MAF 131/170b (1960) 'Badgers: Proposals for control', letter to G. R. Hill, 27 July.

NA PRO: MAF 459/12 (1983a) 'Badger Steering Group (to co-ordinate MAFF work on badger-borne tuberculosis): Meetings and papers', Badger-borne Bovine Tuberculosis, E. F. G. Smith, 14 July.

NA PRO: MAF (1983b) 'Badger Steering Group: Meetings and Papers', JA Colmer, TB and Badgers—authorisation for public speaking, 5 May.

NA PRO: MAF 458/26 (1984) 'Quangos review 1979: Consultative Panel on badgers and tuberculosis', Reappointment of Consultative Panel on Badgers and Tuberculosis, submission to the Management Board.

NA PRO: MAF 459/12 (1982) Badger Steering Group (to co-ordinate MAFF work on badger-borne bovine tuberculosis): meetings and papers. 'Badger management objectives, strategies and manpower', a paper by D. C. Drummond.

NA PRO: MAF 459/14 (1985) 'Bovine tuberculosis: Methods of badger control; discussion on need to research other methods following suspension of gassing, June 1982', Views of interested organisations on methods of badger control.

NA PRO: MAF 459/16 (1987a) 'Consultative Panel on Badgers and Tuberculosis: Membership', Letter to Margaret Thatcher from the Minister of Agriculture, 23 February 1987, 'Appointment of chairman of Consultative Panel on Badgers and Tuberculosis'.

NA PRO: MAF 459/16 (1987c) 'Consultative Panel on Badgers and Tuberculosis: Membership', Brief for meeting with Mr Mark Thomasin-Foster, Chairman Designate of the Badger Panel.

NA PRO: MAF 459/17 (1986a) 'Consultative Panel on Badgers and Tuberculosis: Membership', Memorandum from J. W. Hepburn, 18 December.

NA PRO: MAF 459/17 (1986b) 'Consultative Panel on Badgers and Tuberculosis: Membership', Appointments.

NA PRO: MAF 459/19 (1986) 'Wildlife and storage biology discipline: Badger management group', Report of the Wildlife and Storage Biology Discipline Management Group to the Tuberculosis in Badgers and Cattle Co-ordinating Group. An Alternative Course of Action for Controlling Badgers.

NA PRO: MAF 459/20 (1984) 'Consultative Paper on Badgers and Tuberculosis: Working papers', Letter from the Parliamentary Secretary to Robert Hicks MP.

NA PRO: MAF 459/22 (1984) 'Lord Zuckerman's report, "Badgers, Cattle and Tuberculosis": Follow-up review of Government policy', Prime minister. Bovine tuberculosis and badgers—review of policy, 3 April.

NA PRO: MAF 459/26 (1984) 'Consultative Panel on Badgers and Tuberculosis: Agenda, briefs and minutes', R. J. Jeffery, Consultative Panel on Badgers and Tuberculosis. Further Briefing for 28th meeting, 29 February.

NA PRO: MAF 459/37 (1985a) 'Badger control policy: Consideration of the recommendations of the Dunnet Report on Badgers and Bovine Tuberculosis', K. Wilkes, Badger Control Policy, 9 October revision.

NA PRO: MAF 459/37 (1985b) 'Badger control policy: Consideration of the recommendations of the Dunnet Report on Badgers and Bovine Tuberculosis', Bovine tuberculosis and badgers—publicity submission to the Minister.

NA PRO: MAF 459/37 (1986b) 'Badger control policy: Consideration of the recommendations of the Dunnet Report on Badgers and Bovine Tuberculosis', Submission to the minister. Badger Panel's views on the Dunnet recommendations.

NA PRO: MAF 459/65 (1990) 'Consultative Panel on Badgers and Tuberculosis: Membership', Note from Ms E. A. J. Attridge, 2 February.

NA PRO: MAF 459/52 (1991) 'Tuberculosis in Badgers and Cattle Co-ordinating Group: Agenda, briefs and minutes', P. M. Phillip, Bovine Tuberculosis: advice on keeping badgers and cattle apart.

Schön, D. A. and Rein, M. (1994) *Frame Reflection: Towards the Resolution of Intractable Policy Controversies* (New York: Basic Books).

Stocks, C. (2008) 'Too risky: Hilary Benn decides against a badger cull', *Farmers Weekly*, 11 July, 6.

Welsh Assembly (2008) *Final Report of the Rural Development Sub-Committee Inquiry into Bovine Tuberculosis* (Cardiff: Welsh Assembly).

Wilkinson, K. (2007) *Evidence Based Policy and the Politics of Expertise: A Case Study of Bovine Tuberculosis* (Newcastle: Centre for Rural Economy).

Woods, A. (2004) *A Manufactured Plague: The History of Foot and Mouth Disease in Britain* (London: Earthscan).

Zuckerman, Lord (1980) *Badgers, Cattle and Tuberculosis* (London: Her Majesty's Stationery Office).

doi: 10.1111/j.1467-856X.2009.00388.x   *BJPIR: 2009 VOL 11, 574–592*

Tracing Foreign Policy Decisions: A Study of Citizens' Use of Heuristics

Robert Johns

Public opinion researchers agree that citizens use simplifying heuristics to reach real, stable preferences. In domestic policy, the focus has been on citizens delegating judgement to opinion leaders, notably political parties. By contrast, citizens have been held to deduce foreign policy opinions from their own values or principles. Yet there is ample scope for delegation in the foreign policy sphere. In this exploratory study I use a 'process-tracing' method to test directly for delegation heuristic processing in university students' judgements on the Iranian nuclear issue. A substantial minority sought guidance on foreign policy decisions, either from parties, international actors or newspapers. This was not always simple delegation; some used such heuristics within more complex decision-making processes. However, others relied on simple delegation, raising questions about the 'effectiveness' of their processing.

Keywords: public opinion; voting behaviour; survey methods

Students of electoral behaviour have tended to regard the 'high politics' of foreign affairs as the preoccupation of political elites, arguing that voters' concerns typically lie closer to home—the economy, taxation, healthcare and so on (Almond 1950; Rosenau 1961; Hughes 1978). However, this orthodoxy has been called into question. Many researchers now argue that voters have genuine policy preferences, that they react sensibly to changing international circumstances and that their preferences can influence government and policy (Aldrich et al. 1989; Page and Shapiro 1992; Anand and Krosnick 2003). Meanwhile, foreign affairs are widely seen—by experts and voters alike—as having been crucial in several recent elections, in the US (Weisberg 2005), the UK (Clarke et al. 2005) and, most vividly, in Spain (Colomer 2005). The question of how citizens make decisions in this field is therefore important for political parties and candidates, and psephologists, as well as researchers into public opinion formation.

This article reports on a process-tracing experiment (see Lau and Redlawsk 2006) designed to lay bare the process of foreign policy decision-making. The unusually direct access to opinion formation offered by this method is relatively new to public opinion research in general, and to the domain of foreign policy opinion in particular. Using the case of Iran's nuclear programme—a relatively obscure issue at the time of the experiment—I explore the bases on which 100 British undergraduate students reached a decision on the policy that they would prefer their government to support. The particular focus of interest is the extent to which citizens reduce the costs of seeking and processing information by 'delegating' the decision to a chosen elite source, such as a political party or newspaper, and the effectiveness of this strategy in leading them to the same decision that they would have made on the basis of a more assiduous cognitive approach. Having reviewed the literature on foreign policy opinion and described the process-tracing method in some detail, I present results suggesting that simple delegation scores a good deal higher on convenience than on effectiveness.

Foreign Policy and Public Opinion

In a previous era of opinion research, the more pressing question was not how but *whether* foreign policy attitudes are formed. Gabriel Almond (1950) found that the American public's stock response to foreign policy questions was indifference; when opinions were reported, they looked like non-attitudes (Converse 1964), lacking intellectual structure, factual content and stability. This tallied with the perennial finding that the average citizen is very short of knowledge on international politics (Erskine 1963; Delli Carpini and Keeter 1996). What Paul Sniderman et al. (1991) call 'minimalism'—the view that the public lacks both political knowledge and meaningful political attitudes—was for decades the received wisdom about public opinion on foreign policy (Isernia et al. 2002, 202; Brewer et al. 2004, 94). Yet, in recent years, minimalism has been strongly and convincingly challenged, such that foreign policy attitudes are now considered much worthier of study. This challenge is based on 'low-information rationality' (Popkin 1991; Sniderman et al. 1991; Lupia and McCubbins 1998). These authors acknowledge the minimalist premises that citizens lack both knowledge and preformed attitudes on foreign affairs. But they reject the minimalist conclusion, arguing that citizens can make a policy decision by finding a link from the issue in question to an existing attitude, value or predisposition of some other kind (Zaller 1992; Tourangeau et al. 2000, ch. 6; Alvarez and Brehm 2002). Consider two survey respondents asked 'do you favour President Bush's policy of bombing Iraq?' The first is a strongly partisan Republican, the second a committed pacifist. Neither needs to know anything at all about Iraq, and both can make a decision very simply: the first can answer 'yes' along partisan lines; the second 'no' along ethical lines. Both respondents have found a simple short cut to judgement that obviates the need for fuller information. Such short cuts are known as heuristics (following Kahneman et al. 1982; Simon 1982).

Contributors to the literature on foreign policy attitudes have specified a range of general guiding principles that citizens can use to lead them to decisions on specific policy issues. Michael Alvarez and John Brehm (2002, ch. 9) list four value dimensions—moral traditionalism, militarism, a sense of the dangerousness of the world, and political trust—and show that the first three at least are clearly related to foreign policy preferences. Jon Hurwitz and Mark Peffley (1987) and Eugene Wittkopf (1990) provide further evidence along the same lines, focusing on an internationalism–isolationism value dimension and its structuring of attitudes towards military interventions, defence spending, overseas aid and trade policy. Similar structuring principles have been identified by Larry Bartels (1994), William Chittick et al. (1995) and Richard Herrmann et al. (1999). And Paul Brewer et al. (2004) demonstrate significant correlations between levels of international trust and a range of foreign policy preferences (see also Popkin and Dimock 2000). International images are also available as guiding principles: Hurwitz and Peffley (1990; Peffley and Hurwitz 1992) compile evidence that US citizens used images of the Soviet Union to simplify the world and to derive attitudes to foreign policies concerning the Soviets (see also Herrmann et al. 1999).[1]

There is an important contrast between the foreign policy studies cited above and research on heuristic processing in political attitudes and behaviour more generally. This contrast hinges on a distinction between two types of heuristic: 'deduction' and 'delegation'. Studies of foreign policy decision-making have *mostly* been based on the first type, with citizens deducing specific issue positions from abstract principles. Yet, in the broader heuristics literature, equal if not more emphasis is placed on the second type, whereby citizens, rather than gathering and assessing lots of information pertinent to a decision, simply adopt the choice made by someone else. In short, the cognitive processing involved in political judgement is delegated. The phrase 'someone else' is deliberately vague, because policy decisions can be delegated to a wide range of actors. Political parties are the pre-eminent example in the literature: it has long been established that partisan voters adopt their party's standpoints on domestic issues, and their party's candidates in elections (e.g. Lodge and Hamill 1986; Rahn 1995; Huckfeldt et al. 1999). But there is also evidence of such delegation to interest groups, to newspapers and to friends or neighbours (see Sniderman 1993; Lupia and McCubbins 1998, 40; Lau and Redlawsk 2001, 953–4).

The contrast between the domestic and foreign policy opinion literatures should not be overdone. John Zaller's (1992) demonstration of citizens' use of partisan cues to form policy opinions was based in part on attitudes to the Vietnam War. More recent work on support for military action has revealed similar findings (Berinsky 2007; Baum and Groeling 2009). Nevertheless, the claim made by the authors of one such recent study—that '[w]ith relatively few partial exceptions ... most theoretical discussions of public opinion and foreign policy do not account for partisan differences in public opinion' (Baum and Groeling 2009, 160)—still holds true. Why, then, has there been this relative neglect of delegation heuristics by those researching into public opinion on foreign policy? The answer probably lies in the fact that foreign affairs were considered relatively remote both from voters and from everyday party politics. Electoral competition in western democracies has been based on economic and social/moral left–right value dimensions, and foreign policy issues do not fit neatly along these dimensions (Dalton 1996, 230, 252; Pierce 1999). As a result, parties have tended not to publicise strong stances on international affairs, and it is less easy for voters to discover and to adopt these standpoints. Hence Peffley and Hurwitz (1992, 433) showed that foreign policy attitudes are not closely related to partisanship. Moreover, other key opinion-formers, like trade unions, churches or newspapers, have also been more concerned with influencing citizens on domestic policy matters. To summarise: in foreign policy, citizens were less often called upon to make decisions, and, when they were called upon, they had fewer heuristic handles to grab on to.

However, there are two reasons why delegation heuristics are worthy of study in the sphere of foreign policy. The first point, noted at the outset, is that international affairs are higher up the political—and therefore the parties' and voters'—agenda. As studies of US public opinion on Iraq have shown, citizens are apt to follow their party's lead when it takes a clear stance on a prominent conflict (Jacobson 2006; Berinsky 2007). And a similar pattern, with partisan heuristics becoming more

© 2009 The Author. Journal compilation © 2009 Political Studies Association
BJPIR, 2009, 11(4)

readily accessible, seems likely in Britain. Tony Blair's Labour became strongly identified with the Iraq War, such that Labour supporters (or opponents) could derive a pro- (or anti-) war position simply from their party identification. Certain newspapers (e.g. *The Independent*) were so forthright as to become likewise readily associated with a stance on the issue. And, in a twist on the Hurwitz/Peffley interpretation of the role of international images, it seems likely that British citizens' attitudes to foreign policy have come strongly under the influence of images of the USA. Polling evidence suggests that, for some, knowing that the Bush administration favours a particular policy may be sufficient for them to reject it (see Asmus et al. 2003; YouGov 2003). This is not quite the same as the Hurwitz/Peffley version, which envisages citizens deducing an attitude to a policy from its likely impact on an international actor that they particularly like or dislike. Here, citizens delegate the decision to that actor. In practice, both approaches are likely to result in the same decision. The difference is that the delegation approach does not require citizens to make any judgements about a policy or its impact: they need only know whether a particular actor favours it or not.

This leads to the second reason why delegation heuristics might be more common in foreign policy reasoning than has been thought: they are simpler to use. Deduction heuristic processing requires at least some cognitive processing, namely that which is required to link the specific decision to the general principle. Sometimes this will be easy—as for pacifists deciding whether to support a war—but sometimes it will be rather harder: it may not be obvious which values are relevant, or these values may conflict (Alvarez and Brehm 2002). Such processing is much quicker and easier where citizens are on familiar territory, but, as noted, this is seldom the case in foreign politics. Partisan heuristics are especially useful where citizens know or care relatively little about the specific issue (Meernik and Ault 2001). Newspaper endorsements are especially useful where, as with foreign policy, many citizens will only experience the issue through the media (as opposed to domestic areas like healthcare and tax rates, in which people can draw on personal experience in forming judgements).

There is, then, ample reason to suppose that citizens use delegation heuristics when making foreign policy decisions. The literature on public opinion formation in this sphere is therefore incomplete, because it is concerned almost exclusively with deduction heuristics. It is important to complete the picture, not just for the sake of completeness, but because the use of delegation heuristics has implications for the *effectiveness* of heuristic processing. Since heuristics are supposed to be a substitute for information, their use is effective in so far as it leads citizens to the same decisions that they would have reached if fully informed (Kuklinski et al. 2001, 410; Lau and Redlawsk 2001, 952). Where political scientists have investigated the effectiveness of heuristic processing, the conclusion is clear: effectiveness cannot be taken for granted (Kuklinski and Hurley 1994; Bartels 1996; Lau and Redlawsk 1997 and 2001; Kuklinski and Quirk 2000; Kuklinski et al. 2001). It is most at risk where citizens rely utterly on short cuts and bring no other information to the decision, which is more or less the definition of delegation heuristic processing. For instance, the UK Labour party's supporters have typically been non-militaristic and internationalist in foreign policy outlook (Seyd and Whiteley 1992, 52–53). Those who relied solely on a partisan heuristic in the run-up to the Iraq War would have supported a policy which, had they heard and read more about the issue, they might well have opposed. Meanwhile, citizens delegating decisions to a particular country will be led astray unless they keep updating their image of that country, because its behaviour could change substantially over time, especially if there is a change of government or regime (Peffley and Hurwitz 1992).

Existing studies of foreign policy decision-making share an optimistic outlook about the effectiveness of heuristics (Holsti 1997; Popkin and Dimock 2000; Brewer et al. 2004, 106–107). This is the more understandable since they focus on deductive processing, which is the province of those able to recognise and apply the relevant abstract principles to specific foreign policies (Zaller 1992, ch. 2; Alvarez and Brehm 2002, ch. 3). However, to the extent that citizens actually use delegation rather than deduction heuristics, such optimism is called into question. We need therefore to address two empirical questions: (1) do citizens use delegation heuristics to reach foreign policy decisions? (2) Do they use these heuristics effectively? Shortly, I report empirical evidence directly addressing the first question and bearing on the second. Before that, however, it is necessary to describe the method employed to measure the use of heuristics.

Methods and Data

Process-Tracing and Direct Measurement of Heuristic Processing

Almost all of the existing studies (as cited just above) follow a correlational design, in which researchers measure association between the dependent variable (the policy decision) and the heuristic variable (such as internationalism, partisanship, level of trust, or image of the country involved). A significant correlation is taken to indicate the use of that heuristic (see Lau and Redlawsk 2001, 957). Yet this is a highly indirect gauge of heuristic processing, and that raises two problems. The first is a possibility that the correlation is spurious: the fact that survey respondents' policy views and broader beliefs covary does not demonstrate that the former are derived from the latter. Most studies involve extensive controls, such that a significant correlation probably does indicate some sort of heuristic processing. But a more direct measure would be more convincing. Further, a direct measure would address the second problem, which is signalled by the words 'some sort' just above. To understand the *nature* of heuristic processing, we need more than measures of association. A strong regression coefficient for partisanship could reflect widespread content-free processing, along the lines of 'Labour favours X, I'm Labour, so I favour X, whatever it is'. The same coefficient could equally reflect a far more thoughtful approach: 'Labour favours X, because Labour tends to support more internationalist solutions, and X is the policy agreed upon by the European Union. I like Labour's internationalism, and in particular their more pro-European approach—these are reasons why I support Labour in the first place. So I'm happy to support my party's endorsement of X'. From now on, I refer to these, respectively, as simple and complex processing. A measure of heuristic processing should be able to distinguish between these two types, not least because the second, more cognitively elaborated approach seems more likely to be effective (Petty et al. 1995). This requires a more direct method of measurement.

© 2009 The Author. Journal compilation © 2009 Political Studies Association
BJPIR, 2009, 11(4)

In this research, I adopt the 'process-tracing' method employed by Richard Lau and David Redlawsk for their (2001) investigation of the use of heuristics to make presidential voting decisions (see also Lau 1995; Lau and Redlawsk 1997). This method is based on the 'information board', an experimental tool whereby participants have access to a wide array of information, but none of it is immediately available: a decision-maker must actively choose the information he or she wants to consult, usually by clicking a box or link on a computer screen (Lau and Redlawsk 2001, 955). Since computers can trace participants' process through the task—by recording whether, at what stage and for how long a user visits each particular page—information boards have become a simple and non-intrusive means of studying the way that participants use information to make judgements (Carroll and Johnson 1990).

Process-tracing is ideally suited to current purposes because it enables the direct measurement of heuristics' use that was lacking from previous studies. Based on the literature, we can identify *a priori* the kinds of information likely to be of heuristic value (e.g. partisan cues). Recording whether that information was consulted or not provides an initial, albeit crude, measure of heuristics use. Another useful facet of the information board technique is that it allows us to measure the use of several different types of heuristic. Unlike prior studies, which have tended to single out one heuristic at a time, process-tracing allows the researcher to offer a range of short cuts to participants, and to judge which are preferred (and by whom).

Decision-Making Task

While Lau and Redlawsk (2001) explored candidate choice in presidential primaries and elections, here we are concerned with foreign policy preferences: specifically, the issue of Iran's developing nuclear programme. Participants were presented with three policy options designed to address this potential problem—air strikes, sanctions and negotiations—and asked to choose that which they would prefer the British government to support. The Iranian nuclear issue is very appropriate for a study like this, for two reasons that work in combination. On the one hand, the issue is important: among elites, the need to restrict Iran's nuclear activities has been the subject of debates and negotiations for some time now (http:// news.bbc.co.uk/1/hi/world/middle_east/4557653.stm); meanwhile, the issue raises major public concerns—nuclear weapons, state-sponsored terrorism, US imperialism and so on. On the other hand, at the time of the experiment the issue remained only *potentially* important to most citizens. This is partly because it remained some way down the political parties' and the media agenda, and partly because, even if and when it achieves this prominence, there will probably be a short delay before citizens react (Jentleson 1992; Knopf 1998). Hence, when participating in this study, the Iran nuclear issue was one on which they were yet to form a view, and on which they were probably short of information.

Structure of the Task

The process-tracing part of the experiment was sandwiched between two questionnaires. (Copies of the questionnaires, and of all the experimental web pages, are available from the author on request.) The questionnaires included measures of political awareness (a six-question quiz on foreign affairs and a political interest question) and—in the post-test—questions about the task undertaken, but were mainly comprised of items tapping participants' openness to the different heuristics on offer: partisanship, newspaper readership and attitudes towards key international players. Having completed the pre-test questionnaire, participants were presented with the three options, and instructed as follows: 'Shortly, we'd like you to select from these the approach that you would like the British government to support. Before that, though, you have the chance to find out a bit more about Iran and about these different options'. Thus they were led into the process-tracing part of the task.

The fulcrum of this part of the experiment was the 'information home page', from which all of the information pages were linked. Each information page offered two links: 'Back to the information home page' and 'Make my choice'. The latter indicates that, at any stage, participants were invited to skip straight to the decision page. Hence the experiment was not fixed in length: participants in this study were able to spend as little or as much time as they wanted collecting information before making their choice. Since, in the real world, citizens' political engagement varies hugely around a low mean (Zaller 1992; Delli Carpini and Keeter 1996), this flexibility is crucial for a realistic simulation of decision-making. The minimally engaged will tend to avoid all but the most basic information concerning political issues, however high up the agenda they rise.

Information Pages

As in Lau and Redlawsk's experiments, participants were offered 'non-heuristic' as well as delegation heuristic information. Non-heuristic information is more detailed, non-normative and designed so as not to offer heuristic handles (Lau and Redlawsk 2001, 957). The more of this information that a participant consults, the less dependent he or she is on heuristic reasoning. Participants were offered two brands of non-heuristic information: six answers to 'frequently asked questions' providing background on the issue; and three 'what the options involve' pages offering detailed descriptions of each policy on offer.

There were three types of delegation heuristic page: party stances, international perspectives and newspaper policy endorsements. The choice of the four parties and six newspapers was guided by two considerations: first, to include the key opinion-formers; second, to ensure that each of the three policy options had at least one advocate.[2] Similar thinking governed the selection of international perspectives: the US (air strikes) and the EU (sanctions) are the two key influences on British foreign policy; Russia (negotiations) was chosen as the most likely opponent of any punitive approach; and Israel was included for its historical involvement with—and likely strong stance (air strikes) on—the issue.

The heuristic pages are designed for delegation reasoning. Process-tracing cannot be used to measure deductive heuristic reasoning, because virtually any information on an issue contains numerous potential links to numerous potential principles. The impossibility of directly measuring the use of deduction heuristics is unfortunate, since they are much referred to in the foreign policy literature, and it would be interesting to explore whether some people prefer deduction over delegation or vice versa. However, this is not an option: only with delegation heuristics is it possible to check whether someone consults the specific information—e.g. the party stance—that is of heuristic value. There remains, though, the question of how, when a participant consults a delegation heuristic page, we can be sure that they are processing and using the information in a heuristic manner (Lau and Redlawsk 2001, 962). There is one straightforward means by which we can be sure: by offering *only* the heuristic-relevant information. Hence, in this study, participants accessing the party or international standpoints were led to a page on which they are simply told what that standpoint is. Then they are given the option of accessing a further page on which that standpoint is outlined and justified in detail. Those who ignore the additional page *must* be using the information in a simple heuristic manner; those who access the extra information, though they may still be said to be using heuristics, are doing so at a more cognitively complex level (and probably therefore more effectively).[3]

Participants

The process-tracing method had not previously been applied in the sphere of citizens' policy decision-making. Moreover, there has been very little research into the use of delegation heuristics to reach foreign policy judgements. For these reasons, this was designed as an exploratory or 'semi-qualitative' study, with an N of 100. I use the term 'semi-qualitative' because, while the study allows for close scrutiny of the way in which individuals build information into foreign policy decisions, it has an N sufficiently large for basic quantitative analysis. The 100 participants were volunteer students from the University of Strathclyde.[4] The major disadvantage of such convenience sampling—that student volunteers do not con- stitute a representative sample—is less of an issue in a small-N exploratory study. Moreover, as Alex Mintz et al. (2006) argue, student samples can serve as a reasonable approximation of the public in a foreign policy context. The diverse social backgrounds of the students, coupled with the fact that volunteers were drawn from the full range of university departments, ensured sufficient variance on political awareness.

Results

Quantity and Type of Information Consulted

The first and most basic empirical question to answer is whether participants accessed the heuristic information pages. Table 1 provides a detailed breakdown of what was on offer and what was chosen by participants. In the table, the informa- tion is divided into three broad categories: non-heuristic, simple heuristic (the bare endorsement of a policy option by a party or international actor) and complex heuristic (more detailed justifications of their stance by parties, international actors or newspapers).

Several results are particularly worthy of note. First, the non-heuristic information was most popular, accounting for more than half of all pages and words read, and

Table 1: Breakdown of Information Consulted by Type

Page type	Information available to participants		Information consulted by the average participant			Number of participants	
	Pages	Words	Pages read	% of available pages read	Words read	Read all the pages	Read none of the pages
Non-heuristic							
FAQs	6	742	2.92	49	361	32	34
What the options involve	3	1,649	1.34	45	737	32	41
Total	9	2,391	4.26	47	1,098		
Simple heuristic							
Parties	4	367	1.50	38	138	24	49
International stances	4	337	0.99	25	83	17	63
Total	8	704	2.49	31	221		
Complex heuristic							
Parties	4	2,078	0.22	6	114	3	88
International stances	4	2,058	0.21	5	108	4	91
Newspapers	6	2,299	0.99	17	379	5	66
Total	14	6,435	1.42	10	602		
Grand total	31	9,530	8.17	26	1,920		

consulted by more than half of the participants. A caveat about potential order effects should be added here, though: non-heuristic information may have been consulted more often because it was listed first on the information home page. In any case, all of the heuristic information offered was consulted by at least some participants—this confirms theoretical expectations about the types of short cut taken by citizens when making foreign policy decisions. Third, among the heuristic information, the simple pages proved markedly more popular. This is probably due in part to the structure of the pages—the detailed party and international perspectives being accessible only via the corresponding basic page—but it also shows that participants do not insist on building heuristic information into more complex cognitive structures. Finally, among the heuristic pages, the party stances proved most popular. Again this may be partly due to order effects, with the party pages listed higher than the other heuristic pages. Nevertheless, there is reason to question the idea that, when it comes to foreign policy decisions, citizens do not seek out partisan guidance. In summary, aggregate patterns of information use suggest that participants were using simple heuristics. To confirm or refute this suggestion, we need to scrutinise more closely those who accessed the heuristic pages.

Users of Heuristic Information

Since short cuts are supposed to be a substitute for information, we would expect consultation of the simple heuristic pages to be relatively common among two (overlapping) groups: those lower on general awareness; and those who consulted little other information during this experiment. There are two approaches to measuring the amount of information consulted: the number of pages of each type accessed, and the amount of time spent on pages of each type. Taking the two approaches in turn, Table 2 reports Pearson correlations between the measures of awareness (knowledge and interest) and the total amount of information consulted on the one hand, and the consultation of different types of information on the other.

Table 2: Political Awareness, Quantity of Information and Dependence on Heuristic Pages

Number of pages	Simple heuristic	Complex heuristic	Non-heuristic	Simple/total
Knowledge	0.244**	0.218*	0.162	0.096
Interest	0.235**	0.148	0.245**	0.177
Total information consulted			0.177	0.149

Amount of time	Simple heuristic	Complex heuristic	Non-heuristic	Simple/total
Knowledge	0.174*	0.195*	0.175*	−0.016
Interest	0.137	0.163*	0.293**	0.115
Total information consulted				−0.229*

* $P < 0.10$; ** $P < 0.05$.

© 2009 The Author. Journal compilation © 2009 Political Studies Association
BJPIR, 2009, 11(4)

Since the better-informed consult more pages anyway, it was predictable that they also read more heuristic pages in absolute terms. The positive correlations in the first column bear out this prediction, but it is noticeable that, at least when measuring by number of pages, the correlations are stronger in this than in the neighbouring columns. That suggests that simple heuristics are not even *relatively* popular among the less aware. To check this, I calculated the importance of simple heuristics in each participant's information search (by simply dividing the number of simple heuristic pages they consulted by the total number of pages they accessed). As the right-hand column shows, there is no evidence of a negative relationship between awareness and dependence on basic heuristic processing. Moreover, only when measuring consultation by time is there any indication that simple heuristics are relatively useful to those consulting less information. The implication of these results is that heuristic information, like other types, is sought by those who *want* it, not by those who *need* it. Heuristics, even in their simplest form, are not used mainly by the otherwise uninformed. This, however, is not quite the key issue. What we really need to know is whether they are used—and used effectively—by at least some uninformed citizens. To address these issues, I turn to an examination of individual decision-making processes.

Types of Information Processing

Here, the dependent variable becomes the entire decision process, rather than simply whether a participant consulted a particular page or type of information. I began by trying to develop a typology of information users. Table 3 sets out six types, along with a count of how many such participants were observed. (Four participants did not fit this typology, and—since they shared nothing else in common—are excluded from these analyses.)

The first thing to note about Table 3 is that delegation heuristic reasoning was a minority pursuit. Twenty-nine participants consulted most or all of the pages on offer, another 29 consulted none of it and 16 studiously avoided the heuristic information. This leaves 22 participants whose pattern of information use is consistent with heuristic processing as posited in the literature. Henceforth, these 22 become the primary focus of this note.

Table 3: A Typology of Information Users

Type	Description	n
Complete	Accessed virtually all of the pages	21
Semi-complete	Accessed most of the pages, of most types	8
Non-heuristic	Accessed only non-heuristic information	16
Complex heuristic	Accessed simple heuristic pages, but also the related complex heuristic and/or non-heuristic information	12
Simple heuristic	Accessed simple heuristic pages and little if anything else	10
Nothing	Accessed none of the pages, or accessed one or two very briefly	29

A second result is that the theoretical distinction drawn above between simple and complex heuristic processing shows up clearly in empirical analysis. At least among these few participants, the two types were about equally common. This distinction is best illustrated through examples. P108, a Labour identifier, began by checking Labour's stance (via the simple endorsement page), then equally briefly looked up the views of the Conservatives, Liberal Democrats and the EU (of which he approved quite strongly, according to the pre-test). This all took just 28 seconds, after which he voted for sanctions.[5] P18 spent 15 seconds checking 'What is the nuclear threat from Iran?', and dwelt for only three and six seconds, respectively— that is, nowhere near enough to read the material—on the detailed descriptions of air strikes and sanctions. He then looked up Respect's stance, and proceeded to decide in favour of negotiations (the one option that he had ignored before). I classified these two participants as simple (partisan) heuristic processors. In contrast, P111, a Liberal Democrat identifier, spent considerable time looking up answers to five of the FAQs, and reading about all three options in detail. Only then did he check the Liberal Democrat stance, and make his decision in favour of negotiations. Meanwhile, P57, a Labour identifier, began with the FAQs and then moved to consult Labour's stance. Having read about Labour's endorsement of sanctions, he read more about that policy; apparently unconvinced, he then turned to detailed descriptions of the two other options. Ultimately, he too chose negotiations. P111 and P57 were classified as complex heuristic processors.

The complex heuristic examples illustrate two important points about that type of processing. First, the more detailed information can be consulted before and/or after the heuristic cue is noted. P111 seemed to use partisanship as a kind of final validation of a decision reached on the basis of non-heuristic information; P57 sought partisan information early, but used it as guidance for further searching. (Or the cues may simply have served as just another piece of information, to be integrated along with the non-heuristic information into a decision (Tourangeau et al. 2000, ch. 6). Second, and crucially, the consultation of additional information provides a basis on which participants could decline to take the heuristic short cut. In learning more about his party's policy, P57 found reasons to seek an alternative, which he found and eventually chose. With complex heuristic processing, the cues may guide participants through the available information, but they do not override it.

The detailed scrutiny of information use yields some more general results about the use of heuristics. While, as the examples above imply, partisanship was the most commonly used cue, there was evidence of participants taking different short cuts. P87, a Labour identifier and *Sun* reader, read answers to the FAQs, briefly checked all four parties' stances and then read the *Sun* comment. In then opting for air strikes, he was adopting his newspaper's rather than his party's stance. P79, a Liberal Democrat who approved quite strongly of the EU, checked the stance of both (as well as reading very briefly about air strikes). He chose sanctions, following an international rather than a party heuristic. Another noticeable feature of the heuristic reasoning observed is that several participants appeared to apply what might be called negative heuristics: that is, they checked the policy preference of an actor that they dislike or distrust, and responded by adopting a different stance. In the case of partisan cues, this is a heuristic application of what has been termed negative party identification (Rose and Mishler 1998). In the absence of a bipolar measure of attitudes towards the parties, we can only identify suggestive examples of negative partisan heuristic processing. P56, a non-identifier, consulted only two pages, the Labour and Conservative stances, and then promptly chose negotiations. The pre-test did include bipolar measures of attitudes towards the different international actors, but there were no obvious instances in which such negative affect guided decision-making. Plenty of participants reported strong dislike for the US in particular, but very few actually consulted that country's stance (probably because they had read it on the air strikes page, or inferred it from parallels with Iraq). This last example illustrates a broader finding, namely that the potential for delegation heuristic reasoning is often unfulfilled. Many participants were party identifiers or regular newspaper readers but were not thereby guided in their use of information—they still read everything (or nothing).

So far, then, we have three main findings. First, although heuristics are supposed to serve as a substitute for information, there is little evidence that the heuristic pages were especially popular among those who were otherwise short of information. Second, individual search histories offered clear evidence of delegation heuristic processing, though it appears to be the practice of a minority: in this case, under a quarter of the participants. Third, delegation heuristic processing is not always the cognitive simplification described in the literature. As often as not, heuristics were integrated into a broader information search and a more complex decision process.

The Effectiveness of Heuristic Processing

As already noted, this study can provide only indicative answers to the research question concerning effectiveness. On the basis of the findings above, these indications are positive. Many citizens avoid the risk of error involved in delegation heuristic reasoning; others minimise this risk by using heuristics in conjunction with other information. Still, some participants seemed to rely on the simplest syllogistic reasoning as described in the literature, and therefore they have no safeguard against error. The empirical section ends with four comparisons of the 12 complex and the 10 simple heuristic processors. All four are set out in Table 4, and all four fuel suspicion that these simple heuristics put effectiveness at risk.

First, the table indicates a slight tendency for simple heuristic processors to be less aware than complex heuristic processors, but the differences are small, as are the numbers, and general awareness is in any case only a very indirect indicator of likely effectiveness. The second comparison employs an alternative measure of awareness, specific to the policy issue in hand: in the post-test, participants were asked whether the information accessed had confirmed or changed an existing attitude, or whether it had produced or failed to produce a new attitude. Table 4 indicates that seven of the 12 complex heuristic processors were sufficiently aware of the issue to have some prior opinion available. This was true of only two of the 10 simple processors. In other words, most of the complex processors were not only taking more time and effort to build judgements, but were building them on firmer foundations. Most of the simple processors, on the other hand, were hastily erecting cognitive structures without any foundations.

© 2009 The Author. Journal compilation © 2009 Political Studies Association
BJPIR, 2009, 11(4)

Table 4: Characteristics of Simple and Complex Heuristic Processors

Awareness		Simple heuristic	Complex heuristic
Knowledge	High	3	5
	Low	7	7
Interest	High	3	6
	Low	7	6
Prior view on the issue			
Had a prior view		2	7
Made up mind		7	4
(Still don't know)		(1)	(1)
Willingness to compare			
Read about at least two options		1	8
Information reported as useful			
Simple heuristic pages		3	1
Other pages		1	8
None		6	3

Heuristic use was classified as complex if a participant supplemented the cue with either a detailed justification from the source, or non-heuristic information about that option. But to ensure effectiveness, defined as making the same decision as if fully informed, requires comparison of different options. (However much information a citizen compiles about option A, he or she cannot be sure that he or she would prefer it to B without learning something about that alternative.) As the third comparison shows, though, eight of the 12 complex heuristic users engaged in such comparison, while only one of the 10 simple heuristic processors did so.

The final comparison is based on participants' dependence on the heuristic information. An open-ended question on the post-test asked respondents which (if any) page or pages they had found particularly useful. Nine complex but only four simple processors specified a page. Of the complex processors, only one mentioned a delegation heuristic page (and that was a broadsheet newspaper). In contrast, three of the four simple processors mentioned delegation heuristic pages. P18 referred to 'the pages regarding the political parties', which must mean the Respect page since that was the only such page he accessed. And P79 mentioned the 'EU's opinion on the matter', in line with the suggestion earlier that he was guided by an international rather than a party heuristic. These results therefore validate some of the inferences about heuristic processing made in the previous section, as well as suggesting that complex processors, by not only using but leaning more heavily on contextual information, will use heuristics more effectively.

The various analyses in this section all point to a fourth main finding: in heuristic processing, there is a clear trade-off between simplicity and effectiveness. While the numbers are small, the differences are so stark that, if the four comparisons in Table 4 are converted to basic 2×2 crosstabs, three of the four indicators of

© 2009 The Author. Journal compilation © 2009 Political Studies Association
BJPIR, 2009, 11(4)

effectiveness—all except general awareness—show a significant relationship ($\chi^2 > 3.84$) with the simple–complex distinction. In the upcoming discussion, I assess the potential implications of this and the other key findings.

Summary and Discussion

The primary contribution of this study is to show that, the preoccupation in the literature with deduction notwithstanding, some citizens do use delegation heuristics to make foreign policy decisions. It is worth re-emphasising that, while correlations can *suggest* the use of short cuts, direct measurement via process-tracing allows for a *demonstration* of delegation heuristic processing. There was evidence of participants using all three delegation heuristics—party positions, international perspectives, newspaper endorsements—that were on offer, though the party cues proved most popular. Admittedly, this type of reasoning was not widespread: many participants were willing to read a great deal more than the basic information needed for delegation processing; many others were not even willing to read those basics. Nevertheless, this study provides an indication that, as far as heuristic processing is concerned, the literatures on foreign and domestic policy opinion have diverged too far.

A second important finding is that heuristic processing varies along a simple–complex dimension: some participants relied solely on simple short cuts; others integrated heuristic information into less rudimentary cognitive structures. The significance of this lies in the connection with effectiveness. Psychologists have generally found that more cognitively elaborated attitudes are stronger and more stable, suggesting that they are in some sense more reflective of a person's real opinion (Petty and Cacioppo 1986; Petty et al. 1995). And it makes intuitive sense that the more information a person takes into account, the more likely he or she is to reach the decision that he or she would have made if fully informed. On the other hand, Lau and Redlawsk (2006)—albeit in their rather different context—find that simpler decision rules are more likely to be effective, on the grounds that complexity stretches voters beyond their cognitive limits. Adjudicating between these conflicting predictions is ultimately an empirical matter. Several of the results from this study tend to imply a negative relationship between simplicity and effectiveness, but more conclusive evidence awaits an explicit test of effectiveness.

With a relatively low N and a student sample, this was primarily a qualitative and exploratory study. The evidence of delegation heuristic processing, and of the variations in complexity of this type of reasoning, call for an extended study, with a larger and more representative sample. The primary purpose of such an investigation would be to quantify delegation heuristic processing; that is, to identify how common it is, to assess the relative popularity of different options for delegation and to measure the distribution of participants' processing along the simple–complex continuum. However, the value of that study would be greatly enhanced if it also incorporated a measure of effectiveness. Lau and Redlawsk (2001, 962–3) offer two means of determining the decision that a participant would have made if fully informed; a third alternative is to convert the current study into a split-half experiment, with a control sample obliged to read all of the information.) That offers the possibility of checking whether the public delegate their decisions to the appropriate sources, and whether particular sources prove more helpful. Furthermore, it allows us to address the question above, concerning the relationship between simplicity and effectiveness.

One advantage of setting the extended study in the same context is that British views on a nuclear Iran form an interesting test of the effectiveness of delegation heuristic processing. As has been emphasised (Lupia and McCubbins 1998; Kuklinski et al. 2001), effectiveness is a function of the institutional context in which citizens are asked to reason. For example, partisan heuristics will work best where a party has long been associated with a particular foreign policy outlook, allowing for parties and their supporters to become more closely aligned. Cues from international actors will work best where general orientations towards those actors are derived from their foreign policy stances. In Britain, research in these areas is conspicuous by its absence, leaving us reliant on impressions. Attitudes to the US look like effective heuristics, since—at least under the Bush administration—they have become closely connected with foreign policy. Partisanship looks likely to be less effective: Labour has become significantly more hawkish over time, the Conservatives—largely for purposes of opposition—have seemed less so, with neither move owing much to changing attitudes among the parties' supporters. The question then becomes: do British citizens recognise the different utilities of these alternatives for delegation, and adjust their behaviour accordingly? An extended version of the current study is well placed to address that question.

Finally, a direct test of effectiveness allows for measurement of the aggregate information effects on foreign policy opinion (see, for example, Bartels 1996). This study has been about *how* people make decisions, rather than *what* decision they make. But this focus on process rather than outcome should not obscure the fact that using heuristics may skew public opinion. For instance, anti-American sentiment might lead British citizens to oppose a campaign of air strikes which, if they knew more about the potential threat from Iran, they would support. Of course, it is equally possible to conceive of scenarios in which heuristics would make citizens more hawkish than they would be if better informed. The key point about future studies is that, by identifying the decisions that participants would have made if fully informed, they can test for such aggregate bias.

About the Author

Robert Johns, Department of Government, University of Strathclyde, 16 Richmond St, Glasgow G1 1XQ, UK, email: *robert.johns@strath.ac.uk*

Notes

I am grateful for support from the University of Strathclyde's Research Development Fund, and for advice from Dr Lori Helene Gronich (Georgetown University) and Dr Graeme Davies (Aberystwyth University).

1. This brief review does not take in the work of Mintz (e.g. 2003 and 2004). While Mintz's 'poliheuristic' theory of foreign policy decision-making has the same theoretical ancestry as the work on heuristics discussed here, he has a different empirical focus: the decisions of policy elites. The task facing elite decision-makers is very different from that confronting ordinary citizens and so, as a consequence, are the heuristics used.

2. The three major national parties—Labour (sanctions), the Conservatives (air strikes) and the Liberal Democrats (negotiations)—were included, along with Respect (the minor party likely to take the strongest (anti-air strikes) stance on the issue). With the newspapers, the ideal would have been to have tabloid and broadsheet newspapers endorsing each of the three policy options, but this was not realistic given the likely political stances of the larger-circulation papers. Nonetheless, a broad coverage was achieved: *The Herald* (broadsheet/sanctions), *The Independent* (broadsheet/negotiations), *The Scotsman* (broadsheet/air strikes), the *Daily Mail* (mid-market tabloid/air strikes), *The Sun* (tabloid/air strikes) and the *Daily Record* (tabloid/sanctions).

3. A final point to note about the information offered to participants is that, of necessity, some of it was invented. The experiment hinges on the key opinion-formers taking a clear stance in favour of air strikes, sanctions or negotiations. That had not happened by the time of the experiment, not because any of these options is unrealistic or unlikely to command support, but simply because the issue was then some way down the foreign affairs agenda. As it rises up that agenda, the parties, other national governments and newspapers are likely to take explicit stands. The information pages were based on predicting those stances. Hence the party pages were hypothetical policy statements, and the newspaper pages mimicked editorial comments. None of the 'factual' information, though—names, quotations, historical details—was fabricated.

4. Participants were paid a small reward, both to encourage volunteers and to ensure that, once embarked on the task, participants would not cut short their information search because they felt unrewarded for their effort.

5. Only six of the 22 heuristic processors were female. One immediate implication of the shortage of female heuristic processors is that most of the example participants in this section are male.

Bibliography

Aldrich, J. H., Sullivan, J. L. and Borgida, E. (1989) 'Foreign affairs and issue voting: Do presidential candidates waltz before a blind audience?', *American Political Science Review*, 83:1, 123–141.

Almond, G. A. (1950) *The American People and Foreign Policy* (New York: Harcourt Brace).

Alvarez, R. M. and Brehm, J. (2002) *Hard Choices, Easy Answers* (Princeton, NJ: Princeton University Press).

Anand, S. and Krosnick, J. A. (2003) 'The impact of attitudes towards foreign policy goals on public preferences among presidential candidates', *Presidential Studies Quarterly*, 33:1, 31–71.

Asmus, R., Everts, P. P. and Isernia, P. (2003) 'Power, war and public opinion: Thoughts on the nature and structure of the trans-atlantic divide', *Transatlantic Trends*. Available online at: http://www.transatlantictrends.org/trends/doc/2003_english_essay.pdf.

Bartels, L. M. (1994) 'The American public's defense spending preferences in the post-Cold War era', *Public Opinion Quarterly*, 58:4, 479–508.

Bartels, L. M. (1996) 'Uninformed votes: Information effects in presidential elections', *American Journal of Political Science*, 40:1, 194–231.

Baum, M. A. and Groeling, T. (2009) 'Shot by the messenger: Partisan cues and public opinion regarding national security and war', *Political Behavior*, 31:2, 157–186.

Berinsky, A. J. (2007) 'Assuming the costs of war: Events, elites, and American public support for military conflict', *Journal of Politics*, 69:4, 975–997.

Brewer, P. R., Gross, K., Aday, S. and Willnat, L. (2004) 'International trust and public opinion about world affairs', *American Journal of Political Science*, 48:1, 93–109.

Carroll, J. S. and Johnson, E. J. (1990) *Decision Research: A Field Guide* (Beverly Hills, CA: Sage).

Chittick, W. O., Billingsley, K. R. and Travis, R. (1995) 'A three-dimensional model of American foreign policy beliefs', *International Studies Quarterly*, 39:3, 313–331.

Clarke, H. D., Sanders, D., Stewart, M. C. and Whiteley, P. (2005) 'The issue agenda and voting', in P. Norris and C. Wlezien (eds), *Britain Votes 2005* (Oxford: Oxford University Press), 146–161.

Colomer, J. M. (2005) 'The general election in Spain, March 2004', *Electoral Studies*, 24, 149–156.

Converse, P. E. (1964) 'The nature of belief systems in mass publics', in D. Apter (ed.), *Ideology and Discontent* (New York: Free Press), 206–261.

Dalton, R. J. (1996) *Citizen Politics* (2nd edn) (Chatham, NJ: Chatham House).

Delli Carpini, M. X. and Keeter, S. (1996) *What Americans Know about Politics and Why It Matters* (New Haven, CT: Yale University Press).

Erskine, H. G. (1963) 'The polls: Exposure to international information', *Public Opinion Quarterly*, 27:4, 658–662.

Herrmann, R. K., Tetlock, P. E. and Visser, P. S. (1999) 'Mass public decisions to go to war: A cognitive-interactionist framework', *American Political Science Review*, 93:3, 553–571.

Holsti, O. R. (1997) *Public Opinion and American Foreign Policy* (Ann Arbor, MI: University of Michigan Press).

Huckfeldt, R., Levine, J., Morgan, W. and Sprague, J. (1999) 'Accessibility and the political utility of partisan and ideological orientations', *American Journal of Political Science*, 43:3, 888–911.

Hughes, B. (1978) *The Domestic Context of American Foreign Policy* (San Francisco, CA: Freeman).

Hurwitz, J. and Peffley, M. (1987) 'How are foreign policy attitudes structured? A hierarchical model', *American Political Science Review*, 81:4, 1099–1120.

Hurwitz, J. and Peffley, M. (1990) 'Public images of the Soviet Union: The impact on foreign policy attitudes', *Journal of Politics*, 52:1, 3–28.

Isernia, P., Juhász, Z. and Rattinger, H. (2002) 'Foreign policy and the rational public in comparative perspective', *Journal of Conflict Resolution*, 46:2, 201–224.

Jacobson, G. C. (2006) *A Divider, Not a Uniter* (New York: Pearson Longman).

Jentleson, B. W. (1992) 'The pretty prudent public: Post post-Vietnam American opinion on the use of military force', *International Studies Quarterly*, 36:1, 49–74.

Kahneman, D., Slovic, P. and Tversky, A. (1982) *Judgment under Uncertainty: Heuristics and Biases* (Cambridge: Cambridge University Press).

Knopf, J. (1998) 'How rational is the "rational public"?', *Journal of Conflict Resolution*, 42:5, 544–571.

Kuklinski, J. H. and Hurley, N. L. (1994) 'On hearing and interpreting political messages: A cautionary tale of citizen cue-taking', *Journal of Politics*, 56:3, 729–751.

Kuklinski, J. H. and Quirk, P. J. (2000) 'Reconsidering the rational public: Cognition, heuristics, and mass opinion', in A. Lupia, M. D. McCubbins and S. L. Popkin (eds), *Elements of Reason* (New York: Cambridge University Press), 153–182.

Kuklinski, J. H., Quirk, P. J., Jerit, J. and Rich, R. F. (2001) 'The political environment and citizen decision making: Information, motivation, and policy tradeoffs', *American Journal of Political Science*, 45:2, 410–424.

Lau, R. R. (1995) 'Information search during an election campaign: Introducing a process tracing methodology for political scientists', in M. Lodge and K. McGraw (eds), *Political Judgment* (Ann Arbor, MI: University of Michigan Press), 179–206.

Lau, R. R. and Redlawsk, D. P. (1997) 'Voting correctly', *American Political Science Review*, 91:3, 585–598.

Lau, R. R. and Redlawsk, D. P. (2001) 'Advantages and disadvantages of cognitive heuristics in political decision making', *American Journal of Political Science*, 45:4, 951–971.

Lau, R. R. and Redlawsk, D. P. (2006) *How Voters Decide* (New York: Cambridge University Press).

Lodge, M. and Hamill, R. (1986) 'A partisan schema for political information processing', *American Political Science Review*, 80, 505–519.

Lupia, A. and McCubbins, M. D. (1998) *The Democratic Dilemma* (Cambridge: Cambridge University Press).

Meernik, J. and Ault, M. (2001) 'Public opinion and support for US presidents' foreign policies', *American Politics Research*, 29:4, 352–373.

Mintz, A. (2003) 'Integrating cognitive and rational theories of foreign policy decision making: A poliheuristic perspective', in A. Mintz (ed.), *Integrating Cognitive and Rational Theories of Foreign Policy Decision Making* (New York: Palgrave Macmillan), 1–10.

Mintz, A. (2004) 'How do leaders make decisions? A poliheuristic perspective', *Journal of Conflict Resolution*, 48:1, 3–13.

Mintz, A., Redd, S. B. and Vedlitz, A. (2006) 'Can we generalize from student experiments to the real world in political science, military affairs, and international relations?', *Journal of Conflict Resolution*, 50:5, 757–776.

Page, B. I. and Shapiro, R. Y. (1992) *The Rational Public* (Chicago, IL: University of Chicago Press).

Peffley, M. and Hurwitz, J. (1992) 'International events and foreign policy beliefs', *American Journal of Political Science*, 36:2, 431–461.

Petty, R. E. and Cacioppo, J. T. (1986) *The Elaboration Likelihood Model of Persuasion* (New York: Academic Press).

Petty, R. E., Haugtvedt, C. P. and Smith, S. M. (1995) 'Elaboration as a determinant of attitude strength', in R. E. Petty and J. A. Krosnick (eds), *Attitude Strength: Antecedents and Consequences* (Mahwah, NJ: Lawrence Erlbaum), 93–130.

Pierce, R. (1999) 'Mass–elite issue linkages and the responsible party model of representation', in W. E. Miller, R. Pierce, J. Thomassen, R. Herrera, S. Holmberg, P. Esaiasson and B. Wessels (eds), *Policy Representation in Western Democracies* (Oxford: Oxford University Press), 9–32.

Popkin, S. L. (1991) *The Reasoning Voter* (Chicago, IL: University of Chicago Press).

Popkin, S. L. and Dimock, M. A. (2000) 'Knowledge, trust, and international reasoning', in A. Lupia, M. D. McCubbins and S. L. Popkin (eds), *Elements of Reason* (New York: Cambridge University Press), 214–248.

Rahn, W. (1995) 'Candidate evaluation in complex information environments', in M. Lodge and K. McGraw (eds), *Political Judgment* (Ann Arbor, MI: University of Michigan Press), 43–64.

Rose, R. and Mishler, W. (1998) 'Negative and positive party identification in post-communist countries', *Electoral Studies*, 17, 217–234.

Rosenau, J. N. (1961) *Public Opinion and Foreign Policy* (New York: Random House).

Seyd, P. and Whiteley, P. (1992) *Labour's Grass Roots* (Oxford: Clarendon).

Simon, H. (1982) *Models of Bounded Rationality* (Cambridge, MA: MIT Press).

Sniderman, P. M. (1993) 'The new look in public opinion research', in A. Finifter (ed.), *Political Science: The State of the Discipline II* (Washington DC: APSA), 219–246.

Sniderman, P. M., Brody, R. A. and Tetlock, P. E. (1991) *Reasoning and Choice* (Cambridge: Cambridge University Press).

Tourangeau, R., Rips, L. J. and Rasinski, K. (2000) *The Psychology of Survey Response* (Cambridge: Cambridge University Press).

Weisberg, H. F. (2005) 'The US presidential and congressional elections, November 2004', *Electoral Studies*, 24, 777–784.

Wittkopf, E. R. (1990) *Faces of Internationalism: Public Opinion and American Foreign Policy* (Durham, NC: Duke University Press).

YouGov (2003) 'Poll on Bush's visit, 20 November 2003', Available online at: http://www.yougov.co.uk/extranets/ygarchives/content/pdf/TEL020101039_3.pdf

Zaller, J. R. (1992) *The Nature and Origins of Mass Opinion* (Cambridge: Cambridge University Press).

doi: 10.1111/j.1467-856X.2009.00373.x   *BJPIR: 2009 VOL 11, 593–612*

The Transition to 'New' Social Democracy: The Role of Capitalism, Representation and (Hampered) Contestation

David J. Bailey

This article argues that existing accounts of the transformation from 'traditional' to 'new' social democracy has thus far only identified the contextual changes that have prompted this move. In doing so, they have failed to account for the motives of social democratic party actors in undertaking the transition to 'new' social democracy in response to those changes. The article draws upon a critical realist method, and Marxist and anti-representational theories, to conceptualise 'traditional' social democratic party relations as suffering from tensions between constituents' demands for decommodification, the attempt by party elites to contain (and thereby 'represent') those demands and the (in)compatibility of this process of containment with the need to recommodify social relations in the light of periodic crises in contemporary capitalism. It argues that these tensions explain the attempt by party elites to promote the move towards 'new' social democracy, the (eventual) acquiescence of party constituents to those attempts and the subsequent exit from social democratic constituencies which has resulted. The argument is made with reference to the British Labour Party and Social Democratic Party of Germany (SPD).

Keywords: social democracy; Labour Party; SPD; centre-left parties

Existing literature seeking to explain the transformation, by social democratic parties, from 'traditional' to 'new' (or 'Third Way') social democracy has tended to focus on either material processes such as the global extension and liberalisation of the international political economy (Gray 1996) and the fragmentation and/or erosion of the industrial working class within contemporary post-Fordist capitalism (Kitschelt 1994), or ideational convergence around neo-liberal norms (Hay 1999). However, these contextual changes cannot by themselves explain the decision by social democratic party actors to promote, and in most cases bring into effect, a transformation from 'traditional' to 'new' social democracy. Indeed, while 'traditional' social democratic parties may have experienced economic, political and/or ideological obstacles in recent decades, these do not, by themselves, explain the abandonment of faith in 'traditional' social democracy by social democratic party actors. Put differently, why have social democratic party actors not adopted a re-emboldened commitment to 'traditional' social democracy in an attempt to overcome the material and/or ideational adversities they face in realising their political and policy goals? In seeking to answer this question, the present article attempts to explain the adoption of 'new' social democracy by social democratic party actors in the light of the contextual changes identified within the existing literature.

Political Studies Association   © *2009 The Author. Journal compilation © 2009 Political Studies Association*

Defining 'Traditional' and 'New' Social Democracy

For the purposes of the present article, the following definitions will be used.

'Traditional' Social Democracy

Despite the use of a variety of terms—including 'revisionist' (Sassoon 1996), 'traditionalist' (Leggett 2007), 'classical' (Pierson 2001) and 'classic' (Thomson 2000)—there is a broad consensus within the literature that between 1945 and the mid-1970s there was, within most developed countries, a broad ideological position adopted by member parties of the Socialist International, which is referred to here as 'traditional' social democracy (for similar terminology, see Kitschelt 1994, 7; Hirst 1999, 94; Bailey 2005). This is an ideological commitment to pursue, through election to office, a gradual reform programme which includes Keynesian demand management of a (full-employment) capitalist economy and the redistribution of resources towards its core (working-class) constituency, particularly through the extension of both the welfare state and a progressive fiscal policy (Callaghan 2000, 11–18; Pierson 2001, 56–58; Przeworski 2001, 319–320). These aims were expressed by a party purporting to act in the interests of an electoral constituency centred around, but seeking to extend beyond, the industrial working class (Moschonas 2002, 215; for more detailed discussion of this definition, see also Bailey 2009, ch. 2).

'New' Social Democracy

In contrast, 'new' (Gamble and Wright 1999)—or 'Third Way' (Giddens 1998; Green-Pedersen and Van Kersbergen 2002)—social democracy accepts much of the neo-liberal critique of 'traditional' social democracy (Przeworski 2001, 320–322). This includes the need for balanced budgets, a focus upon low inflation in macro-economic policy, a reduction in the level of disincentivising income transfers, the limiting of economic intervention to the supply-side of the economy (in order for macroeconomic policy to facilitate (rather than temper) the role of the market) and 'the association between collective provision and bureaucratic inertia' (Sassoon 1996, 735; Thompson 1996; Thomson 2000, 156–157; Stammers et al. 2001, 36–37). Political intervention in the economy is focused on public service provisions that benefit the *national* interest (such as health and education), in contrast to those that are specifically in the interest of the working class (Thomson 2000, 157). Economic policy is geared towards ensuring the supply of a skilled and flexible labour force in order to ensure equality of opportunity, rather than equality of outcome, through the meritocratic effects of education and training (Sassoon 1996; Powell 2004).

In sum, the transformation from 'traditional' to 'new' social democratic parties has witnessed a move away from direct interference in the economy, away from an attempt to ease economic imperatives experienced by individuals and away from a focus on the redistribution of resources towards the working class. As such, the transformation to 'new' social democracy has witnessed social democratic parties ending (or considerably downscaling) their historical pursuit of the 'decommodification' of labour (on the importance of decommodification for 'traditional' social democracy, see Esping-Andersen 1990; Huo et al. 2008). Moreover, while national variation in the extent and form of this transition to 'new' social democracy clearly exists (Hall 2002), there is nevertheless a discernible trend towards 'new' social democracy which can be observed across social democratic parties (Volkens 2004). Indeed, this transition has also occurred in cases, such as Sweden, where 'traditional' social democracy was more deeply entrenched, although in those cases the abandonment of decommodification as a policy aim has been less thoroughgoing (Ryner 2004).

Globalisation, Neo-liberalism and the Decline of Social Democracy

Existing attempts to model this transition from 'traditional' to 'new' social democracy can be placed into one of two broad approaches. The first, materialist, approach views the transition from 'traditional' to 'new' social democracy as the result of changes in the contemporary (international) political economy. From this perspective, the shift to post-Fordist production techniques, the internationalisation of finance and trade, the shrinking of the organised manual working class and the diversity, flexibility and complexity of contemporary organisational practices have each reduced both the viability and the desirability of 'traditional' social democratic goals. This process, it is argued, has created a shift in the political opportunity structure faced by social democratic parties, which has resulted in a shift in the range of feasible policy options available to those parties. The new range of feasible alternatives includes training and education, gender and racial equality, citizens' rights and civil liberties, and efficiency-oriented market reforms which seek a more viable welfare state (Kitschelt 1994; Pontusson 1995; Giddens 1998; Klitgaard 2007; Merkel et al. 2008). Thus, Michael Klitgaard (2007, 173–174) claims that 'if social democratic strategists have reason to perceive particular policy problems as a threat to welfare state legitimacy, they may be prepared to implement market-type reforms if these are believed to prevent loss of legitimacy and declining welfare state support'. 'New' social democratic parties have therefore moved towards the promotion of those policies that remain feasible within the current (international) political economy, in order to remain electorally viable, and so that those more long-standing goals that remain practicable can continue to be implemented. This process is portrayed in Figure 1.

The second, 'ideational', approach to social democratic modernisation emerged in part as a reaction to the determinism of the 'materialist' account. Crucially, scholars within the ideational camp claim that, as political opportunity structures are themselves defined in part by the ideas held by members of a political community, they are invariably contestable and, therefore, mutable. As such, it is the *perception* that international economic constraints impinge upon social democratic parties' scope for activity within the post-Bretton Woods era (held by both social democratic voters and social democratic political actors) that determines political feasibility. Indeed, the constraints that result from the contemporary structure of the international political economy have been exaggerated by actors who are

Figure 1: Modernisation as the Result of Material Changes in the International Political Economy

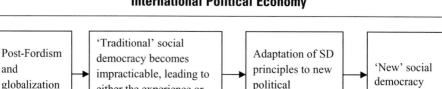

ideologically committed to the erosion of 'traditional' social democratic policies (Hay 2004 and 2006). For instance, Colin Hay (2006, 20) argues that 'the *idea* that globalization entails neo-liberalization has become something of a self-fulfilling prophecy and, as such, an *independent* driver of neo-liberalization in contemporary Europe' (emphases added). Thus, in discussing developments within the British Labour Party, Hay claims that it 'has sought to appeal to the pre-formulated sensitivities of the electorate, viewed as a fixed constraint to which policy appeals must be oriented ... making the party at least somewhat complicit in [Thatcherism's] dubious achievements' (Hay 1999, 67). According to this 'ideational' model, therefore, the transition to 'new' social democracy results from the internalisation, by social democratic actors themselves (be it party actors or social democratic voters), of a prevalent 'logic of no alternative' which has resulted in the absence of a viable alternative political programme (see Figure 2).

While this ideational account rightly points to the need to incorporate ideas in explaining the transition to 'new' social democracy, it nevertheless fails to explain why the 'new' social democratic response to this 'neo-liberal' ideational consensus occurred (rather than, for instance, an attempt to reverse the consensus). What we need, therefore, is to be able to explain the (neo-liberal) direction of social democratic ideas, while seeking to avoid a reintroduction of the determinism of the materialist approaches.

Method

The present article adopts a critical realist method (Bhaskar 1997 [1975] and 1998). This involves the development of relational theories which seek to understand and explain outcomes in terms of the structured relations between individuals. These relations are viewed as containing particular properties, or mechanisms, that are causally efficacious. Moreover, critical realism recognises that the effect of these properties/mechanisms might not be immediately perceptible, both because they interact with multiple other properties/mechanisms within an open system (and are therefore invariably manifested in a mediated form), and also because reality cannot be perceived other than through a mediating conceptual framework. As a result, the process whereby the real causal properties/mechanisms that constitute particular social relations are identified is an unavoidably conceptual process.

Figure 2: Modernisation as Ideational Adaptation to Neo-liberalism

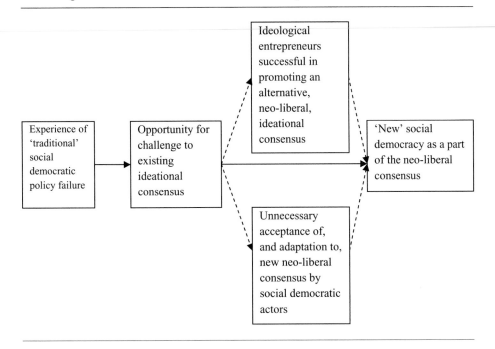

Accordingly, critical realism views social science as a process whereby real causal properties and social relations are conceptualised, and real social outcomes are explained in terms of those conceptualisations. In contrast to positivist tests of particular hypotheses, therefore, the critical realist method enables us 'to "grasp" or "see" empirical evidence of the existence of social objects, and the manner of their functioning' through the positing, identification and clarification of causal mechanisms, their effects and the processes through which they operate (López 2003, 78). It is this method of conceptualising social relations and causal mechanisms in order to produce increasingly plausible explanations for empirical outcomes that is employed in the present study.

A Critical Relational Theory of 'Traditional' Social Democratic Party Decline

The present article draws upon two theoretical approaches: Marxist theories of the capitalist economy, and anti-representational theories of representative-democratic political institutions. These are chosen due to their focus on social relations (and therefore their compatibility with a critical realist method) and for their critical focus on potential sources of failure and decline (which we are arguably witnessing in the transition from 'traditional' to 'new' social democracy (Thomson 2000, ch. 2)). As such, what follows is a critical relational theory of 'traditional' social democratic party decline.

© 2009 The Author. Journal compilation © 2009 Political Studies Association
BJPIR, 2009, 11(4)

The Marxist Critique of Social Democracy

The Marxist critique of 'traditional' social democracy views the attempt to manage, and thereby co-exist with, capitalism as an act that (indirectly or otherwise) consolidates capitalist relations of exploitation (Berman 2006, chs 2 and 3). Thus, social democratic strategy relies upon outcomes 'which the *state*, not the worker, *"calls into being"'*, and as a result the working class 'expresses its full consciousness that it neither rules nor is ripe for ruling!' (Marx 1978 [1875], 24, emphases in original) In seeking a co-existence with capitalism, therefore, 'traditional' social democracy fails to develop the revolutionary potential of the working class to transcend capitalist relations. Moreover, as capitalism is susceptible to recurrent crises—as capitalists exhaust opportunities for profit-making (for a good discussion, see Harvey 2006, 183–203)—the management of capitalist relations requires the attempt to resolve such crises. This is largely achieved through the expansion of the capital–labour relation, as 'crises of capitalism are less intense under conditions of rapid increase in the labour force' (Harvey 2006, 434), due to the increased opportunities for profitable investment which such expansion presents. This expansion, moreover, constitutes an attempt to commodify (or re-commodify) previously un-commodified areas of social life. Those seeking to manage capitalist relations, therefore, will experience recurrent pressures to promote the commodification, or re-commodification, of social life.

This pressure for commodification therefore threatens those social democratic achievements that have thus far had a de-commodifying effect upon society. Such pressures cannot, however, be presumed necessarily to lead to the erosion of social democratic achievements. The question we need to answer, therefore, is whether, faced with pressures for re-commodification, 'traditional' social democratic parties can, and/or will, be expected to act as effective vehicles of resistance. While empirical experience would suggest an answer in the negative, an inductive approach alone is insufficient. The article now turns to anti-representational critiques of (social democratic) political parties in seeking to obtain a more plausible response.

The Critique of Representation

As noted above, one of the defining elements of 'traditional' social democratic parties was their attempt to represent an 'enlarged coalition of the working class' (Moschonas 2002, 50–52), meaning a constituency centred upon the working class, but extending into the 'radical-liberal' sections of the middle class. In conceptualising this representative function, we can turn to an anti-representational branch of political theory which highlights the coercive nature of representation. Thus, Todd May (1994) identifies such an argument in the writings of both classical anarchists, particularly Bakunin and Kropotkin, and post-structuralists such as Gilles Deleuze. Thus, post-structuralist theories 'must be seen as carrying through the anarchist critique of representation', and 'post-structuralism has completed that critique by showing where political representation fails' (May 1994, 98).

Mikhail Bakunin, a key classical anarchist, claimed that representational political relations unavoidably empower one group of actors (the representative elite) and disempower another (the represented). Thus, he argues,

> *Irrespective of their democratic sentiments or intentions*, the rulers by virtue of
> their elevated position look down upon society as a sovereign regarding
> his subjects. But there can be no equality between the sovereign and the
> subject ... Political power means domination ... and subjects will naturally
> hate their rulers, who will then naturally be forced to subdue the people
> by even more oppressive measures, further curtailing their freedom
> (Bakunin 2002 [1870], 221, emphasis added).

The process of representation should therefore be considered a repressive and
coercive act. Adopting a similar argument, Deleuze argues that representation seeks
to posit sameness, or identity, between the represented and representative, despite
their inherent differences (Deleuze 2004 [1994], 67). As such, representation is
viewed as 'a site of transcendental illusion', which seeks 'the subordination of
difference to resemblance' (Deleuze 2004 [1994], 334–335). In denying difference,
therefore, representation is also viewed by post-structuralists as ultimately repressive (Buchanan 2008, 22–23). Thus, Deleuze (2004 [1994], 64) speaks of

> the politician, who is above all concerned to deny that which 'differs', so
> as to conserve or prolong an established historical order, or to establish a
> historical order which already calls forth in the world the forms of its
> representation.

Informed by such an account, therefore, we can conceptualise the representative
role of 'traditional' social democratic parties as an attempt by a representative party
elite to repress and contain the demands of the 'enlarged coalition of the working
class', in order that those demands might be 'represented'.

Conceptualising 'Traditional' Social Democratic Party Relations

Based on the foregoing discussion, the relations that constitute(d) 'traditional'
social democratic parties can be conceptualised in terms of a representative party
elite which seeks/sought to ensure the successful containment of the demands for
decommodification of its predominantly working-class constituency, while simultaneously seeking to manage capitalist relations of production (requiring the
recommodification of those same constituents in the light of periodic capitalist
crises). There existed, therefore, clear tensions at the centre of 'traditional' social
democratic party relations, between the demands of constituents for decommodification, the ability of party elites to contain those demands and the extent to which
these demands, and their partial realisation, were compatible with the necessary
expansion of capital–labour relations. Figure 3 seeks to depict these tensions, and
the process of social democratic party transformation they prompted. Schematically,
'traditional' social democratic parties initially experienced a period of relative stability, during which the representation/repression of their extended working-class
constituency was relatively straightforward as demands for decommodification
were partially realised and partially contained. However, capitalist crises created
pressures for the further recommodification of labour, which undermined social
democratic party elites' ability to contain the demands of their 'enlarged' working-
class constituency, thereby incentivising those elites to seek to dampen those
demands. This included the attempt to inculcate the (ideational) view that this

Figure 3: The Contestation and Transformation of 'New' Social Democracy: A Critical Relational Theory of Decline

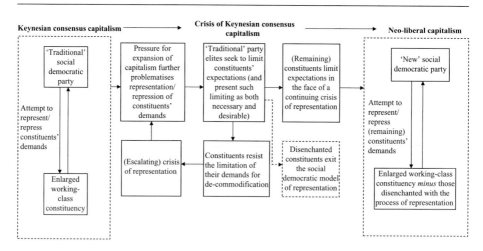

limiting of demands was both necessary and desirable. Moreover, constituents seeking to resist this process were faced with a choice between exit, acquiescence and party failure, with those opting to stay within social democratic party relations presumably preferring acquiescence to failure. Thus, while social democratic parties with a constituency more trenchantly committed to 'traditional' social democracy might be expected to experience greater resistance, and therefore a more prolonged process of transformation, the claim of the present article is that those parties will nevertheless ultimately be expected to move towards 'new' social democracy rather than face ongoing party failure.

This critical relational approach to the trajectory of social democratic transformation explains both the motives of social democratic party elites in promoting the abandonment of 'traditional' social democracy and their ability to realise this aim. In contrast to the materialist and ideational accounts outlined above, therefore, it considers the role and contestation of ideas, the motives of social democratic party elites in framing the dampening of demands for decommodification as necessary and desirable and the likely outcome of any contestation that may ensue.

The Cases of the British Labour Party and Social Democratic Party of Germany

The present article turns now to consider the recent history of British and German social democratic parties in an attempt to assess the ability of the critical relational account outlined above to provide a more plausible explanation for social democratic transformation than that provided by the existing literature (for a more thorough comparison of cases of social democratic party transformation, see Bailey 2009, ch. 3). In an attempt to aid comparison, the different claims of the materialist, ideational and critical relational accounts are outlined in Table 1. The cases are

Table 1: Alternative Conceptualisations of Social Democratic Party Transformation

	Materialist	Ideational	Critical relational
Initial catalyst	International political economic change produces a shift in the political opportunity structure	Policy failure prompts the emergence of a new ideational consensus within society	Inability for capitalism to expand problematises the representation/repression of 'traditional' social democratic constituents
Transition	Party elite attempts to change policy to meet new societal preferences	Party elite and constituents adopt the new (neo-liberal) ideational consensus	Party elite seeks to further repress and contain the demands of its 'enlarged working-class' constituency
Outcome	'New' social democratic parties as more representative of voter preferences	'New' social democratic parties as expressive of the new 'neo-liberal' ideational consensus	'New' social democratic parties as more repressive towards its 'enlarged working-class' constituency (alongside an exit from the party constituency by those disaffected with the social democratic mode of political activity)

chosen using a most-different systems design (Przeworski and Teune 1970), comparing, on the one hand, a 'traditional' social democratic party, located within a liberal market economy, which underwent a relatively rapid, wide-ranging and complete transition to 'new' social democracy (British Labour Party) with, on the other hand, a 'traditional' social democratic party, located within a co-ordinated market economy, which has only falteringly and in an incomplete way begun moves towards a 'new' social democratic agenda (Social Democratic Party of Germany). In doing so, we are able to assess whether the claims of the critical relational approach apply within contexts both more (UK) and less (Germany) amenable to neo-liberal transformation.

Social Democratic Party of Germany (SPD)

Initial Catalyst

There were three distinct events that prompted moves towards 'new' social democracy within the SPD: the period in opposition which began in 1982; the experience of a prolonged period of economic stagnation during the 1990s, alongside continued opposition; and the experience of ongoing, high and apparently irresolvable unemployment between 1998 and 2003 while in office.

© 2009 The Author. Journal compilation © 2009 Political Studies Association
BJPIR, 2009, 11(4)

The SPD's period in opposition, between 1982 and 1998, was prompted by the exit of the Free Democratic Party (FDP) from the governing coalition the two parties had formed since 1969. This was a decision made by the FDP leadership on the basis of an analysis that viewed the leadership of the SPD as too greatly encumbered by internal party opposition to implement (what it viewed as) necessary government spending cuts in the light of a contracting national economy and a public deficit of nearly 4 per cent of GNP (Giersch et al. 1992, 189–194; Meyer 2001, 76). Indeed, this view might well have been an accurate one, given that five of the 15 ministers in the SPD–FDP government between 1974 and 1978 were labour officials, and given that Schmidt and his ministers were increasingly forced to defend themselves against criticism from the German Confederation of Trade Unions (DGB) over the government's refusal to provide sufficient support to organised labour (Braunthal 1983, 113–122; Giersch et al. 1992, 156–157, 213–215). During its period in opposition, moreover, the SPD leadership sought, but was unable, to move the party away from a 'traditional' social democratic programme which they viewed as electorally unviable (Padgett 1993).

The second catalyst for reform came during the 1990s, while the SPD was still in opposition. German reunification led to a sharp rise in wages in the new Länder, which in turn resulted in job losses in the less productive former East Germany, a steep rise in unemployment across the German economy (from 4.2 per cent in 1991 to 9.2 per cent in 1997), and a significant rise in government debt (from 37.9 per cent in 1991 to 62.2 per cent in 1998). Under such conditions, firms were increasingly unable to identify opportunities for profitable investment, resulting in stagnant growth (GDP growth per annum averaged 1.3 per cent between 1995 and 1997, compared to 2.6 per cent for the Organisation for Economic Development and Co-operation (OECD) developed economies) (Manow and Seils 2000, 285–286; Huber and Stephens 2001, appendix; OECD.stat, http://stats.oecd.org/wbos/Index.aspx?usercontext=sourceoecd). These economic problems ultimately resulted in the SPD's selection of Gerhard Schröder as its business-friendly candidate for chancellor in the 1998 general election.

Finally, the third catalyst for change came in the light of ongoing pressure to reform the German economy following the SPD–Green coalition's narrow re-election in 2002. German per capita growth per annum between 1990 and 2000 was lower than all its major competitors except Japan and its growth in exports was lower than its four major competitors (US, UK, France and Japan), including in manufactured goods (where it was strongest), in part reflecting (and resulting from) a relatively low level of investment and foreign direct investment. As a result, the German system of labour market regulation, which makes job dismissal difficult, and its welfare regime, which encourages early retirement over redundancies and/or part-time work (both of which represented key 'traditional' social democratic achievements), were viewed as key factors producing an inflexible, low-growth economy (Kitschelt and Streeck 2003). Economic growth declined to 0.06 per cent in 2002 and unemployment remained above the government's target of 3.5 million unemployed. This, together with poor election results in 2002 and the inability of the corporatist Alliance for Jobs to propose any obvious alternative solutions prompted more substantive moves towards a 'new' social democratic programme from 2003 onwards, including the introduction of the Agenda 2010 reforms (Dyson 2005, 126; Merkel et al. 2008, 85).

Comparing the three alternative explanations presented in Table 1, it is the claim of this article that the critical relational account provides the most plausible explanation for these initial moves towards 'new' social democracy. Thus, it was the inability of the SPD leadership to manage the demands of its own constituency in 1982, and the impact that this pressure had upon attempts to restore growth to the national economy, that eventually led to (the appearance of) policy ineffectiveness and, ultimately, the end of the coalition government. Similarly, it was the inability of the party leadership to overcome internal opposition to the substantive revision of the party programme, alongside a stagnating economy, that in part explained the inability of the SPD to gain re-election between 1982 and 1998. Finally, it was experience of ongoing economic difficulties in the early 2000s that resulted in the more aggressive attempt by the Schröder leadership to move towards 'new' social democratic measures (in the face of internal party opposition) from 2003 onwards. Thus, while the materialist approach correctly identifies the apparent difficulties faced by social democratic party elites in presenting a viable economic programme to a post-Fordist electorate, it nevertheless fails to account for the representational problems associated with attempts to overcome these difficulties. Similarly, while the ideational account rightly points to the attempt by the SPD leadership to encourage its constituency to accept the necessity (and desirability) of the move towards 'new' social democracy, it nevertheless fails to identify the real material factors which influenced the party elite to undertake such aims.

Transition

Following its ejection from office in 1982, the SPD party elite sought (although largely failed) to ensure support for a moderation of policy demands across its constituency. For instance, after its 1987 election defeat, the SPD's internal review claimed that, 'so long as important sections of the electorate do not trust the SPD for the tasks of economic modernisation but only for ensuring that social safeguards are maintained it will be very difficult for us to build a majority' (quoted in Padgett 2003, 41). However, such analyses prompted further divisions between the party elite and its constituency. For example, in 1989 the SPD drew up a new Basic Programme, during which revisionists (grouped around Lafontaine) sought to introduce a commitment to more flexible working arrangements, but were successfully blocked by trade unionist opposition within the party (Padgett 1993).

The second attempt by the party elite to move towards 'new' social democracy witnessed Schröder becoming the SPD's candidate for chancellor in the 1998 general election. This move, however, was rather uncertain as Schröder sought *both* to support economic innovation and business *and* to commit the SPD to the reversal of welfare retrenchment and labour market liberalisation measures of the incumbent Kohl government (Meyer 2001, 80; Merkel et al. 2008, 71). This ambiguity was also reflected in the initial policies implemented by Schröder's Red–Green coalition government upon its election to office. For instance, its first budget included a reduction in corporate tax, although this was offset by a reduction in subsidies and a broadening of the tax base, thereby increasing the net tax burden on large corporations (Merkel et al. 2008, 75). However, following Lafontaine's resignation as finance minister in 1999, Schröder sought to adopt a more consistently liberal economic policy. This was a move initially marked by the publication of the now infamous Third Way/*Neue Mitte* document in 1999. In the same year, the government introduced an austerity programme which sought to cut pensions and unemployment benefits (Harlen 2002, 69). Following a series of poor regional election results and a hostile reception from many within the SPD, however, Schröder hesitated in his attempt at party transformation. In 2001, for instance, he rejected the report commissioned by the Alliance for Jobs due to its overly liberal approach to labour market regulation (Harlen 2002, 77).

Finally, as noted above, Agenda 2010 represented a clear break with previous policy, witnessing a turn towards a far more consistently 'new' social democratic position (Dyson 2005, 126). This largely focused on labour market flexibility and reducing non-wage labour costs. Thus, the Hartz reforms, which were at the core of Agenda 2010, would merge unemployment benefits with social welfare benefits, creating a new Basic Income for Job Seekers. This would reduce the level of benefit generosity, reduce entitlements to benefits by taking into consideration alternative sources of income available to the claimant (including a claimant's spouse's and parents' income) and increase conditionality upon efforts to secure employment (Kemmerling and Bruttel 2006).

In espousing this liberal message, Schröder sought repeatedly to emphasise the economic necessity of his proposed reforms, particularly the way in which they could salvage those 'traditional' social democratic goals that remained feasible: 'we must ensure that the macroeconomic risks do not derail the entire world economy, especially to the detriment of the poor and poorest of the world'. Moreover, Agenda 2010 would 'ensure that equity is maintained between the generations' and produce 'a healthy welfare state and a functioning social market economy' (Schröder 2003). Finally, the reforms represented 'the right approach to retaining the substance of the social security system under radically changed international economic conditions' (quoted in *Financial Times*, 2 May 2003). However, resistance grew within the SPD constituency, and particularly among the organised labour section of that constituency, with trade union opposition resulting in mass demonstrations and the chairman of the DGB describing Agenda 2010 as the 'dismantling of the welfare state' (quoted in *Financial Times*, 23 May 2003). Eventually opposition within the party led to an Extraordinary Party Congress being called for June 2003, prior to which there was considerable speculation that the Agenda 2010 reforms would be overturned. However, in threatening to resign should the Congress vote against him, Schröder managed to turn the vote into a more general question of his role as party leader. This, combined with fears that internal instability would be electorally damaging to the party, convinced the majority of SPD members to support Schröder within the Congress. Thus, faced with the option of acquiescence or party failure, the party membership ultimately opted for acquiescence and maintained their support for Schröder. As a result, the Extraordinary Party Congress adopted a resolution stating that Agenda 2010 represented the best possible alternative available to the SPD: 'Merely to defend the status quo would be to jeopardize what has been achieved so far. Changing the status quo through comprehensive innovation, on the other hand, means opening up new prospects for greater prosperity, freedom and cohesion (SPD 2003, 2).

Thus, in the terms of the critical relational theory outlined above, in the light of an ongoing capitalist crisis and the problems it created for the SPD party elite's attempt at representation, that elite sought to inculcate the view among its constituency that moves towards 'new' social democracy were both necessary and desirable. Moreover, while resistance to this claim occurred, faced with the choice between acquiescence and party failure, constituents ultimately opted for the former.

Outcome

The adoption, by the June 2003 Extraordinary Party Congress, of the resolution welcoming Agenda 2010 can be considered the point at which the SPD completed its transition to 'new' social democracy. Thus, in proceeding to form a Grand Coalition as a junior partner with the Christian Democratic Union/Christian Social Union (CDU/CSU) following the 2005 general election, the SPD adopted a coalition agreement that was considerably to the right of the preceding 2002 agreement on economic policy, and adopted (under SPD finance minister Peer Steinbrück) a policy firmly committed to fiscal balance (Paterson and Sloam 2006, 242; Debus 2008, 219). Following this Extraordinary Party Congress, however, the SPD experienced a decline in electoral support, a decline in membership and the emergence of a splinter party, the Alternative for Work and Social Justice (WASG) (which has since merged with the Party of Democratic Socialism (PDS) to become the Left Party) (Debus 2008, 206). Thus, having secured formal party backing for his 'new' social democratic reforms, Schröder was faced with considerable exit from his social democratic constituency. Electoral support fell by 8 per cent to 19.6 per cent in the Bavarian Land elections in September 2003, and party membership was estimated to have fallen by 23,000 between January and June 2003, all of which was widely viewed as a result of Agenda 2010. While the SPD leadership sought to convince the public of the necessity of economic reforms, such moves apparently failed to appease constituents' dissatisfaction. Elections to Hamburg's Land elections on 29 February 2004 witnessed the worst SPD performance since 1945, handing victory to the CDU in a traditionally left-leaning city. This result was perceived across the board as part of the continued reaction against Agenda 2010, with Münterfering himself acknowledging that 'we have made mistakes in *explaining* our reform agenda' (quoted in *The Independent*, 1 March 2004, emphasis added). This trend was repeated in June, with the SPD gaining only 21.5 per cent of the national vote in EP elections and 14.5 per cent in Thuringa Land elections. Further, on 22 May 2005 the SPD lost the North Rhine Westphalia elections to its CDU opponents by an 8 per cent margin, losing 5.7 per cent of its vote share for the region (with the WASG gaining 2.2 per cent). In response, Schröder announced an early general election in which the SPD's vote declined by 4.2 per cent from the 2002 election and the Left party gained 8.7 per cent of the vote (more than double the 2002 performance of the PDS (Pulzer 2006)).

In contrast with alternative accounts, therefore, the critical relational approach is able to explain both the adoption by the SPD of a 'new' social democratic programme *and* the subsequent exit from the party constituency that occurred. While the materialist and ideational accounts both view the process of transformation as one of adaptation, therefore, it is the merit of the critical relational approach that it is also able to account for the exit from party relations which resulted from the increased repression characterising 'new' social democracy.

British Labour Party

Initial Catalyst

In the case of the British Labour Party, the initial catalyst for the transformation to 'new' social democracy can be traced back to the period in office between 1974 and 1979, during which it proved unable to achieve a successful balance between the demands of its core constituency and the requirements of the British capitalist economy. Thus, following a fall in GDP by 2.5 per cent in 1974, the government chose to implement major spending cuts (of nearly £1 billion) in its April 1975 budget, including reductions in subsidies for nationalised industries, food and housing (Coates 1980, 13–24). This was followed by a flat-rate £6 wage rise limit, further public expenditure cuts and a further restriction in wage rises in 1976. As these measures could not convince international currency markets that the British capitalist economy, and therefore sterling, represented a profitable investment opportunity, the Callaghan government was famously forced to introduce a further round of cuts in July 1976, and again in September when it applied to the International Monetary Fund (IMF) for an emergency loan. These measures each represented an attempt to recommodify labour in Britain in an attempt to reverse economic decline. However, each of the measures also exacerbated tensions between the party leadership and its constituency. In 1977 the trade union leadership was increasingly unable to maintain its support for the government's ongoing attempts at wage restraint, seeing, for instance, the Transport and General Workers Union (TGWU) conference reject General Secretary Jack Jones' recommendation for a waiting period of 12 months between pay-rise claims (Holmes 1985, 109–110). Similarly, in 1978 the government's 5 per cent pay limit was immediately broken when an industrial dispute at Ford settled for 15 per cent, prompting a series of industrial disputes in which workers sought to catch up on previous pay claims. This 1978–79 'winter of discontent' witnessed strike numbers rise from 1 million to 4.5 million (Rhodes 2000, 35), and left the Labour government unable to contain successfully the demands of its constituency.

As is well known, once out of office in 1979 the Labour Party experienced a radicalisation that witnessed the left, led by Tony Benn, successfully mobilising around three interconnected goals: internal party democracy through the ascendant Campaign for Labour Party Democracy (CLPD); national economic democracy in the form of a political-economic programme which came to be known as the Alternative Economic Strategy (AES); and withdrawal from the European Community (Seyd 1987). The result of these developments, however, was a major defeat in the 1983 general election, which witnessed the Labour party gain only 27.6 per cent of the vote (its lowest since 1918), and lose 60 seats in the process. This in turn resulted in the extended period in opposition that eventually witnessed

Tony Blair's election as party leader on 21 June 1994, at which point the party moved rapidly towards a 'new' social democratic programme. Perhaps the most immediate events leading to the transformation to 'new' social democracy, therefore, were the two consecutive electoral defeats, in 1987 and 1992, both of which occurred despite significant attempts by the party leadership to moderate party policy following the 1983 defeat. It was these defeats that ultimately enabled Blair to gain ascendance within the Labour party.

The merit of the critical relational approach in considering factors that prompted the British Labour party's move towards 'new' social democracy, therefore, is that it highlights the incompatibility between the requirements of the British capitalist economy and those of the maintenance of a 'traditional' social democratic constituency. As such, it can explain the crisis in party relations that occurred, both during the 1974–79 government and between 1979 and 1983, as a result of the attempts by the party elite to successfully manage British capitalist relations. In contrast, the materialist approach highlights policy failure, without accounting for internal party discord, while the ideational approach points towards a new 'neo-liberal' ideational consensus, which was markedly absent among 'traditional' social democratic constituents during this period.

Transition

The Labour party's transition to 'new' social democracy lasted from 1983, with the election of Neil Kinnock as the first modernising party leader, to 1995, when new party leader, Tony Blair, was able to acquire the assent of the Party Conference to the adoption of the new Clause IV of the party constitution. Throughout this transition there occurred an observable attempt by the party leadership to dampen constituent demands for decommodifying policies. Thus, beginning with Kinnock's attack on the Militant Tendency within the Labour Party at the Party Conference of 1985, all potential opponents to the moderation of party policy were classified as members of the 'hard left' in an attempt to ostracise and stigmatise dissent within the party (Panitch and Leys 2001, 227). Following the 1987 general election defeat, moreover, the party leadership undertook a concerted effort to downscale policy ambitions with regard to the interventionist and redistributive aims of the party's economic policy. Thus, in launching the policy review process, comprising seven policy review groups, the party leadership (and particularly the leadership office) took a firm hand in steering the party towards embracing much of the neo-liberal critique of 'traditional' social democracy, particularly the view that the market was a better allocator of resources than the state (Taylor 1997; Motta and Bailey 2007, 123). For instance, in the 1990 policy review document, *Looking to the Future*, the party stated: 'We welcome and endorse the efficiency and realism which markets can provide' (Labour Party 1990, 6). Similarly, in seeking to highlight the necessity with which such views should be held, the Labour Party leadership was successful in espousing the view that 'In very many areas of the economy ... the market and competition are *essential* in meeting the demands of the consumer, promoting efficiency and stimulating innovation, and *often the best means* of securing all the myriad, incremental changes which are needed to take the economy forward' (Labour Party 1989, quoted in Shaw 1993, 119, emphases

added). Further still, in advancing the case for reduced state provisions for traditional social democratic constituents, Blair repeatedly argued for the undesirability
and/or impossibility of maintaining a 'traditional' social democratic commitment to
state-led decommodification of the economy:

> *in a global economy* the old ways won't do. Of course a fair tax system is
> right. But really a life on benefit—dependent on the state—is *not what most
> people want*. They want independence, dignity, self-improvement, a
> chance to earn and get on (Blair 1996, 292–293, emphases added).

The process of transition, in the case of the British Labour Party, therefore, was
characterised by the promotion, by the party leadership, of the view that 'new' social
democracy was both necessary and desirable. This observation has already been very
effectively made by those adopting an ideational approach (Watson and Hay 2003).
However, the critical relational account of these developments is also able to explain
the motives of the party elite in their attempt to reconcile the now moderated demands
of their constituency with the pressures for re-commodification being exerted by the
capitalist economic context within which they were located. Thus, following the 1983
general election defeat, the view that ideological moderation was necessary was
increasingly accepted by the Labour party's grass-roots membership. This allowed the
party leadership to draw upon an anxiety that already existed among members of the
Labour party left—'that the rank and file of the labour movement do not want to put
at risk the survival (or, by implication, the possibility) of a Labour government'—in
order to ensure the moderation of constituents' ambitions (Panitch and Leys 2001,
175). As a result, internal discussion and dissent were often effectively silenced, in the
name of maintaining representational credibility, with arguments such as: 'You will
have a ready ear in the media to attack the Labour government. But I will tell the
Labour Party where that leads. It leads to twenty years of Tory government' (Blair, NEC
meeting, 17 November 1997, quoted in Davies 2001, 35; see also Motta and Bailey
2007).

Outcome

The Labour party leadership under Blair was largely successful in its attempt to
moderate constituents' demands and steer the party towards the promotion of
recommodifying public policies. As already noted, this was marked by the adoption
by the 1995 Extraordinary Party Conference of the new Party Constitution, and
particularly the new Clause IV, which committed the party to 'a dynamic economy
... the enterprise of the market and the rigour of competition'. As a result, since
entering office in 1997 the Labour Party leadership has implemented a policy
agenda in which 'minimal-provision standards are far lower [than other social
democratic governments], redistribution has no priority'. Moreover, 'in most
instances New Labour favoured private-sector solutions. The understanding of the
state is minimalist and liberal' (Merkel et al. 2008, 66).

However, signs of malaise among the core party constituency have emerged
as a result of the transformation to 'new' social democracy. The Labour Party
experienced a decline in support between the elections of 1997 and 2005, from
43 per cent of the vote in 1997 to 35 per cent in 2005. Although this might be

understandable following eight years in office, it occurred alongside a more serious decline in electoral turnout which led to the Labour Party's share of the electoral support of the entire electorate (including non-voters) declining from 30.8 per cent in 1997, through 24.18 per cent in 2001, to 21.6 per cent in 2005. Indeed, calculated in these terms, the 2005 general election victory saw the Labour Party gain only slightly above the total electoral support that it achieved in 1983 (20.1 per cent), and considerably lower than it did in 1979 (28.1 per cent). The extent to which this decline in total support can be explained in terms of the transformation from 'traditional' to 'new' social democracy can be inferred from data examining voters' perceptions. Most notably, the ability of the Labour Party to mobilise voter interest in areas typically associated with decommodifying public policies appears to have declined considerably. For instance, Harold Clarke et al. (2006, 5) show how voter interest in social services, an area in which the Labour Party is traditionally able to out-compete the Conservative party, has declined from 38 per cent in 2001 to 25 per cent in 2005 (measured in terms of those viewing health and education as the most important issues facing the country). As a result, a number of commentators argued that, rather than being able to appeal to the British electorate on the basis of its policy programme, the Labour Party was only able to win the 2005 general election as a result of the unpopularity and perceived ineffectiveness of the Conservative opposition (Clarke et al. 2006; Quinn 2006). Similar trends can also be witnessed among the party membership. Thus, Labour Party membership rose significantly up until 1997. However, following the Labour Party's period in office, and particularly since the early 2000s, membership levels have consistently fallen, from 405,000 in 1997 to their lowest ever level of 176, 891 in 2007 (Kirkup and Prince 2008).

In contrast to existing materialist or ideational approaches, therefore, the critical relational approach is able to explain *both* the ability of the Labour party leadership to oversee a move towards a 'new' social democratic programme *and* the subsequent apparent disaffection and exit from party relations by significant sections of the party constituency which characterised much of the post-1997 experience within the Labour party (due to the increased focus on repression and recommodification of the party during its 'new' social democratic stage).

Conclusion

Existing approaches to the transformation from 'traditional' to 'new' social democracy rightly identify the impact of material and ideational changes upon the contexts facing social democratic actors. They are unable, however, to account for the transition to 'new' social democracy which occurred in response. This article has sought to draw upon Marxist and anti-representational critiques of 'traditional' social democratic parties to derive an explanation for their failure. In particular, the article argues that the concern of 'traditional' social democratic party elites was to contain the demands of their predominantly working-class constituents within a capitalist economic context, and that by implication those constituents who consented to such a process of containment could not be expected to develop the potential to challenge those capitalist relations within which they were based. As such, once capitalism required the recommodification of existing social relations, 'traditional' social democratic party elites sought to secure the acquiescence of their constituency to a *further* limiting of their demands. Moreover, given that the alternatives available to social democratic constituents were exit, acquiescence or party failure, those constituents who chose to remain within social democratic party relations ultimately chose (and/or will choose) acquiescence over failure. Thus, while not denying the importance of contestation and ideas, it is the claim of this article that the result of the process of contestation, and the ideas that eventually emerge(d), ultimately witnessed the adoption of 'new' social democracy due to the properties of social democratic party relations themselves. While the pace and extent of the transition to 'new' social democracy might vary across national cases, therefore, the article argues for the unlikelihood of sustaining (or returning to) 'traditional' social democracy in the longer term.

Acknowledgements

The author acknowledges the helpful comments of Sara Motta, Colin Hay, Philippe Marlière, Lasse Thomassen, Neil Robinson, Stephen Gill, the two anonymous reviewers, and the editorial advice of Adam David Morton.

About the Author

David J. Bailey, Lecturer in Political Science, Department of Political Science and International Studies, University of Birmingham, Edgbaston, Birmingham B15 2TT, UK, email: *d.j.bailey@bham.ac.uk*

Bibliography

Bailey, D. J. (2005) 'Obfuscation through integration: Legitimating "new" social democracy in the European Union', *Journal of Common Market Studies*, 43:1, 13–35.

Bailey, D. J. (2009) *The Political Economy of European Social Democracy: A Critical Realist Approach* (London: Routledge).

Bakunin, M. (2002 [1870]) 'Representative government and universal suffrage', in S. Dolgoff (ed.), *Bakunin on Anarchism* (London: Black Rose Books), 218–224.

Berman, S. (2006) *The Primacy of Politics: Social Democracy and the Making of Europe's Twentieth Century* (Cambridge: Cambridge University Press).

Bhaskar, R. (1997 [1975]) *A Realist Theory of Science* (2nd edn) (London: Verso).

Bhaskar, R. (1998) *The Possibility of Naturalism: A Philosophical Critique of the Contemporary Human Sciences* (3rd edn) (London: Routledge).

Blair, T. (1996) *New Britain: My Vision of a Young Country* (London: Fourth Estate).

Braunthal, G. (1983) *The West German Social Democrats, 1969–1982: Profile of a Party in Power* (Colorado: Westview).

Buchanan, I. (2008) 'Power, Theory and Praxis', in I. Buchanan and N. Thoburn (eds), *Deleuze and Politics* (Edinburgh: Edinburgh University), 13–34.

Callaghan, J. (2000) *The Retreat of Social Democracy* (Manchester: Manchester University Press).

Clarke, H., Sanders, D., Stewart, M. and Whiteley, P. (2006) 'Taking the bloom off New Labour's rose: Party choice and voter turnout in Britain, 2005', *Journal of Elections Public Opinion and Parties*, 16:1, 3–36.

Coates, D. (1980) *Labour in Power? A Study of the Labour Government, 1974–1979* (London: Longman).

Davies, L. (2001) *Through the Looking Glass: A Dissenter inside New Labour* (London: Verso).

Debus, M. (2008) 'Unfulfilled promises? German social democrats and their policy positions at the federal and state level between 1994 and 2006', *Journal of Elections Public Opinion and Parties*, 18:2, 201–224.

Deleuze, G. (2004 [1994]) *Difference and Repetition* (trans. P. Patton) (London: Continuum).

Dyson, K. (2005) 'Economic policy management: Catastrophic equilibrium, tipping points and crisis interventions', in S. Green and W. E. Paterson (eds), *Governance in Contemporary Germany: The Semisovereign State Revisited* (Cambridge: Cambridge University Press), 115–137.

Esping-Andersen, G. (1990) *The Three Worlds of Welfare Capitalism* (Cambridge: Polity).

Gamble, A. and Wright, T. (1999) 'Introduction: The new social democracy', in A. Gamble and T. Wright (eds), *The New Social Democracy* (Oxford: Blackwell), 1–9.

Giddens, A. (1998) *The Third Way: The Renewal of Social Democracy* (Cambridge: Polity Press).

Giersch, H., Paqué, K. H. and Schmieding, H. (1992) *The Fading Miracle: Four Decades of Market Economy in Germany* (Cambridge: Cambridge University Press).

Gray, J. (1996) *After Social Democracy—Politics, Capitalism and the Common Life* (London: Demos).

Green-Pedersen, C. and Van Kersbergen, K. (2002) 'The politics of the "Third Way": The transformation of social democracy in Denmark and the Netherlands', *Party Politics*, 8:5, 507–524.

Hall, P. A. (2002) 'The comparative political economy of the "Third Way" ', in O. Schmidtke (ed.), *The Third Way Transformation of Social Democracy: Normative Claims and Policy Initiatives in the 21st Century* (Aldershot: Ashgate), 31–48.

Harlen, C. M. (2002) 'Schroeder's economic reforms: The end of reformstau?', *German Politics*, 11:1, 61–80.

Harvey, D. (2006) *The Limits to Capital* (new and fully updated edn) (London: Verso).

Hay, C. (1999) *The Political Economy of New Labour: Labouring under False Pretences?* (Manchester: Manchester University Press).

Hay, C. (2004) 'The normalizing role of rationalist assumptions in the institutional embedding of neo-liberalism', *Economy and Society*, 33:4, 500–527.

Hay, C. (2006) 'What's globalization got to do with it? Economic interdependence and the future of European welfare states', *Government and Opposition*, 41:1, 1–22.

Hirst, P. (1999) 'Has globalisation killed social democracy?', in A. Gamble and T. Wright (eds), *The New Social Democracy* (Oxford: Blackwell), 85–96.

Holmes, M. (1985) *The Labour Government, 1974–1979: Political Aims Economic Reality* (London: Macmillan).

Huber, E. and Stephens, J. D. (2001) *Development and Crisis of the Welfare State: Parties and Policies in Global Markets* (Chicago, IL: University of Chicago Press).

Huo, J., Nelson, M. and Stephens, J. D. (2008) 'Decommodification and activation in social democratic policy: Resolving the paradox', *Journal of European Social Policy*, 18:1, 5–20.

Kemmerling, A. and Bruttel, O. (2006) ' "New politics" in German labour market policy? The implications of the recent Hartz reforms for the German welfare state', *West European Politics*, 29:1, 90–112.

Kirkup, J. and Prince, R. (2008) 'Labour party membership falls to lowest level since it was founded in 1900', *Daily Telegraph*, 30 July 2008.

Kitschelt, H. (1994) *The Transformation of European Social Democracy* (Cambridge: Cambridge University Press).

Kitschelt, H. and Streeck, W. (2003) 'From stability to stagnation: Germany at the beginning of the twenty-first century', *West European Politics*, 26:4, 1–34.

Klitgaard, M. B. (2007) 'Why are they doing it? Social democracy and market-oriented welfare state reforms', *West European Politics*, 30:1, 172–194.

Leggett, W. (2007) 'British social democracy beyond New Labour: Entrenching a progressive consensus', *British Journal of Politics & International Relations*, 9:3, 346–364.

López, J. (2003) 'Critical realism: The difference it makes, in theory', in J. Cruickshank (ed.), *Critical Realism: The Difference it Makes* (London: Routledge), 75–89.

Manow, P. and Seils, E. (2000) 'Adjusting badly: The German welfare state, structural change, and the open economy', in F. W. Scharpf and V. A. Schmidt (eds), *Welfare and Work in the Open Economy: Volume II. Diverse Responses to Common Challenges* (Oxford: Oxford University Press), 264–307.

Marx, K. (1978 [1875]) *Critique of the Gotha Programm* (Moscow: Progress Publishers).

May, T. (1994) *The Political Philosophy of Poststructuralist Anarchism* (Pennsylvania: Pennsylvania State University Press).

Merkel, W., Petring, A., Henkes, C. and Egle, C. (2008) *Social Democracy in Power: The Capacity to Reform* (London: Routledge).

Meyer, T. (2001) 'From Godesberg to the Neue Mitte: The new social democracy in Germany', in A. Giddens (ed.), *The Global Third Way Debate* (Cambridge: Polity), 74–85.

Moschonas, G. (2002) *In the Name of Social Democracy: The Great Transformation: 1945 to the Present* (London: Verso).

Motta, S. C. and Bailey, D. J. (2007) 'Neither pragmatic adaptation nor misguided accommodation: Modernization as domination in the Chilean and British left', *Capital and Class*, 92, 107–136.

Padgett, S. (1993) 'The German social democrats: A redefinition of social democracy or bad Godesberg mark II', in R. Gillespie and W. E. Paterson (eds), *Rethinking Social Democracy in Western Europe* (London: Frank Cass), 20–38.

Padgett, S. (2003) 'Germany: Modernising the left by stealth', *Parliamentary Affairs*, 56:1, 38–57.

Panitch, L. and Leys, C. (2001) *The End of Parliamentary Socialism: From New Left to New Labour* (2nd edn) (London: Verso).

Labour Party (1990) *Looking to the Future* (London: Labour Party).

Paterson, W. and Sloam, J. (2006) 'Is the left alright? The SPD and the renewal of European social democracy', *Germany Politics*, 15:3, 233–248.

Pierson, C. (2001) *Hard Choices: Social Democracy in the Twenty-First Century* (Cambridge: Polity Press).

Pontusson, J. (1995) 'Explaining the decline of European social democracy: The role of structural economic change', *World Politics*, 47:4, 495–533.

Powell, M. (2004) 'Social democracy in Europe: Renewal or retreat?', in G. Bonoli and M. Powell (eds), *Social Democratic Party Policies in Contemporary Europe* (London: Routledge), 1–20.

Przeworski, A. (2001) 'How many ways can be third?', in A. Glyn (ed.), *Social Democracy in Neoliberal Times* (Oxford: Oxford University Press), 312–333.

Przeworski, A. and Teune, H. (1970) *The Logic of Comparative Social Inquiry* (New York: Wiley).

Pulzer, P. (2006) 'Germany votes for deadlock: The federal election of 2005', *West European Politics*, 29:3, 560–572.

Quinn, T. (2006) 'Choosing the least-worst government: The British general election of 2005', *West European Politics*, 29:1, 169–178.

Rhodes, M. (2000) 'Restructuring the British welfare state: Between domestic constraints and global imperatives', in F. W. Scharpf and V. A. Schmidt (eds), *Welfare and Work in the Open Economy: Volume II. Diverse Responses to Common Challenges* (Oxford: Oxford University Press), 19–68.

Ryner, J. M. (2004) 'Neo-liberalization of social democracy: The Swedish case', *Comparative European Politics*, 2:1, 97–119.

Sassoon, D. (1996) *One Hundred Years of Socialism: The West European Left in the Twentieth Century* (London: Fontana Press).

Schröder, G. (2003) 'Courage for peace and courage for change', speech to the German Bundestag, 14 March.

Seyd, P. (1987) *The Rise and Fall of the Labour Left* (Basingstoke: Macmillan).

Shaw, E. (1993) 'Towards renewal? The British Labour party's policy review', *West European Politics*, 16:1, 112–132.

SPD (2003) 'The courage to reform', Resolution passed by the Extraordinary Party Congress on 1 June 2003 in Berlin.

Stammers, N. (2001) 'Social Democracy and Global Governance', in L. Martell et al. (eds), *Social Democracy: Global and National Perspectives* (Basingstoke: Palgrave), 27–48.

Taylor, G. R. (1997) *Labour's Renewal? The Policy Review and Beyond* (London: Macmillan).

Thompson, N. (1996) 'Supply side socialism: The political economy of New Labour', *New Left Review*, 216, 37–54.

Thomson, S. (2000) *The Social Democratic Dilemma: Ideology, Governance and Globalization* (London: Macmillan).

Volkens, A. (2004) 'Policy changes of European social democrats, 1945–1998', in G. Bonoli and M. Powell (eds), *Social Democratic Party Policies in Contemporary Europe* (London: Routledge), 21–42.

Watson, M. and Hay, C. (2003) 'The discourse of globalisation and the logic of no alternative: Rendering the contingent necessary in the political economy of New Labour', *Policy and Politics*, 31:3, 289–305.

doi: 10.1111/j.1467-856X.2009.00384.x   *BJPIR: 2009 VOL 11, 613–633*

Labour and Epistemic Communities: The Case of 'Managed Migration' in the UK

Alex Balch

How do new ideas flow through networks to reframe policy questions, and what role is played by the growing world of think tanks and policy experts? This article takes the remarkable shift in UK labour migration policy since 2000 and demonstrates how policy was redesigned by networks of actors working between and within the worlds of think tanks and government, including the Prime Minister's Policy and Innovation Unit (PIU), the Treasury, the Home Office and the Institute for Public Policy Research (IPPR). The article shows how different kinds of ideas and knowledge flowed through different actors and networks to influence the reframing of policy, using the epistemic communities hypothesis (ECH) as a theoretical framework for the analysis.

Keywords: immigration policy; epistemic communities; Labour party; managed migration

Introduction

This article takes the opportunity to assess the forms and means by which ideas and knowledge play a role in policy change in the UK by looking at a particular area—labour migration[1]—over a decade of policy development: 1997–2007. The central puzzle is about the adoption of a new policy on labour migration under the narrative of 'managed migration' and how to explain this change, its timing and its tempo. Of particular use here is the epistemic communities hypothesis (ECH) as outlined by Peter Haas (1992, 2001 and 2004), which provides a framework that proposes a role for experts in the change of policy addressing why, when, how and with what effects governments turn to expertise.

The choice of approach is driven by gaps in our understanding of immigration policy, particularly with respect to the role of ideas and expertise. The policy area of labour migration is one that has experienced dramatic change since the late 1990s as the UK has lurched from a country struggling to keep a lid on immigration to one opening its arms to extraordinary levels of inward flows. Aspects of immigration policies have traditionally provided a strong explanatory challenge for theoretical accounts, which have tended to focus on outcomes and a narrow range of variables exogenous to the political process, betraying an under-conceptualisation of that process. International accounts of policy, for example, have emphasised the role of business interests (Freeman 1995), internationalisation and states' reduced control

over borders (Soysal 1994; Sassen 1996) or the liberal influence of courts and bureaucracies (Guiraudon 2000a), but these offer little understanding of the policy-making process, and do not offer a good fit with the UK, long described as a 'deviant' case (Freeman 1994). We know, for example, that the UK has relatively weak courts, and has retained its own border regime within the EU (in contrast to Schengen states). In addition, political elites in the UK are known to enjoy relative isolation from the 'organised public' and lobbying over immigration and conduct policy in a relatively autonomous way (Statham and Geddes 2006, 266).

Some help is offered by those that emphasise national paradigms in terms of the links between identity politics and migration policies (Brubaker 1992; Hollifield 1994). In the case of the UK, Randel Hansen's excellent study of post-war immigration counters some of the weaknesses of traditional accounts. By bringing political processes back into the analysis, Hansen was able to reject the thesis that politicians were attempting to 'whitewash' Britain (Paul 1997), arguing strongly that their actions could be considered responsible issue management under the constraints of the peculiar implications associated with the post-war dismantling of empire (Hansen 2000). Building on Hansen's approach and looking at the 'new era' of policy post-2000 I reject the thesis that the UK 'lost control' over immigration policy, leading to unprecedented levels of inflows. Instead I argue that policy was redesigned and redeveloped by a government in the thrall of new ideas about governance, with epistemic communities assuming a more central role in policy change. Furthermore, by adopting this perspective, the article addresses the rise and rise of think tanks and 'policy experts' in the sphere of immigration, which to date has been largely ignored by those seeking to explain policy change.

I argue that research on immigration has been driven by the interest in (suboptimal) outcomes, which has created what could be described as an epistemic 'gap' into which political processes are assumed, subsumed or reified (e.g. Castles 2004), and where the political sociology of policy-making is relatively unknown (Sciortino 2000). This gap extends to our understanding of the kinds of ideas and knowledge that drive policy. There has been some work done on how research fits with policy in the field of immigration, which confirms a range of problems (Brans et al. 2004; Martiniello and Florence 2005). The work of Christina Boswell should be mentioned here as she has looked in detail at the legitimising and instrumental functions of knowledge utilisation in debates over immigration in the EU (Boswell 2008) and in the UK between 2002 and 2004, and the political dilemmas regarding expertise (Boswell 2009). This very useful analysis could be complemented by thinking about why, how and when expertise provides a framing or agenda-setting role, directing and shaping the debate—that is, consideration of the preconditions for knowledge utilisation. The argument here is that the discussion over research usage should take into account the reasons why certain types of knowledge (macroeconomic data, criminal statistics, demographic data, etc.) become more (or less) salient in the policy debate in the first place.

Finally, the approach taken here is especially apposite considering the legacy of more than a decade of Labour governments since 1997. On taking office, the new government was very keen to associate itself with bringing new ideas into policy and to connect with a youthful and fresh mode of politics that was more open. This was illustrated once in office by the creation of new epistemic networks with nodes at the centre of government—where researchers joined the other 'bright young things' already plucked from the world of academia, think tanks and the media and rapidly promoted within the Labour party as politicians or special advisers. More than a reflection of the meritocratic society of which Tony Blair spoke,[2] the incoming government's approach was presented as a deliberate marriage between technocracy and managerialism. Labour wanted to put forward the appearance of being a progressive, modernising and reforming government (Hay 1999; Finlayson 2003). This was summed up in a narrative of evidence-based policy-making (EBPM): a style of governance supposedly characterised by an enhanced knowledge dimension; expanded research budgets across Whitehall; greater strategic capacity at the centre; and more input into policy-making from expertise outside government, that is, NGOs and think tanks (Davies et al. 2000; Bullock et al. 2001).

1. The Epistemic Communities Hypothesis and Policy Change

The proposal of this article is that in order to investigate the use of knowledge in the policy process, and to explain the time, timing and tempo of change, we need to pay closer attention to what kinds of ideas and knowledge, and types of actor, play a role in policy development. To do this, the article applies the ECH as a theoretical framework. The ECH has been used to explain why politicians make apparently brave decisions to relinquish political control of certain policy levers, for example the decision by the Labour government to give control of monetary policy to the Bank of England (King 2005).[3] It specifies how certain types of people and their ideas can influence policy change under particular conditions and with observable effects. Specifically, epistemic communities are identifiable groups or networks of experts with shared analytic and normative beliefs or ideas about a particular issue (Haas 1992, 16). Their currency is consensual knowledge which contains ideational structures that provide the source of paradigmatic policy change. The process of change via epistemic communities involves a causal chain of uncertainty, interpretation and institutionalisation (Haas 1992, 3–4). First there is the production of the initial demand or appetite from policy-makers, thought to be a function of uncertainty brought about by exogenous and endogenous factors (Haas 1992, 12). This demand can then be met by epistemic communities that have a shared interpretation of the issue. The extent of their impact is determined and can be observed by the extent to which they can embed their influence in mechanisms that institutionalise the use of expert knowledge.

The next sections present the empirical material, first mapping out the key moments and decisions in the story of labour migration policy change in the UK (1997–2007), and then identifying how certain ideas informed these decisions. In particular I am interested in the role of ideas and their journey in the policy process—focusing on how a new approach was developed and became part of policy. The subsequent section revisits the central tenets of the ECH, linking it with the particular case of labour migration policy change in the UK. The evidence is drawn from a mass of data incorporating policy statements, documents, parliamentary records and more than 20 elite in-depth interviews carried out with key actors

© 2009 The Author. Journal compilation © 2009 Political Studies Association
BJPIR, 2009, 11(4)

involved in policy during the period. This research (presented in greater detail elsewhere; see Balch (forthcoming)) combines to flesh out a kind of 'intellectual history' of policy change on labour migration in the UK.

2. Policy Change over Labour Migration 1997–2007: Key Moments and Decisions

In one of the few reviews of immigration policy under New Labour, Will Somerville (2007, 29) confidently declared that for economic migration the government 'comprehensively changed policy and marked a decisive break with the previous policy model'. He is, however, less certain about the precise timing of this policy change, admitting that 'the exact date when a new, more pro-active economic migration policy was introduced is difficult to judge', and concluding that 'the benefit of hindsight suggests that late 2000 and early 2001 was a crucial period' (Somerville 2007, 29).

The reorientation of labour migration policy in the UK since the late 1990s has certainly been eye-catching. Figures from the Office of National Statistics show net immigration more than tripling from well under 100,000 in 1997 to nearly 300,000 in 2006.[4] This contrasts sharply with the main theme of restriction that dominated UK policy throughout the 1960s, 1970s and 1980s and into the mid-1990s (Holmes 1988; Layton-Henry 1994; Hansen 2000; Flynn 2005). The restrictive paradigm has the classic features of a policy of 'muddling through' (Lindblom 1959), well illustrated by the response of a Home Office civil servant when asked about immigration policy development. He replied that 'immigration law in this country has developed mainly as a series of responses to, and attempts to regulate, particular pressures, rather than as a positive means of achieving preconceived social or economic aims'.[5]

An early sign in 1997 that the new Labour government might change things was provided by the almost instant announcement abolishing the Primary Purpose rule.[6] However, the 1998 White Paper confirmed Jack Straw's pre-election 'cigarette paper' metaphor[7]—there was to be no abrupt shift in policy on immigration following the election victory (Layton-Henry 2004). The 1998 White Paper focused on process and efficiency rather than an overhaul of the system, and dashed the hopes of campaigners and activists hoping for a radical departure in terms of policy (Flynn 2003, 4).[8]

It would be broader commitments to modernisation across government that enlarged the potential for a re-evaluation of policy, resulting in reviews of the whole control system—from initial applications through to permanent settlement (HMSO 1998, 4.2), and the work permit system, based in the Department for Education, led by the Treasury in 1998/99. This was followed in late 2000 by the announcement of a new policy direction, based on a concept of 'managing migration' for the benefit of the UK economy.

In a clear case of preaching to the converted, Home Office Minister Barbara Roche[9] made a speech on economic migration at an Institute for Public Policy Research (IPPR) conference held at the British Bankers Association in London. The new direction announced by Roche was all about recognising the 'potentially huge benefits' of migration and changing policies to adapt to the global economy by bringing in new ideas, including from other countries, and carrying out more research on migration in the UK (Roche 2000). This 'new' thinking echoed many of the conclusions of a seminar organised by Sarah Spencer at the IPPR some seven years earlier (Spencer 1994a).

However, there was an important difference—the 'positive' approach to refugees outlined by Spencer was largely forgotten in favour of her economic arguments. For the wider policy community around immigration, the injection of utilitarian ideas, although a step change from the restrictive policy that had existed for so long, represented a 'virtuous Dr Jekyll to the vicious Mr Hyde of asylum policy' (Flynn 2004, 1). The instrumental linkage between labour migration and national economic interest reflected a commodification of migrant labour that could never fully satisfy the agenda of a rights-based approach (Ryan 2005, 4–5).

I argue that the construction of the concept of 'managed migration' can be likened to a policy frame (Entman 1993; Schoen and Rein 1994), or paradigm (Hall 1993). Frames provide signposts and guidance for policy-makers, shape perceptions and influence political outcomes. Hall defines a policy paradigm as 'a framework of ideas and standards that specifies not only the goals of policy and the kinds of instruments that can be used to attain them, but also the very nature of the problem they are addressing'. A policy paradigm becomes embedded and 'is influential precisely because so much of it is taken for granted' (Hall 1993, 279). Thus, the managed migration frame helps us to understand key moments in the years that follow, particularly the decision not to impose transitionary arrangements on A8 nationals[10] in 2002.[11] This was arguably the most significant moment in terms of labour migration policy in the period 1997–2007. The policy decision was based on (as it turns out, wildly inaccurate) evidence about potential inflows (Dustman et al. 2003), and so can be directly linked to the managed migration narrative announced by Roche and repeated by Home Office ministers ever since.[12]

The relative inertia of the first few years under Labour stands in contrast to the government's second and third terms in office. Home Office and Immigration and Nationality Directorate (IND) reorganisation gathered pace after 2001 with the incorporation of Work Permits UK signalling a more business-friendly cultural and organisational shift (Duvell and Jordan 2003). Incremental change to the incredibly complex system of labour migration (see Morris 2004) from the late 1990s was significantly geared up under the 'Five-Year Plan' (HMSO 2005) and subsequent 2006 Act. This was an attempt to reconstruct the system from the managed migration perspective: systemic streamlining with skills-based selection to maximise economic benefits.

The large inflows related to the 2002 decision on A8 nationals have clearly had a significant political and institutional impact. The effect of institutional, political and organisational pressure can be seen in the decision to restrict access for A2 nationals[13] before the subsequent (2007) enlargement. In contrast to 2002 this decision was taken against expert opinion. Here the managed migration frame was displaced by a political imperative to respond to public concerns over immigration levels (despite the likelihood that A2 migration would be on a different scale to A8 migration).

© 2009 The Author. Journal compilation © 2009 Political Studies Association
BJPIR, 2009, 11(4)

Institutional and organisational crisis was finally recognised in 2006 with John Reid's comment that the IND was 'not fit for purpose'. This resulted in a convulsive institutional reaction—the IND scrapped and replaced by the Border and Immigration Agency (BIA),[14] and the creation of the Migration Advisory Committee (MAC)[15] and the Migration Impacts Forum (MIF)[16] in 2007. These changes, with immigration regulated by an 'agency' rather than a 'directorate', along with new structures to incorporate and regulate expert knowledge flow into the policy process, conform at least at surface level to the evidence-based, depoliticised agenda outlined by Barbara Roche in 2000. Many of the important decisions on labour migration taken post-2001 can therefore be traced to the paradigm shift.

Given the crucial 'framing' role this therefore assigns the narrative of 'managed migration',[17] that narrative's genesis and genealogy become of great interest for our understanding of policy change, and the role of ideas in the policy process. Roche's 'landmark' speech did not arrive fully formed from the top of her head. It was heavily trailed and prepared, and can be linked with similar ideas from other times and places. The question is how this particular configuration of ideas about labour migration—the specific flavour provided by this narrative—arrived, took shape and then successfully dominated the policy debate.

3. 'Managed Migration': The Narrative of a Narrative

The ideas presented in Roche's speech owed a great debt to a report titled 'Migration: An economic and social analysis' (Portes et al. 2001), a joint research effort from the Home Office and Cabinet Office (Policy and Innovation Unit (PIU)). The research emphasised the positive benefits of immigration to the UK economy, and outlined the linkages between migration, supply-side economics, labour market policy and social exclusion. As one of those academics seconded to the Cabinet Office to advise the PIU points out:

> I think that [the 2001 PIU/Home Office report] is probably the most single important thing to pay attention to ... I have spoken to others about this, and for me, here is a shifting of both policy and an intellectual framework (Interview, Shamit Saggar, Professor of Political Science, Sussex University, July 2006).

Roche was appointed as 'sponsor minister' for the research, and according to Jonathan Portes, who led the research team that wrote the report, she had become a keen supporter:

> When she read it [the 2001 PIU/Home Office report] she became very enthusiastic, and insisted on doing a speech, which was a couple of months before it was actually published, but a lot of stuff that was in her speech was taken pretty directly (Interview, Jonathan Portes, Chief economist, Department of Work and Pensions, November 2006).

The report emerged from the 'strategic challenges' PIU research programme, started in late 1998, and the review of the work permit system in 1999 led by the Treasury. Given the large number of policy areas that could conceivably be re-examined and rethought, why did the PIU and the Treasury choose to tackle immigration—an area identified as a vote-loser for Labour (Crossman 1977)?[18]

In electoral terms, the weakness of the Conservative opposition certainly meant that the political landscape was more favourable for a departure in policy. In the case of the Treasury, healthy economic growth in the UK had also led to a number of sectors, such as health, construction and IT experiencing labour shortages and subsequent demands for migrants (Geddes 2005). Under Labour, the Treasury played a key role in the domestic policy agenda, perceived as part of the deal to maintain the awkward 'marriage' between the chancellor and the prime minister (Naughtie 2002). The Treasury showed an interest in streamlining the work permits system, particularly for employees of multinational companies. This was a response to pressure from law firms such as Cameron McCenna, which give advice on work permits for big companies. Juliet Cole, chair of the Immigration Law Practitioners' Association (ILPA) work permits sub-committee, for example, was in constant dialogue with the Treasury and Home Office about reforms on policy. There are also links between the Treasury-led review and another New Labour metanarrative— the 'be friendly to business' agenda. As Sarah Spencer explains:

> I remember going to a CBI conference round about 1999 when Margaret Hodge [then employment minister] was bending over backwards, effectively saying 'tell me what you need and I will do it—which red tape don't you like—tell me what it is and it is gone ...'. And they were saying this and that about how the [work permits] system was still, despite the reforms, too slow and so on. What Labour did was bring in a private sector person to run Work Permits UK (Interview, Sarah Spencer, Associate Director of Centre on Migration, Policy and Society (COMPAS), March 2006).

However, I would argue that this type of policy-making is more akin to the old ways of 'muddling through'—tinkering with the system in the interests of business. The narrative provided by the PIU is central to creating the new policy landscape— something the Treasury was less interested in at the beginning, as Portes explains:

> It was a lower level issue at the Treasury at that point—they were helpful but they didn't put any effort behind it or give us resources or any great analysis—there was a junior economist in the Treasury who had done some useful work, but later on they got much more into it (Interview, Jonathan Portes, November 2006).

The PIU decision to look at migration can be traced to the Unit's remit to take a broader perspective than that allowed by the demands of individual departments and to cut across issues. Migration was one of 10 'strategic challenges' identified by a group set up in the PIU and led by Jonathan Portes to look at issues not well addressed by existing policy structures.

> It is not accidental that the strategy unit goes back to look at migration again and again—because it is a long-standing problem area where almost every front-line politician is of the view that there has been too much symptom-treating and not enough looking at underlying causes (Interview, Shamit Saggar, July 2006).

Portes, working with Suma Chakrubati, was to lead the team looking at migration. As he explains, it was personal, rather than political, interest that drove the project forward:

> Migration was the one that I was personally most interested in and most excited about, and Suma was also very keen on it, although there was not a great deal of appetite from the political masters of the PIU—they said if you really want to you can do it, but it wasn't that everyone was saying: 'this is a great idea please go away and do this for us' (Interview, Jonathan Portes, November 2006).

The research set out to calculate macroeconomic impacts, concluding that in the financial year 1999/2000, the net fiscal contribution of immigrants to the UK was £2.6 billion (Portes et al. 2001). Another government report closely followed (carried out jointly by the PIU, IPPR and Home Office), specifically looked at the fiscal effects of migration and confirmed the first report's findings (Gott and Johnson 2002). In the UK context, this approach of locating migration within macroeconomic indicators was novel and has hitherto become a central theme in the debate (Geddes 2005, 196–197; Boswell 2009). It might seem that the criss-cross of claim and counter-claim regarding the positive (e.g. Siskandarajah et al. 2005), or negative (MigrationWatch 2004; HMSO 2008) effects of immigration sometimes resembles an exercise in counting angels dancing on the head of a pin—but it strongly illustrates the power of the original research to re-frame the debate.

This impact was created by a combination of a coherent narrative and the willingness of the 'political masters' or gatekeepers to be associated with the research, providing the window of opportunity (Kingdon 1995) for a paradigm shift to take place. One of the crucial elements influencing the successful transmission of the ideas was the ability to bring people on board at all stages. This was first of all by getting the Home Office to take 'ownership' of the research before it was released, and secondly to get the support of political masters once it was produced. In the first case, this meant overcoming internal Home Office politics. As Spencer explains:

> There were people in the Home Office who were saying 'come on, we've got to change policy—the old approach of simply keeping people out is not tenable', and there were the operational people in the Home Office at IND who were effectively saying 'there is only one political imperative: keep people out!', but the people at Queen Anne's Gate were arguing that it is more complex than that, more nuanced (Interview, Sarah Spencer, March 2006).

The research was essentially produced by a team gathered together under the auspices of the PIU, and with very little in terms of personnel or resources provided by other government departments, but the presentation of the final publication as a joint PIU–Home Office project was key. This strategic co-ordination can be traced to networks of specific individuals in important decision-making positions:

> There was actually a surprisingly positive response from the Home Office—we were expecting them to be very much 'get off our turf' and it wouldn't have happened without Stephen Boys-Smith[19] who was then

the secretary general for IND—Stephen actually recognised that there was a gap and the Home Office didn't have the capacity to do this itself. Home Office policy officials at working level were never too keen on this, but Stephen was, and the head of economics at the Home Office—Richard Price (whose name also appears on the report) who was an old friend of mine from the Treasury—and we are very much of a mind on this—so there was an alliance between Richard, Stephen and I to say that we can work with the Home Office on this (Interview, Jonathan Portes, November 2006).

Despite Home Office co-operation, the PIU was Blair's creature—research results could have been buried if they were not to the liking of the prime minister. Reports can easily be 'handled' by assigning greater or lesser weight through classification.[20] It is perhaps surprising that it ever saw the light of day given Straw's pre-election 'cigarette paper' analogy. One (unnamed) source suggested that the report arrived at the in-tray of the prime minister without the usual 'health warning' or briefing note supplied by special advisers. The story goes that without the hindrance of political considerations Blair was convinced by the arguments for managing migration in the economic interest of the country and recommended that the report be published. Clearly, the narrative chimed elegantly with the pro-business agenda, and openness to cultural diversity and so-called 'Third Way' global capitalism (Flynn 2003, 19–20).

Whichever way publication was eventually sanctioned, there was then a political clamour to champion the new approach and assume ownership—chiefly through packaging and delivering it to the public. In her speech, Roche criticised the previous policies of successive governments as seeking to reduce numbers of immigrants without any justification (Flynn 2003, 6). She was very keen to differentiate the question of policy towards asylum seekers from a new policy of 'managed migration'. This new policy focus would be open and responsive to evidence and expertise on migration in general, but the question this research was supposed to address was clearly formulated in purely economic terms:

> In the past we have thought purely about immigration control ... Now we need to think about immigration management ... The evidence shows that economically driven migration can bring substantial overall benefits for both growth and the economy (Roche 2000).

The speech reflected the shift within government from tough measures for asylum seekers to a focus on work permits and other labour migration schemes (Duvell and Jordan 2003, 302). Although Roche promised 'modernisation' of the work permit system, the review over the preceding year had already led to an almost instant rise in permits granted in 1999 (see Figure 1).

As one of the top civil servants in Work Permits UK confirmed:

> The real changes that influenced size and changed both the policy and organisation were: there was an economic Cabinet Office committee-led review of work permit arrangements at the very end of the 1990s, the beginning of 2000, chaired by the then chancellor, Gordon Brown. The economic Cabinet Committee encompassed all government departments,

Figure 1: Work Permits Issued per Year (1947–2005)

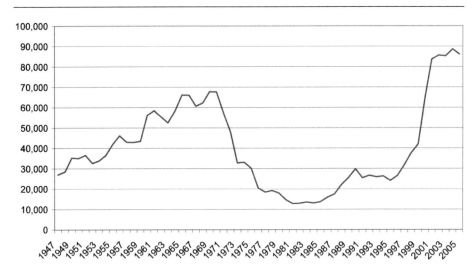

Source: Work Permits (UK) (Clarke and Salt 2003; Salt and Millar 2006).

with key leads being the Department of Education and Skills, who held responsibility then for the Work Permit Schemes and the Home Office with responsibility for immigration (Interview, Steve Lamb, Deputy Director, Work Permits UK, March 2006).

The term 'managed migration' provided the essential framework or narrative for communicating a new approach by incorporating ideas regarding positive economic benefits of migration, while also maintaining a dimension of control. The full fanfare for the new approach was reserved for a government-funded conference on migration research convened in 2001.[21] Here the full results of the PIU–Home Office project were presented as the centrepiece of a new research agenda. Later with the 2006 Act and its overhaul of instruments for labour migration there was again to be the quiet hand of PIU expertise guiding policy on labour migration. After 'Migration: An economic and social analysis', the work of the Unit continued with a team, headed by Mark Kleinman, producing a second report. Unlike its predecessor, this project was in the 'private' category, but conversations with officials from the PIU have confirmed that much of the work of that project subsequently formed the basis of the Home Office 'Five-Year Plan' (HMSO 2005).

In conclusion, the evidence presented here shows how a relatively small number of actors in the PIU, IPPR and Home Office were therefore able to construct and enable the launch of a paradigm shift in policy on labour migration. As Portes confirms:

> It [the PIU report] is an illustration of the way I think that personalities and people matter—and the fact that because I had a good relationship with Richard that this worked. But also Jitinder Kohli,[22] who was then at the PIU doing a completely different project but became head of produc-

tivity at the Treasury and pushed migration then because from the PIU he had been quite interested (Interview, Jonathan Portes, November 2006).

4. The ECH and Labour Migration Policy Change in the UK (1997–2007)

The 'fit' between the ECH and labour migration policy change in the UK (1997–2007) at first glance seems good. Haas postulated that when epistemic communities play a role in policy change there are three basic elements in the causal chain: uncertainty, (re)interpretation and institutionalisation (Haas 1992, 4): uncertainty over a policy area prompts policy-makers to turn to epistemic communities for consensual knowledge that contains alternative interpretations; these interpretations provide a new frame for understanding policy; this frame can then become concretised into a new policy settlement via institutional processes and constructions.

It is not much of a stretch then to say that from 1997 to 2007 we can observe conditions of uncertainty over immigration and then a reinterpretation of labour migration policy more closely following the consensus held by a network of experts, including several associated with the IPPR. The think tank is not shy in encouraging this interpretation of events, underlining its role in introducing ideas and knowledge into the policy process and helping to change the approach to labour migration.

> IPPR very much welcomes the recognition in the White Paper of the many benefits that migrants bring to Britain and the need for a holistic, consistent, evidence based policy that embraces entry controls through to integration and social cohesion. That approach reflects the argument first put forward in IPPR's 1994 report Strangers and Citizens: a positive approach to migrants and refugees, the subsequent contribution that we made to the PIU/Home Office study Migration, an economic and social analysis (2001), and many of the issues raised at our current seminar series on future migration policy.[23]

According to this initial account, then, there appears to be a resemblance between labour migration policy in the UK between 1997 and 2007 and the three different stages of policy change as laid out in the ECH. Such an assertion does not mean we should throw out traditional explanations of migration policy that highlight business interests (e.g. Freeman 1995), path-dependent effects (e.g. Hansen 2002), foreign policy concerns (Meyers 2002) or the liberal features of legal and bureaucratic systems (Guiraudon 2000a). Introducing the influence of ideas into the policy process instead contributes to these accounts by shedding light on the political sociology of immigration policy-making (Sciortino 2000).

When applying a framework such as the ECH to a new policy area there are inevitably challenges and points of weakness, however. One of the key issues, and common to all approaches foregrounding ideational factors, is the difficulty in separating an independent causal influence of ideas from the role of interests: in this case demands from Labour's clients regarding the underlying business case for increased immigration. Gary Freeman's model of immigration politics in liberal democratic states (Freeman 1995), for example, emphasises the role of business interests in securing more expansive immigration policies through client politics. However, I argue that this falls short of explaining timing in this case—there had been such calls for a more rational approach to admissions since the mid-1990s (*The Economist*, for example, demanded a change to a more positive approach in 1996).[24] The needs of business therefore need to be seen as one set of interests among others in terms of pressure for an opening of the debate about economic migration.

> Yes, there was lobbying and in a situation such as this when you are getting more or less the same line from the big employers, the TUC, when they are all coming along to government and there is this stuff happening in the EU at the same time, it meant that we were starting to have a proper discussion about what should be the rules about managed migration (Interview, Neil Gerrard, MP, Labour party, April 2006).

Research looking at the relationship between political elites and the 'organised public' over immigration suggests that policy-makers are insulated from pro-migrant lobbying and conduct policy in a relatively autonomous way (Statham and Geddes 2006, 266). Although business clearly played a role in terms of exerting pressure for change, it could be argued that it was more a case of pushing towards a 'tipping point', feeding the political desire to change policy. Certain sectors and industries wanted more migrant labour in the late 1990s, but the construction of a new policy in a sensitive area requires more than a response to a simple list of demands. After the new policy frame had been constructed, it proved relatively easy to get agreement from unions and employers on how then to develop that system, as shown by the joint statement in 2005.[25]

Thinking more closely about the timing and tempo of change can provide clues as to the explanatory power of the ECH in this case. This leads us to different questions related to each of the three dimensions. First, regarding uncertainty: why did the change of approach happen when it did (a full three years after the change of government, and seven years after the IPPR campaign)? Second, how did the new interpretation actually come to find its way into policy: how closely does the PIU–IPPR–Home Office network identified here, for example, fit the description of an epistemic community? Third, do subsequent developments and the new institutional constructions represent the final stage of the ECH?

First, concerning the timing, the secondment of Sarah Spencer as a policy expert from the IPPR into the PIU in 1999 is potentially significant in terms of the sequence of change. Although Spencer modestly claims that her move into government reflected the fact that a change in thinking had *already* occurred, the connection with the 1994 work at the IPPR is clear:

> At that point when they decided they wanted to do the study, they looked around to see who had said anything about the social and economic impact, and that was why I was seconded into the Cabinet office—on the basis of that 1994 report—I was asked to contribute to that study because it was the only thing that was there that was saying the kind of things that by now they were interested to hear (Interview, Sarah Spencer, March 2006).

In order to understand the timing of policy change, institutional factors and the governing style of Blair need to be brought in, particularly his motivation to push and stretch the policy capacity of the office of the prime minister, sometimes to the detriment of other cabinet ministers (Foley 2000, 301–314; Kavanagh 2001, 3). Within the British form of cabinet government, there is traditionally a delicate balance between the various departments and the role of the prime minister. The decision of the PIU to commission a study on migration therefore becomes crucial, and central to this decision was the perception of immigration as a policy problem, or as an area where there existed a high degree of uncertainty, supporting the ECH. This was one of the findings of the Strategic Challenges project, and the choice of immigration was coloured by the personal interest of key players in the PIU rather than their political masters. Personal links and shared beliefs with key policy actors within the Home Office allowed the report to be issued through this department. This served to distance the prime minister but also fulfilled the PIU aim of building capacity in government departments and involving the network of policy-makers. The team leader, Jonathan Portes, was an ex-Treasury economist, and the inclusion of Sarah Spencer gave the project a frame that was likely to focus on the potential for immigration to provide part of the solution to the aim of greater labour market flexibility.

Second, central to the ECH is the identification of an epistemic community (as opposed to activists, for example) which produces consensual knowledge and provides a new non-political interpretation of the policy issue for policy-makers (Haas 2001). Migration experts and labour market economists are typically thought to believe that migration provides net fiscal benefits, especially for receiving countries (see Simon 1989). The shift in labour migration policy in the UK since 2000 follows this expert interpretation by advocating an increase in legal routes of entry and the management of migration in the interest of national economic growth. We need only look at the Home Office's presentation of its own aims and objectives regarding immigration. In the mid-1990s there was a restrictive rhetoric, with the main aim to keep those coming to work and live in the UK to 'an irreducible minimum'. By the early 2000s this had been replaced by a more expansive logic of labour migration being used to 'boost the economy'. This certainly reflects the expert opinion gathered by Sarah Spencer at the IPPR in the early 1990s (Spencer 1994b).

However, there are some problems here: to begin with, the individuals gathered to produce 'Migration: An economic and social analysis' were not all exactly experts in labour migration. The team, recruited by the PIU, included not only people from think tanks and the media, but also actors who held significant positions in the Home Office policy network. In addition to this, there should be some doubt over whether IPPR can be considered an epistemic community considering its political links with the Labour party.

Think tanks regularly make claims to objectivity but it is a fairly straightforward task to demonstrate an incredibly close relationship between the IPPR and the Labour party. The IPPR has sometimes been referred to in the press as 'Labour's civil service'.[26] After Labour's 1997 election victory, 15 members of staff moved into government jobs.[27] The IPPR–Home Office connection was further underlined when David Blunkett's special adviser Nick Pearce (2001–03) became head of the think tank. How far is this description from that given by Haas, where epistemic communities are 'unlike other organised interest groups active in politics and policymaking' because they are 'bound by the truth tests to which they were socialised, and thus are more likely to provide information that is politically untainted' (Haas 2001, 11580)?

I would argue that the IPPR as a think tank has a certain level of autonomy from government—it finds its own funding, and claims to be driven by 'progressive' values: 'to build a fairer, more democratic and environmentally sustainable world'.[28] While the closeness to Labour is an important caveat to its designation as a non-political epistemic community, it is nevertheless difficult to claim that the IPPR is an entirely political organisation. In some ways the network identified here resembles an advocacy coalition (Sabatier and Jenkins-Smith 1999), including experts and non-experts, but I argue that with the PIU research it operated as an epistemic community.

Third, with respect to the institutionalisation of expert intervention and interpretation (Haas 1992, 30), there was no instant or dramatic shift in the institutional framework around labour migration in 2000–01. In concrete policy terms the second White Paper (HMSO 2002) signalled incremental rather than radical change, despite the fact that the focus of the government had shifted to recruitment schemes and the process of labour migration (Duvell and Jordan 2003, 303). The new routes of entry were actually more of a reworking of older schemes, for example an overhaul of the Working Holidaymaker Scheme (WHS)[29] and the expansion of the Seasonal Agricultural Workers Scheme (SAWS) to other sectors under the Sector-Based Scheme (SBS).

In institutional terms, change came with the incorporation of the newly streamlined work permit system, Work Permits UK, into the Home Office in 2001 and the creation of a new 'managed migration' department. Targets were revised to speed up turnarounds in applications from weeks and months to days. The mechanism for deciding the numbers of immigrants entering each year to work in the UK was no longer the government, but the market. This is best illustrated by David Blunkett's comment in 2003 that there was 'no obvious upper limit' on migration. Over and above institutional movement, this also represented an injection of change into the organisational culture of the Home Office (Duvell and Jordan 2003).

The follow-ups to the first PIU report published through the Immigration Research and Statistics Service (IRSS) within the Home Office looked at labour market outcomes (Haque et al. 2002) and fiscal effects (Gott and Johnson 2002) to present a new level of detail regarding immigration and the UK economy. This was part of the PIU strategy of building up parallel research capacity within the different departments, in this case through the IRSS and the Strategic Policy Team (SPT).

The creation of MAC and MIF can be seen as part of a decidedly technocratic turn and an attempt to depoliticise decisions over admissions. MAC is made up of 'independent experts'[30] who 'provide independent, transparent and evidence-based advice to government on where labour market shortages exist that can sensibly be filled by migration'. At least one of those appointed to MAC (Diane Coyle) provides a human thread in the story of policy change, being directly involved in the drawing up of the 2001 PIU report (see Appendix I). MIF also brings together experts to discuss evidence regarding 'the wider social impacts of migration'. This is something the IPPR has pressed for and in its response the think tank welcomed the proposals (although suggesting that the MAC should take on more policy functions) (Cooley et al. 2005). This represents one of the 'endgames' for members of the epistemic community around labour migration policy—a place on the advisory board and the opportunity to guide and control labour migration policy.

Conclusions

Research on the role of ideas and knowledge in political science has tended to focus either rather narrowly on (expert) knowledge utilisation, or in a more grand fashion on big epoch-changing policy shifts such as the move from Keynesian to monetarist economics (Hall 1993; Blyth 2002a) or the causal effects of ideas about globalisation (Hay 2004). Policy on labour migration in the UK provides an excellent case to study the causal effects of ideas precisely because the shift from a restrictive paradigm illustrates 'the contingent and open-ended nature of social and political processes and dynamics—especially those conventionally seen as fixed' (Hay 2003, 2). In addition this time period is particularly appropriate to this kind of research, given Labour's commitment from the late 1990s, through the rhetoric of EBPM, to tap into scientific knowledge and expertise through the production of evidence to reform and modernise public policy (HMSO 1999).

The evidence presented here shows how ideas about the macroeconomic impacts of migration came to frame a new policy on labour migration. The elaboration of these ideas can first be traced to the PIU–Home Office publication 'Migration: An economic and social analysis' (Portes et al. 2001), and then a political journey structured in part by Blair's strategy as prime minister. Although often described as practically presidential (Foley 2000), the Blair era had as one of its central planks the building up of policy resources at the centre of government. This had two main implications for policy on labour migration: a challenge to the monopoly of thinking on the issue in the Home Office, and the recruitment and inclusion of experts into immigration policy-making.

When considering the shift to managed migration after 2000 it is impossible to ignore Spencer's campaign on a positive approach to immigration policy at the IPPR in the early 1990s. Not only did this produce a coherent policy framework with an emphasis on evidence-based policy, it was also very similar to the discourse that the shift to managed migration adopted several years later. Would a change in thinking have occurred if Spencer had not earlier developed a coherent discourse around a positive approach to immigration at the IPPR? Although we might never know, it is possible that elements of the Labour government had at least partially assimilated the recommendations outlined by Spencer in 1994—Blair was shadow home secretary at that point (before he was elected Labour party leader and replaced by Straw). What is more likely however is that Spencer's work influenced others working in the same field. As described in the ECH (Haas 1992) the crucial point is when a government turns to narratives available through epistemic communities rather than actions within those communities. In the case of labour migration policy change we need to take account of the levels of uncertainty in Labour's ranks, and how the discourse made available via the PIU–Home Office report tied in with two overarching narratives of EBPM and business-friendly macroeconomic management. This only provides the background, however, to a story dominated by personalities and contacts between like-minded individuals in the PIU, Home Office and IPPR.

Was the epistemic community used in an instrumental way to serve interests? Yes to an extent, because the narrative of managed migration satisfied a need—namely to present a competent and convincing 'story' of how the government is dealing with a traditionally difficult issue. The point here is that, in line with the ECH, the consensual knowledge provided by experts contained new ideas about immigration (as a driver of macroeconomic growth), which had implications for later policy decisions. Identifying an independent causal influence for ideas does not mean dismissing interests as irrelevant—interest-based accounts correctly identify the motivation for change but neglect the path-dependent ways in which a new policy frame can subsequently affect future decisions (Hansen 2002). The decision to allow free movement for A8 nationals is a good example—the new policy framework that led the government to use expertise in its decision-making had far-reaching (if perhaps unintended) consequences, leading to over a million Eastern Europeans coming to the UK between 2004 and 2007 (Pollard et al. 2008). By incorporating the influence of ideas as well as interests we can better understand why the new policy led to the creation of institutional structures to incorporate experts into the policy process, for example through MAC and MIF.

One of the key points that emerged during the research was the difficulty in designating networks of actors and organisations identified here as unequivocally epistemic communities in the same way that Haas describes (Haas 2001, 11580). I therefore resort to describing the network as *operating as* an epistemic community. Future research should focus on the political function and dimension of organisations such as the IPPR and PIU, but also look in detail at the way in which new structures such as MAC and MIF provide evidence of the institutionalisation phase of the ECH.

The ECH proves to be a useful framework for investigating the role of ideas in policy change. While one of the main problems with using this approach is the difficulty in disaggregating the role of ideas with those of interests, the approach here was to pay closer attention to the timing and tempo of change. On this basis, in the case of labour migration policy in the UK it is argued that in a contingent and conjunctural way a limited opening or 'window' for change occurred around 2000. This allowed a specific network of actors in the policy community, operating as an epistemic community, to dislodge the dominant restrictive policy paradigm or 'frame', and open the debate around policy. This suggests that to understand policy change we should pay attention to how the political appetite for new policy ideas can be fuelled by uncertainties over policy performance, and the role of expertise in the reframing of policy.

© 2009 The Author. Journal compilation © 2009 Political Studies Association
BJPIR, 2009, 11(4)

About the Author

Alex Balch, The Department of Politics, University of Sheffield, Elmfield, Northumberland Road, Sheffield S10 2TU, UK, email: *a.r.balch@sheffield.ac.uk*

Notes

1. It should be noted that this article is concerned with labour migration and so does not touch upon related policies on asylum, family reunion, immigrant integration, etc.

2. In 1997, shortly after gaining office, Blair declared of the UK: 'The Britain of the elite is over. The new Britain is a meritocracy'; quoted in *The Guardian*, 14 February 2001, 'Satirical fiction is becoming Blair's reality'. Available online at: http://www.guardian.co.uk/Archive/Article/0,4273, 4135949,00.html

3. For example, the decision by the Labour government to give control of monetary policy to the Bank of England (King 2005).

4. Office of National Statistics, http://www.statistics.gov.uk/cci/nugget.asp?id=260

5. Home Office evidence to the Select Committee on Race Relations and Immigration, 1971, quoted in Spencer (1994a).

6. Introduced in the early 1980s, in the first Thatcher government, the Primary Purpose rule regulated entry for spouses who were not British citizens. Couples needed to prove that the primary purpose of the marriage was not to settle in the UK. Once the rule was removed couples still needed to prove that the marriage was genuine.

7. Jack Straw was responding to Michael Howard's attempt to put 'clear blue water' between Labour and the Conservative party on immigration (*The Guardian*, 3 March 1995).

8. It should be noted that there was reduced room for manoeuvre for the incoming Labour government because of pre-election promises to stick to Tory spending plans for the first two years. These plans included a reduction in staffing levels at the Home Office, based on the (with hindsight, absurdly optimistic) expectation that a new IT system would streamline casework, reduce backlogs and cut running costs.

9. Roche was Home Office minister 1999–2001. Before that she was financial secretary to the Treasury.

10. A8 = the Czech Republic, Estonia, Hungary, Latvia, Lithuania, Poland, Slovakia and Slovenia (2004 enlargement of the EU).

11. Announced on 10 December 2002 during the negotiations leading to the accession of the new member states at the Copenhagen European Council (2002).

12. The 'managed migration' narrative was more fully laid out in an official publication in the second immigration White Paper, 'Secure Borders, Safe Haven—Integration with Diversity' (HMSO 2002), put together by David Blunkett and Nick Pearce (ex-IPPR) as his special adviser.

13. A2 = Romania and Bulgaria (2007 enlargement).

14. Eventually becoming the UK Border Agency (UKBA) in April 2008.

15. Migration Advisory Committee (MAC): http://www.bia.homeoffice.gov.uk/aboutus/workingwithus/indbodies/mac/

16. Migration Impacts Forum (MIF): http://press.homeoffice.gov.uk/press-releases/forum-migration-impacts

17. Although it is difficult to establish when this phrase was first coined, it has been attributed to Stephen Boys-Smith, secretary-general of the IND (1998–2002).

18. See, for example, Andrew Lansley's article in *The Guardian* (3 September 1995): 'Immigration, an issue which we raised successfully in 1992 and again in the 1994 Euro-elections campaign, played particularly well in the tabloids and has more potential to hurt'.

19. 1998–2002—then took up the post of Director General of the Organised Crime, Drugs and International Group at the Home Office. Succeeded by Bill Jeffrey.

20. For example, a report can be made public in two ways: 'to' government—where an outside research group reports findings, or 'of' government—where research is presented as being government produced. A third option is when the report is kept private, for internal use only. Given the controversial nature of immigration this report might have remained private, but instead ended up being 'to' government.

© 2009 The Author. Journal compilation © 2009 Political Studies Association
BJPIR, 2009, 11(4)

21. Bridging the Information Gap: A Conference of Research on Asylum and Immigration in the UK, March 2001.

22. Head of productivity and structural reform team at the Treasury. Moved in 2004 to head the Home Office's Active Communities Directorate—the voluntary sector's main contact point with the government. http://society.guardian.co.uk/charitymanagement/story/0,8150,1271623,00.html

23. IPPR website: http://www.ippr.org/research/teams/project.asp?id=949&tID=85&pID=949

24. *The Economist*, 4 May 1996.

25. 'Managed migration: Working for Britain—A joint statement from the Home Office, CBI and TUC'. Available online at:http://www.tuc.org.uk/international/tuc-10485-f0.cfm

26. *The Observer*, 7 September 2003, 'Ideas Man' (profile of Matthew Taylor). Available online at: http://observer.guardian.co.uk/comment/story/0,,1036999,00.html

27. Some of the most high-profile moves between the IPPR and the Labour government include: Tessa Blackstone, the IPPR's first chair, was appointed minister of Education in 1997; Patricia Hewitt, IPPR director from 1989–1994, became a minister of state for the Department of Trade and Industry in 1999; Matthew Taylor, director of the IPPR from 1998, was seconded to become head of policy for Labour (at the No. 10 Policy Directorate) in September 2003; Nick Pearce moved in the other direction, replacing Taylor as IPPR director by leaving his job as special adviser to David Blunkett.

28. IPPR website: http://www.ippr.org/aboutippr/

29. The Working Holidaymaker Scheme (WHS) allowed citizens from commonwealth countries to work in Britain for up to two years. Before the changes in 2002 New Zealand, Australia, Canada and South Africa had accounted for 96 per cent of successful applications.

30. MAC member biographies (see also Appendix I): http://www.bia.homeoffice.gov.uk/aboutus/ workingwithus/indbodies/mac/aboutthemac/memberbiographies/

31. Information taken from http://www.bia.homeoffice.gov.uk/aboutus/workingwithus/indbodies/mac/ (accessed 28 April 2008).

Bibliography

Balch, A. (2010) *"Mamaging labour migration in Europe: ideas, knowledge and policy change"*, Manchester: Manchester University Press.

Blyth, M. (2002a) *Great Transformations: Economic Ideas and Institutional Change in the Twentieth Century* (Cambridge: Cambridge University Press).

Boswell, C. (2008) 'The political functions of expert knowledge: Knowledge and legitimation in European Union immigration policy', *Journal of European Public Policy*, 15:4, 471–488.

Boswell, C. (2009) 'Knowledge, legitimation and the politics of risk: The functions of research in public debates on migration', *Political Studies*, 57:1, 165–186.

Brans, M., Jacobs, D., Martiniello, M., Rea, A., Swyngedouw, M., Adam, I., Balancier, P., Florence, E., Van Der Straeten, T. (2004) *Recherche et politiques publiques: le cas de l'immigration en Belgique (Research and Public Policy: The Case of Immigration in Belgium)* (Gent: Academia Press).

Brubaker, R. (1992) *Citizenship and Nationhood in France and Germany* (Cambridge, MA: Harvard University Press).

Bullock, H., Mountford, J., Stanley, R. (2001) *Better Policy Making* (London: Centre for Management and Policy Studies).

Castles, S. (2004) 'Why migration policies fail', *Ethnic and Racial Studies*, 27:2, 205–227.

Clarke, J. and Salt, J. (2003) 'Work permits and foreign labour in the UK: A statistical review', *Labour Market Trends*, November, 563–574.

Cooley, L., Farrant, M., Sriskandarajah, D. (2005) *Selecting Wisely: Making Managed Migration Work for Britain* (London: Institute for Public Policy Research (IPPR)).

Crossman, R. (1977) *Diaries of a Cabinet Minister, Vol. 3: Secretary of State for Social Services 1968–1970* (London: Hamish Hamilton/Jonathan Cape).

Davies, H., Nutley, S., Smith, P. (Eds.) (2000) *What Works? Evidence-Based Policy and Practice in Public Services* (Bristol: The Policy Press).

Dustman, C., Casanova, M., Fertig, M., Preston, I., Schmidt, C. (2003) 'The impact of EU enlargement on migration flows', *Home Office Online Report 25/03*. www.homeoffice.gov.uk/rds/pdfs2/rdsolr2503.pdf

© 2009 The Author. Journal compilation © 2009 Political Studies Association
BJPIR, 2009, 11(4)

Duvell, J. and Jordan, B. (2003) 'Immigration control and the management of economic migration in the UK: Organisational culture, implementation, enforcement and identity processes in public services', *Journal of Ethnic and Migration Studies*, 29:2, 299–336.

Entman, R. (1993) 'Framing: Toward a clarification of a fractured paradigm', *Journal of Communication*, 43:4, 51–58.

Finlayson, A. (2003) *Making Sense of New Labour* (London: Lawrence & Wishart).

Florence, E. and Martiniello, M. (2005) 'The links between academic research and public policies in the field of migration and ethnic relations: Selected national case-studies', *International Journal on Multicultural Societies (UNESCO)*, 7:1, 3–10.

Flynn, D. (2003) 'Tough as old boots? Asylum, immigration and the paradox of New Labour policy', Immigration Rights Project (IPR), Joint Council for the Welfare of Immigrants (JCWI).

Flynn, D. (2004) 'Forward: "The control of rights" by Lydia Morris', Joint Council for the Welfare of Immigrants (JCWI).

Flynn, D. (2005) 'New borders, new management: The dilemmas of modern immigration policies', *Ethnic and Racial Studies*, 28:3, 463–490.

Foley, M. (2000) *The British Presidency: Tony Blair and the Politics of Public Leadership* (Manchester: Manchester University Press).

Freeman, G. (1994) 'Britain: The deviant case', in W. Cornelius, P. Martin and J. Hollifield (eds), *Controlling Immigration: A Global Perspective* (Stanford, CA: Stanford University Press), 297–300.

Freeman, G. (1995) 'Modes of immigration politics in liberal democratic states', *International Migration Review*, 29:4, 881–902.

Geddes, A. (2005) 'Country report: United Kingdom', in J. Niessen and Y. Schibel (eds), *Immigration as a Labour Market Strategy: European and North American Perspectives* (Brussels: Migration Policy Group), 191–211.

Gott, C. and Johnson, K. (2002) 'The migrant population in the UK: Fiscal effects (RDS 77) (London: Home Office, PIU, IPPR).

Guiraudon, V. (2000a) 'The Marshallian triptych reordered: The role of courts and bureaucracies in furthering migrants' social rights', in M. Bommes and A. E. Geddes (eds), *Immigration and Welfare: Challenging the borders of the Welfare State* (London and New York: Routledge), 71–89.

HMSO (1998) *Fairer, Faster, Firmer: A Modern Approach to Immigration and Asylum* (London: UK Home Office).

HMSO (1999) *Modernising Government* (London: UK Cabinet Office).

HMSO (2002) *Secure Borders, Safe Haven: Integration with Diversity* (London: Home Office).

HMSO (2005) *Controlling Our Borders: Making Migration Work for Britain, Five Years Strategy for Asylum and Immigration* (London: Home Office).

HMSO (2008) 'The Economic Impact of Migration', *1st Report of Session 2007–08*. House of Lords Select Committee on Economic Affairs.

Haas, P. (1992) 'Knowledge, power and international policy co-ordination', *International Organization*, 46:1, 1–35.

Haas, P. (2001) 'Epistemic communities and policy knowledge', *International Encyclopedia of Social and Behavioural Sciences*, 11578–11586.

Haas, P. (2004) 'When does power listen to truth? A constructivist approach to the policy process', *Journal of European Public Policy*, 11:4, 569–592.

Hall, P. (1993) 'Policy paradigms, social learning, and the state: The case of economic policy making in Britain', *Comparative Politics*, 25:3, 275–296.

Hansen, R. (2000) *Citizenship and Immigration in Post-war Britain* (Oxford: Oxford University Press).

Hansen, R. (2002) 'Globalization, embedded realism, and path dependence: The other immigrants to Europe', *Comparative Political Studies*, 35:3, 259–283.

Haque, R., Dustmann, C., Fabbri, F., Preston, I., Wadsworth, J., Shields, M., Wheatley, S. (2002) 'Migrants in the UK: Their characteristics and labour market outcomes and impacts (RDS 82) (London: Home Office).

Hay, C. (1999) *The Political Economy of New Labour* (Manchester: Manchester University Press).

Hay, C. (2003) 'Social constructivism as (a tool of) critical political analysis'. Paper presented at the annual conference of the Political Studies Association, University of Leicester, 15–17 April.

Hay, C. (2004) ' "Taking ideas seriously" in explanatory political analysis', *British Journal of Politics & International Relations*, 6:2, 129–164.

Hollifield, J. (1994) 'Europe's immigration crisis', *Harvard International Review*, Summer94, 16:3, 26–33.

Holmes, C. (1988) *John Bull's Island: Immigration and British Society* (Basingstoke: Macmillan).

Kavanagh, D. N. L. (2001) 'New Labour, new millennium, new premiership', in A. Seldon (ed.), *The Blair Effect* (London: Little, Brown & Co), 3–20.

King, M. (2005) 'Epistemic communities and the diffusion of ideas: Central Bank reform in the United Kingdom', *West European Politics*, 28:1, 94–123.

Kingdon, J. (1995) *Agendas, Alternatives, and Public Policies* (Harlow: Longman).

Layton-Henry, Z. (1994) 'Britain: The would-be zero-immigration country', in W. Cornelius, P. Martin and J. Hollifield (eds), *Controlling Immigration: A Global Perspective* (Stanford, CA: Stanford University Press), 273–295.

Layton-Henry, Z. (2004) 'Britain: From immigration control to migration management', in W. Cornelius, T. Tsuda, P. Martin and J. Hollifield (eds), *Controlling Immigration* (2nd edn) (Stanford, CA: University Press), 297–333.

Lindblom, C. (1959) 'The science of "muddling through" ', *Public Administration Review*, 19:2, 79–88.

Meyers, E. (2002) 'The causes of convergence in western immigration control', *Review of International Studies*, 28:1, 123–141.

MigrationWatch (2004) 'The fiscal impact of immigration to the UK', *Briefing paper 1.2 (Economic)*, MigrationWatch UK.

Morris, L. (2004) *The Control of Rights: The Rights of Workers and Asylum Seekers under Managed Migration* (London: JCWI).

Naughtie, J. (2002) *The Rivals: The Inside Story of a Political Marriage* (London: Fourth Estate).

Paul, K. (1997) *Whitewashing Britain: Race and Citizenship in the Postwar Era* (Ithaca, NY: Cornell University Press).

Pollard, N., Latorre, M., Sriskandarajah, D. (2008) *Floodgates or Turnstiles? Post-EU Enlargement Migration Flows to (and from) the UK* (London: Institute for Public Policy Research (IPPR)).

Portes, J., Glover, S., Gott, C., Loizillon, A. (2001) *Migration: An Economic and Social Analysis* (RDS 67) (London: Home Office).

Roche, B. (2000) 'Migration in a global economy', Speech at IPPR conference (British Bankers Association), 11 September. Available online at: http://www.gnn.gov.uk/Content/Detail.asp?ReleaseID=25402&NewsAreaID=2&print=true

Ryan, B. (2005) 'Introduction: Perspectives on labour migration', in B. Ryan (ed.), *Labour Migration and Employment Rights* (London: Institute of Employment Rights), 1–8.

Sabatier, P. and Jenkins-Smith, H. (1999) The Advocacy Coalition Framework: An Assessment. *Theories of the Policy Process*. Sabatier, P. Boulder, Westview Press.

Salt, J. and Millar, J. (2006) 'Foreign labour in the United Kingdom: Current patterns and trends', *Labour Market Trends*, 114:10, 335–355.

Sassen, S. (1996) *Losing Control? Sovereignty in an Age of Globalization* (New York: Columbia University Press).

Schoen, D. and Rein, M. (1994) *Frame Reflection* (New York: Basic Books).

Sciortino, G. (2000) 'Toward a political sociology of entry policies: Conceptual problems and theoretical proposals', *Journal of Ethnic and Migration Studies*, 26:2, 213–228.

Simon, J. (1989) *The Economic Consequences of Immigration* (Cambridge, MA: Basil Blackwell).

Siskandarajah, D., Colley, L., Reed, H. (2005) *Paying Their Way: The Fiscal Contribution of Immigrants in the UK* (London: Institute for Public Policy Research (IPPR)).

Somerville, W. (2007) *Immigration under New Labour* (Bristol: The Policy Press).

Soysal, Y. (1994) *Limits of Citizenship: Migrants and Postnational Membership in Europe* (Chicago, IL: University of Chicago Press).

Spencer, S. (1994a) *Strangers and Citizens: A Positive Approach to Migrants and Refugees* (London: IPPR/Rivers Oram Press).

Spencer, S. (ed.) (1994b) *Immigration as an Economic Asset* (London: Trentham Books).

Statham, P. and Geddes, A. (2006) 'Elites and the "organised public": Who drives British immigration politics and in which direction', *West European Politics*, 29:2, 248–269.

© 2009 The Author. Journal compilation © 2009 Political Studies Association
BJPIR, 2009, 11(4)

Appendix I

MAC (Migration Advisory Committee)[31]
Chair: Professor David Metcalf

Members:
Dr Diane Coyle
Dr Martin Ruhs
Professor Jonathan Wadsworth
Professor Robert Wilson
Professor Mike Campbell (ex officio member)
Paula Higson (government)
Secretariat:
Mark Franks (secretary)
Stephen Earl
Vanna Aldin
Andrew Watton
Anna Downs
Anne Ball
Observer:
Andy Honeyman (Border and Immigration Agency)

© 2009 The Author. Journal compilation © 2009 Political Studies Association
BJPIR, 2009, 11(4)

doi: 10.1111/j.1467-856X.2009.00382.x   *BJPIR: 2009 VOL 11, 634–651*

From Social Contract to 'Social Contrick': The Depoliticisation of Economic Policy-Making under Harold Wilson, 1974–75[1]

Chris Rogers

The 1974–79 Labour governments were elected on the basis of an agreement with the TUC promising a redistribution of income and wealth known as the Social Contract. However, the government immediately began to marginalise these commitments in favour of preferences for incomes policy and public expenditure cuts, which has led the Social Contract to be described as the 'Social Contrick'. These changes were legitimised through a process of depoliticisation, and using an Open Marxist framework and evidence from the National Archives, the article will show that the Treasury's exchange rate strategy and the need to secure external finance placed issues of confidence at the centre of political debate, allowing the government to argue that there was no alternative to the introduction of incomes policy and the reduction of public expenditure.

Keywords: depoliticisation; Social Contract; economic policy; Labour government

Introduction

It is a common conception that a depreciating currency reflects a lack of market confidence in the sustainability of a nation's economic policy, and disciplines governments by forcing them to adopt policies to restore faith. However, a depreciating currency can also offer political opportunities for governments when it is desired for reasons of industrial competitiveness and attributed to market forces, by placing issues of confidence and credibility at the centre of political debate. The need to stabilise exchange rates, and for countries in deficit as Britain was in the 1970s, the need to secure external finance, can therefore help to justify deflationary counter-inflationary and fiscal policies, because market logic acts as a buttress between the government and the consequences of unpopular policy changes.

The idea that the 1974–79 Labour government was engaged in the politics of depoliticisation has often been asserted with reference to the 1976 International Monetary Fund (IMF) crisis (see Clarke 1988, 314–315; Holloway 1995, 128; Bonefeld and Burnham 1998, 41); however the intention of this article is to demonstrate that this was not an isolated example of depoliticisation that occurred during a moment of acute crisis. Rather, it is possible to demonstrate that the events in the autumn and winter of 1976 were the logical extension of the Labour government's statecraft that had been pursued since as early as December 1974. By using an Open Marxist framework of analysis and evidence from the National Archives, this article will demonstrate how the government used issues of credibility and confidence in order to shape domestic political preferences by encouraging perceptions of crisis, firstly in the foreign exchange markets, and secondly in external financing.

Firstly, a return to incomes policy was justified by citing pressure on the sterling rate, which was attributed to a lack of confidence in the government's counter-inflationary credibility, despite the fact that it was favoured by the Treasury to help improve industrial competitiveness, and was allowed to occur, if not actually engineered, by a passive intervention strategy in the foreign exchanges when sterling came under pressure. Secondly, public expenditure cuts were justified by the possibility that Britain would need to secure substantial external financing in early 1976. This culminated in borrowing from the IMF's oil facility, which helped to stifle support for the Labour movement's Alternative Economic Strategy (AES), and lock British policy into multilateral solutions to balance of payments correction. This helped legitimise the argument that immediate public expenditure cuts were essential if more severe and externally imposed reductions were to be avoided in the future.

The State and the Politics of Depoliticisation

It has been common to view globalisation and capital mobility as processes that have given power to markets over states (see *inter alia* Helleiner 1992; Strange 1994; Pauly 1997; Cohen 1998). However, Peter Burnham (2001a, 135) has noted that an alternative 'would be to see the reregulation of financial markets as providing the strongest possible public justification governments can muster for maintaining downward pressure on wages to combat inflation'. As such, the supposed imperatives of markets can be identified as tools that help governments to 'restructure (that is, lower) expectations and improve its credit rating' (Burnham 2001a, 147). Therefore, Burnham (1994, 221–222) has suggested that analyses focusing on the constraints imposed by the deregulation of financial markets represent 'a vulgar and fraudulent discipline [that fails] to grasp the complex organic set of social relations which is the global political economy'.

Understanding this complex set of social relations is therefore of key importance in understanding the nature of the state. In order to achieve this, John Holloway suggests that it is necessary to 'understand the state not as a thing in itself, but as a social form, a form of social relations', which appears 'in the form of something external to social relations' (Holloway 1995, 122; see also, *inter alia*, Bonefeld, 1992; Burnham 1995, 2001b and 2006). Conceived in this way, it should be understood that the state 'is not autonomous, or *simply related to* "the economy", rather it is an integral aspect of the set of social relations whose overall form is determined by the manner in which the extraction of surplus from the immediate producer is secured' (Burnham 1995, 93, emphasis in original). Or rather, states 'are not to be thought of as "thing like" institutions losing power to the market' (Burnham 2001b, 108 and 2006, 76).

© 2009 The Author. Journal compilation © 2009 Political Studies Association
BJPIR, 2009, 11(4)

Such Open Marxist understandings of the state are also framed by the inherently unstable and crisis-prone nature of the capitalist mode of production, of which Marx (1973, 410) hypothesised that the 'universality to which it irresistibly strives encounters barriers in its own nature, which will, at a certain stage of its development, allow it to be recognized as being itself the greatest barrier to this tendency, and hence will drive towards its own suspension'. The fact that the conditions for successful capital accumulation are not naturally occurring means that state intervention in and regulation of the economy are constantly required in order both to offset crises of over-accumulation and to contain the class antagonisms that this inherently creates. Therefore, 'the behaviour of a state is conditioned ... by a need to attract and retain globally mobile capital in order to secure domestic social reproduction' (Kettell 2004, 23). In order for this to be achieved, a number of conditions must be met. As Simon Clarke (2001, 96–98) notes, postponing the onset of crises of overproduction and over-accumulation is intrinsically linked to impoverishing and deskilling workers, which exacerbates class struggle with a political character on a national scale. Or as Werner Bonefeld (1992, 112) phrases it, 'the compulsion on each individual capital, if its devaluation is to be avoided ... forces upon each capital the necessity of expelling living labour from the process of production'.

Economic crises, therefore, should not be seen as disciplinary aspects of an international state system in which power has been increasingly transferred to markets, but rather as fundamental features of the capitalist system, the inevitability of which drives the formation of preferences for policies that increase the command of capital over labour. However, as this also magnifies class antagonisms, and given that a government's prospects for political success are dependent on the maintenance of popular domestic support, the question remains of how governments are able to act according to their preferences without undermining their domestic political legitimacy. The answer can be found in the concept of depoliticisation.

Claus Offe (1975, 26, emphasis in original) long ago contended that 'the *existence* of a capitalist state presupposes the systematic *denial* of its nature as a *capitalist* state'. In many respects, strategies of depoliticisation are attempts at just that, and have been employed by various governments in the United Kingdom.[2] As a concept, depoliticisation does not refer to the removal of the political from politics as it may imply. As Burnham (2001a, 136) notes, the politics of depoliticisation should be understood as a highly political governing strategy, and as Steve Kettell (2008, 631) usefully asserts, 'in a democratic polity, where the political legitimacy of government derives from the pursuit of the "national interest" ... policy-making must ... display at least a semblant of a connection to the views and wishes of the electorate'. Rather, depoliticisation is a statecraft strategy through which governments try to achieve a level of governing competence in economic management (Burnham 2001a, 127–128). As such Matthew Flinders and Jim Buller (2006, 295–296, emphasis in original) define depoliticisation as '*the range of tools, mechanisms and institutions through which politicians can attempt to move to an indirect governing relationship and/or seek to persuade the demos that they can no longer reasonably be held responsible for a certain issue, policy field or specific decision*'; or as Burnham (1999, 47 and 2001a, 128) writes, depoliticisation is 'the process of placing at one remove the political character of decision making'.

Despite the fact that strategies of depoliticisation cannot remove the inherent crisis-prone tendencies of accumulation or categorically prevent an economic crisis from becoming a political crisis, but only smooth class antagonisms temporarily, their benefits are clear. By removing issues from the political agenda, or reducing the perceived importance of these issues in the view of the public, governments can 'change expectations about the effectiveness and credibility of decision making' (Burnham 1999, 47), and make it less likely that they will have their legitimacy questioned when economic policy choices mean that additional social and economic costs have to be accepted by the general population (Kettell 2008, 631).

Methods of depoliticising economic policy-making have often been framed in terms of the debate surrounding 'rules' versus 'discretion'; however Flinders and Buller (2006) have moved the debate beyond this dichotomy and outlined three ways in which governments may employ depoliticisation. The first is *institutional depoliticisation*. This occurs when 'A formalised principal–agent relationship is established in which the former (elected politician) sets broad policy parameters while the latter (appointed administrator or governing board) enjoys day-to-day managerial and specialist freedom within the broad framework set' (Flinders and Buller 2006, 298). The second is *rule-based depoliticisation*, in which state managers adopt 'a policy that builds explicit rules into the decision-making process that constrain the need for political discretion' (Flinders and Buller 2006, 303–304). The final strategy is *preference-shaping depoliticisation*. This involves 'recourse to ideological, discursive or rhetorical claims in order to justify a political position that a certain issue or function does, or should, lie beyond the scope of politics or the capacity for state control' (Flinders and Buller 2006, 307).

The use of an Open Marxist framework in order to demonstrate the origin of governing elites' preferences to depoliticise difficult aspects of policy is, however, not universally accepted. The position has been criticised for a tendency to 'project a "totalising" theory, rooted in central organising principles, capable of accounting for the myriad of contradictory forms of relations between capital, the state and labour' (Bieler and Morton 2003, 473). Ian Bruff (2009, 337) likewise argues that 'Open Marxism's ontology totalises human social practice by way of its focus on capitalist social relations', and notes that the assumption that capitalist social relations are constituted of essential properties means that 'the *epistemological modesty* proclaimed by Open Marxists ... is in fact an assertion of *epistemological austerity*' (Bruff 2009, 337, emphasis in original).

These criticisms have led for calls to examine a broader range of social relations through an understanding of the reciprocal relationship between ideas, material capabilities and institutions (see Cox 1981; Bieler and Morton 2003, 476). Or as Bruff (2009, 341) phrases it, there is a 'need to move beyond the Puritanism of Open Marxism and embrace richer accounts of human social practice in capitalist societies'. John Michael Roberts (2002, 88) has likewise noted that 'open Marxists have yet to develop a set of categories which usefully allow us to explore the distinct ideological characteristics of social forms of life which, at first glance, seem to have nothing whatsoever in common with capital and labour'.

The notion that Open Marxism is a totalising or deterministic theory can, however, be contested. As Bonefeld (2009, 357) notes, Open Marxism does not elevate laws of historically specific social organisations into general laws of history, but 'seeks to dissolve the autarky of things by revealing their social constitution in human practice'. He notes that the appearance of 'things' in their fetishised forms 'does not make [them] any less "human", as if the world of things were a world apart' (Bonefeld 2009, 357). As such, the state and the tendency to depoliticise should not be conceived as determined aspects of a 'closed' theory. Simply because the social relations of capitalist production appear in an inherently crisis-prone form which may make governing strategies of depoliticisation *appear* imperative, it does not determine their deployment. As Bonefeld (2009, 357) phrases it, 'the anatomy of man can explain the anatomy of the ape, but ... the anatomy of the ape does not explain the anatomy of man'.

Open Marxism therefore retains significant explanatory value because it applies a theory of economic action that allows for the examination of its premises with reference to empirical evidence based on a number of simple research questions: do governments favour the imperatives of accumulation? Do these preferences have the potential to intensify class antagonisms? And if so, what governing strategies do governments use to attempt to achieve these objectives? By looking at the depoliticisation framework in the nuanced way suggested by Flinders and Buller, it is possible to see how, during 1974–75—a period often categorised by indecision in economic policy-making and highly politicised modes of governing—the Treasury and the Labour government acted strategically in order to pursue policies that diverged from those implied by its electoral mandate. Instead, they pursued objectives that were geared towards renewing conditions for profitable accumulation, principally through the politics of *preference-shaping* depoliticisation, in such a way that closely accords with an Open Marxist explanatory framework. It is to demonstrating this that the remainder of this article is dedicated.

From Social Contract to 'Social Contrick'

The Labour government was elected in 1974 on the basis of manifesto commitments that were firmly rooted in the Social Contract, which emerged out of the meetings of the TUC/Labour Party Liaison Committee, and first met in January 1972 on the initiative of the General Secretary of the Transport and General Workers' Union, Jack Jones. According to Robert Taylor (2000, 209), his principal motivation was to rebuild the relationship between the two groups after it had been badly damaged in the dispute over the previous Labour government's attempts to reform the structure of British industrial relations with *In Place of Strife* (Cmnd 3888, 1969). The meetings allowed the Labour party and the Trades Union Congress (TUC) to exploit the unpopularity of the Heath government's record on industrial relations, and the key document on the new strategy that emerged from the meetings was *Economic Policy and the Cost of Living* (TUC/Labour Party Liaison Committee (TUC/LPLC) 1973). The document called for statutory measures to control food prices as part of 'a wide-ranging' system of price controls, the expansion of subsidies for house building and public transportation and the redistribution of incomes and wealth (TUC/LPLC 1973, 313). A prompt return to voluntary collective bargaining was also one of the key commitments outlined in the document (TUC/LPLC 1973, 313–315).

© 2009 The Author. Journal compilation © 2009 Political Studies Association
BJPIR, 2009, 11(4)

Thomas A. Koelble (1987, 257) notes that the document 'established a deal in which the unions would support the Government's attempts to fight inflation by curbing their wage demands [in return for] favourable industrial policy, unemployment relief and structural modernization', while Mark Harmon (1997, 56) suggests that the document represented a quid pro quo between the party and the unions—a common theme in a relatively sparse literature on the Social Contract, with Jim Tomlinson (1990, 301) also describing the initiative as the 'most systematic attempt ever in Britain to make an agreement between the governing parties and the trade unions'. However, it has been noted that 'no specific commitment to incomes policy was included in this document, reflecting trade unions' wariness of such policies' (Tarling and Wilkinson 1977, 395), which also indicated a de facto commitment to refrain from introducing incomes policy while in office. This has resulted in Taylor (2000, 211) arguing that the document was 'little more than a shopping list of TUC demands', to which the Labour party had committed itself without having received a tangible demonstration of a similar intention to make concessions from the TUC. As such, the claim that the Social Contract was 'an arrangement whereby the TUC agreed to collaborate with a voluntary incomes policy in return for the repeal of the 1971 [Industrial Relations] Act and some modest economic benefits' (Sheldrake 1991, 77) is an overstatement of what the TUC had offered in return for substantial commitments from a future Labour government.

Given that British trade unionism had proved resilient enough to defeat the Heath government on the issue of 'Who Governs Britain?' after showing widespread discontent with industrial relations reform and incomes policies, it is necessary to ask how the Wilson government felt able to introduce the £6 pay limit in July 1975, and agree cuts in expenditure of £3,750 million from the 1976 public expenditure White Paper in December 1975, without provoking widespread discontent from the TUC. The depoliticisation framework is a useful tool for this purpose, and shows that despite the recognition of the trade union movement's hostility to any measures that implied a reduction in the standard of living of its members and the ability of unions to create conditions of political crisis through industrial action, the government consistently favoured increases in competitiveness over the social wage. The period between the 1974 general elections was the platform from which it was able to pursue these objectives more aggressively by employing the principles of depoliticisation during 1975.

The Short Parliament of February–October 1974

Denis Healey (2006, 392) recalls that on taking office he had been left with 'an economy on the brink of collapse'. The balance of payments was £3.3 billion in deficit in 1974 (Central Statistical Office (CSO) 1977, 46), the Retail Price Index stood at 12.8 per cent in the first quarter of 1974 (CSO 1976, 96–97) and unemployment was rising, reaching 628,000 by August 1974 (Butler and Butler 1994, 218). Given the government's commitments under the Social Contract, and its dependence on the support of the trade unions for its political success, it would have been unsurprising if the government had acted to reflate demand. However, it was not unemployment, but a shift of resources into the balance of payments, that took priority throughout 1974 and 1975.

© 2009 The Author. Journal compilation © 2009 Political Studies Association
BJPIR, 2009, 11(4)

This was reflected in the March Budget, which only made small concessions on pensions, food prices and the distribution of wealth, in favour of diverting resources into exports in an attempt to try and eradicate the balance of payments deficit and reduce the burden of Britain's external debt servicing until North Sea Oil came on-stream. The key problems in formulating the Budget had been outlined to the chancellor at a meeting in early March with the permanent secretary of the Treasury, Sir Douglas Allen. He informed the chancellor that 'it would first be necessary to offset the extra spending proposals [and] if the Chancellor still wanted to go hard for an improvement in the balance of payments, the Budget should be mildly deflationary' (The National Archives (TNA) T 171/1053, Note of a Meeting, 7 March 1974, 2). When the chancellor took his public expenditure plans to the cabinet, he informed his colleagues that it would be imperative to show 'how the extra expenditure, and the effects on demand of all these additional commitments, are going to be met by increased taxation' (TNA CAB 129/175, C (74) 4, 12 March 1974, 2).

The kind of Keynesian fiscal expansion to reduce unemployment and improve the lot of the least well off in society was therefore not forthcoming, and in the context of Britain's balance of payments deficit, the government's Central Policy Review Staff (CPRS) was sceptical about the prospects for the delivery of the government's manifesto commitments, suggesting that it should act quickly to prevent a further deterioration in the balance of payments position and improve company liquidity, noting that the tax yield was unlikely to be sufficient to allow for the promised increase in pensions and child cash allowances. As such, the CPRS argued that it would be essential to question 'how quickly can or should other Manifesto proposals involving higher expenditure be implemented' (TNA CAB 130/726, Misc 9 (74) 2, 12 March 1974, 8).

By the middle of March, therefore, the consensus was that the Budget should take about £200 million out of demand annually (TNA T 171/1053, Note of a Meeting, 15 March 1974, 6). There was to be no 'giveaway' Budget on the basis of the Social Contract. The chancellor's Budget speech on 26 March included a 3 per cent increase in the basic and higher rates of income tax, increases in personal and child tax allowances and a £500 million commitment to additional food subsidies. However, it also included £50 million of defence cuts and the extension of VAT at a rate of 10 per cent to confectionery and petroleum.

Healey (2006, 393) recalls that the Budget was 'received with rapture'; however the reality is much more modest. At a meeting between the TUC Economic Committee and the government on 27 March it was simply noted that 'there was approval of what the Government had already done, and an understanding that the Government was going in the right direction' (University of Warwick Modern Records Centre (MRC) MSS.292.D/560.1/10, Econ Ctee 10/1, 27 March 1974), while others were not as sympathetic. Tony Benn (1989, 127) noted that it was a Budget that would 'undoubtedly disappoint the Party and the movement, one which, as I was listening to it, I was convinced was written by the Treasury and not by Ministers'. Barbara Castle (1980, 51) felt that this view was shared by the chancellor of the Duchy of Lancaster, Harold Lever, recording in her diary that Lever believed that 'the essence of our policy was the Social Contract, which, above all, was based on reducing unemployment and going for growth. He thought the Budget would inevitably increase unemployment and we should be in trouble with the trade unions'.

In anticipation of the autumn election, the government offered some concessions to the working people in the form of a July mini-Budget, which reduced VAT by 2 per cent, gave relief to ratepayers, committed an extra £50 million to food subsidies and added a little under £200 million to demand by the end of 1974; however this occurred in the context of growing concern from the Bank of England and the Treasury about the size of the package as the date of the proposed announcement approached (Dell 1991, 79–80). These concerns quickly hardened into a robust Treasury view calling for an immediate and substantial review of the government's economic strategy.

Edmund Dell (1996, 410) notes that 'the official Treasury had at last concluded that existing policies were not sustainable' by October 1974. This view was reflected in a paper written for the chancellor by Sir Douglass Wass[3] in December, which informed Healey that 'there is no longer any official support for existing policies' (TNA T 277/3053, PCC (74) 4, 20 December 1974, 5). The Treasury analysis argued that the government needed simultaneously to address the problem of inflation and the structural imbalance of resources by deflating domestic demand and intervening directly in the wage bargaining process (TNA T 277/3053, PCC (74) 4, 20 December 1974, 3). This would be achieved by increasing taxation and reducing expenditure, which would necessarily and desirably involve some increase in the level of unemployment, and by laying down a norm for the rate of pay increases, which would be made effective either through government leadership, or statutory requirement (TNA T 277/3053, PCC (74) 4, 20 December 1974, 3). The recommendations struck to the very heart of the Social Contract in a way that was not unappreciated by Wass, who noted:

> I do not by any means underestimate the political costs of such a policy, which I would regret as much as the Chancellor himself and the most careful thought would have to be given to the industrial and social programmes required. But I now believe that the economic costs of clinging to the existing policy outweigh the political costs of abandoning it (TNA T 277/3053, PCC (74) 4, 20 December 1974, 5).

However, Wass also noted that while the political costs of the strategy appeared high, this only held 'without the external crisis that would justify it' (TNA T 277/3053, PCC (74) 4, 20 December 1974, 5).

By the end of 1974, therefore, a coherent picture of economic strategy which recognised that perceptions of crisis could help to alter political expectations had emerged. On the one hand, the Labour government had to manage the demands of organised labour, which had proven both in 1968 and 1974 that it was able to mobilise effectively to defeat legislation or create social conditions that translated into a significant political crisis through industrial action. The Treasury had also identified the need for social objectives to be sidelined while the decline of the British economy and its associated effects were dealt with, and noted that an

© 2009 The Author. Journal compilation © 2009 Political Studies Association
BJPIR, 2009, 11(4)

external crisis would have the potential to nullify trade union militancy, which would allow for a return to incomes policy and help justify a reduction of the public sector's claim on resources.

Exchange Rate Strategy and the £6 Pay Policy

The competitive position of British industry had been a long-standing issue, and the Treasury noted that the classic way to bring about an improvement was to depreciate the currency. After the collapse of the Bretton-Woods system, however, this posed several problems. The most notable of these was the absence of any mechanism to adjust the rate downwards in an orderly fashion, which meant that the authorities would not be able to take credit for any benefits gained from a slide in the rate (TNA T 277/3054, PCC (75) 33 Revise, 26 February 1975, 4), and that in the event of an overt attempt to shift the rate down, British policy would be directly responsible for the erosion of £5 billion of official reserves and £2.5 billion of private holdings (TNA T 358/207, Walker to Barratt, 11 March 1975, 1). Depreciation would also place increasing pressure on the wage bargaining process because employers would be pressured into granting greater wage increases to compensate for the rise in the cost of living (TNA T 358/207, Walker to Barratt, 11 March 1975, 2), and expose Britain to criticisms of international misconduct that could be seen as 'the first link in a chain reaction of possible competitive depreciations' (TNA T 277/3055, PCC (75) 41, 13 March 1975, 4). So despite preferences for devaluation, it was widely felt that it was unworkable under the floating rate system. However, the emergence of market pressure on the rate provided the conditions under which exchange rate strategy and preferences for incomes policy became mutually reinforcing, as the government argued that a new incomes policy was absolutely essential if confidence in the counter-inflationary credibility of British policy was to return and the slide of the pound halted, despite its preference to see sterling fall.

Pressure on the sterling rate in 1975 first significantly emerged in anticipation of the Budget in the spring, when the transactions of a Middle Eastern seller forced the rate to $2.37 by 8 April, for which the Treasury authorised the Bank of England to spend up to $80 million in reserve-switching operations (see TNA T 358/207, Note for the Record, 7 April 1975, 1–2; TNA T 358/207, Note for the Record, 8 April 1975, 1). However, it remained the Treasury's intention to bring about a depreciation of around 10 per cent within 12 months, and it had been decided that to achieve this it would be 'desirable to rely to the maximum extent possible on autonomous factors ... so that the main responsibility for depreciation is seen to lie elsewhere than with HMG' (TNA T 358/207, Walker to Mitchell, 11 April 1975, 1). As a result, the Bank's intervention strategy was kept under constant review, and is aptly described as parsimonious.

When pressure re-emerged on 22 April, and the Governor of the Bank of England requested $200 million to assert control over the markets, it was noted that as 'it is indeed our policy to get the rate down. ... we ought not to slog away spending money to try and stop this happening' (TNA T 358/207, Barratt to Wass, 22 April 1975, 1). As this pressure continued to unfold, the Treasury remained steadfast, with the Head of Overseas Finance, Sir Derek Mitchell, arguing that to arrest the decline through intervention would put Britain's foreign reserves under unjustified strain (TNA T 358/208, Note of a Meeting, 5 May 1975, 1), and Wass noted that 'there need not be a commitment to massive intervention when [sterling] reached a particular level' (TNA T 358/208, Note of a Meeting, 5 May 1975, 2).

The continuation of a strategy of parsimonious intervention had seen sterling fall by nine cents from $2.38 to $2.29 between April and June at a cost of £641 million to the foreign reserves (see TNA T 354/416, Reserves Objectives, 11 August 1975, 3). The extent of the slide was clearly affected by the Treasury's reluctance to intervene, but the persistent pressure had created an impression of crisis, and began to alter expectations about the kind of policies that were legitimate and necessary for the maintenance of external confidence. As such, the Treasury offered the following argument:

> There has developed an expectation that the Government is 'going to act'. For as long as this expectation is disappointed, 25 per cent [below Smithsonian] will not be regarded by outside observers and operators as sustainable. If the exchange rate accordingly is going to be pulled down by market forces, mere money, as opposed to policy change, will not succeed in offering a sufficient opposing force (TNA T 358/208, Hedley-Miller to Wass, 11 June 1975, 1).

When the chancellor reported the events on the foreign exchange markets in June, he noted that pressure on sterling had occurred 'against a background where British wage settlements were being made at four times the level of settlements in West Germany, and where British inflation was likely to run at more than double the rate in our principal competitor countries', and as such informed his colleagues that 'there was an urgent need for a new incomes policy' (TNA CAB 128/56, CC (75) 27th Conclusions, 12 June 1975, 4–5).

The ability for pressure on the sterling rate to act as leverage with the trade unions and to absorb the political ramifications of imposing an incomes policy was clearly recognised. At a meeting between the chancellor and the TUC on 20 June, despite the Treasury's intention to let the pound slide, and the fact that events on the foreign exchange markets had been allowed to occur, if not actively engineered, through the employment of a parsimonious intervention strategy, Healey informed the TUC that they were forcing him to take action, and that if confidence was to be restored and extensive diversification of sterling was to be prevented, it would be absolutely necessary for a 10 per cent wage norm to be introduced at the earliest opportunity (TNA PREM 16/342, Note of a Meeting, 20 June 1975, 1–2).

While union leaders Hugh Scanlon and Jack Jones were anxious not to be framed for a policy they could not deliver, and were sceptical about achieving a 10 per cent norm (TNA PREM 16/342, Note of a Meeting, 20 June 1975, 3–5), they had been engaged in productive discussions with the government (see TNA PREM 16/342, Pay Policy—Mr Murray's initiative, 4 June 1975, 1), and by 19 June, the Prime Minister's Office was referring to the £6 flat rate proposal as the 'Jack Jones' formula (TNA PREM 16/342, Hunt to Wilson, 19 June 1975, 2). When the pound fell four cents against the dollar on 30 June, and both Kuwait and Saudi Arabia indicated that they would move out of sterling imminently (TNA T 358/209, Note of a Meeting, 30 June 1975, 1), the stage was set for the Treasury to propose an early announcement of incomes policy with confidence that union leaders were onside, with market events appearing to drive policy.

At cabinet the following day it was agreed that the chancellor would make an early announcement to the House indicating his determination to get inflation down to 10 per cent by the third quarter of 1976, and that if agreement could not be reached with the TUC, it would be prepared to legislate (TNA CAB 128/57, CC (75) 31st Conclusions, 1 July 1975, 6–7). Within the Prime Minister's Office, Bernard Donoughue and Joe Haines felt compelled to write to Wilson noting that the cabinet was being faced 'with an attempt by the Treasury to stampede it into a statutory pay policy' (TNA PREM 16/343, Donoughue and Haines to Wilson, 1 July 1975, 1); however the reality was a far more sophisticated expression of economic strategy. The Treasury had effectively reconciled the TUC's objection in principle to incomes policy with its own preferences by associating the slide in the rate with a lack of confidence in counter-inflationary credibility, despite its wishes to see the pound fall. Therefore, the external crisis used to justify the £6 pay policy is more appropriately described as a 'non-crisis', which was used in order to shape broader expectations about policy. A similar 'non-crisis' was used in order to justify cuts from the 1976 public expenditure White Paper in December 1975.

External Financing and the 1976 Public Expenditure White Paper

The second pillar of the Treasury's revised economic strategy was a reduction in the public sector's claim on resources. However, given the government's commitments under the Social Contract, expenditure issues were highly sensitive, and the appearance of crisis was once again used in order to foster support for policies to which the organised labour movement was opposed in principle. The expected financing gap was used in order to argue that it was necessary to draw from the IMF's 1975 oil facility, and that expenditure cuts were essential if Britain was to avoid a conditional drawing from the Fund, with more severe consequences for public expenditure. This case was made despite the view that 'ways would inevitably be found to mobilise sufficient resources for last resort lending in the event of need' (TNA T 354/347, Walker to Hedley-Miller, 17 May 1974, 2), the large degree of uncertainty over forecasts and the fact that it had been doubted, even by Fund officials, that it was necessary for Britain to draw.

As Steve Ludlam (1992, 716–717) notes, prudence in public expenditure under Harold Wilson began in February 1974, when Healey informed the third cabinet of the government that public expenditure would not be able to rise. However, the UK's Public Sector Borrowing Requirement (PSBR) had been increasing substantially, and had virtually doubled fiscal year on fiscal year between 1971–72 and 1974–75, reaching nearly £8 billion (CSO 1977, 52). Not only was this a concern to hawkish international opinion informed by monetarist economic theory, which saw public expenditure as actively driving inflation, but there was concern within the UK on the grounds that 'the UK's external debt [was] increasing at a rate roughly equivalent to the value of a full year's North Sea Oil production in 1980 at

1974 prices' (TNA T 354/414, Walker to Hedley-Miller, 22 January 1975, 6). Regardless of any credibility constraint in terms of international financial markets, therefore, it was clear that levels of public sector borrowing were unsustainable. The problem was whether any reduction was saleable at home.

In the April Budget of 1975 Healey had announced cuts of £1,000 million in planned expenditure at 1974 survey prices, which Wass (2008, 98–99) recalls was based on views that were rather more political than economic. As such, the Treasury began making the case for further reductions on the basis of a slower-than-expected rate of growth of GDP and a shortened acceptable time frame for the correction of the balance of payments because of Britain's deteriorating credit rating (TNA T 277/3055, PCC (75) 49 (revise) 8 May 1975, annex, 1–4). The Treasury argued that these deteriorating forecasts meant that the government would have to make 'a very substantial reduction in public expenditure for the year 1979— perhaps rather more than £3 billion at 1974 prices' (TNA T 277/3055, PCC (75) 49 (revise) 8 May 1975, annex, 6) if the tax burden was to be kept relatively constant. The view was put to cabinet on 22 May in what Wass (2008, 119) describes as 'a long and argumentative meeting', and although Tony Benn argued that 'a wholly feasible alternative policy based on import controls' existed, Wilson concluded by suggesting that it was 'only by asking officials to proceed with the expenditure survey on the basis put forward ... could they ensure they would have available sufficient options later in the year should major cuts have to be made' (TNA CAB 128/56, CC (75) 25th Conclusions, 22 May 1975, annex, 5).

The preference for expenditure cuts therefore faced two problems. The first was the general objection to cuts *on principle*. The second was the fact that the Labour left had proposed an alternative that may have been objectionable because of Britain's commitments under the GATT and EEC membership, but was presented as a workable option *in practice*. However, the external financing situation was used in order to make the case that public expenditure cuts were the only feasible option *in practice*, and that the AES was more objectionable *on principle*.

The possibility of drawing on the IMF oil facility to finance the external deficit was first discussed by Treasury and Fund officials on 14 and 15 August, and the most striking thing to come out of the meetings was that the Fund was unsure that Britain could show a demonstrable need to borrow from the oil facility, which would require evidence of a substantial reserves loss (TNA T 354/416, Cassell to Fogarty, 18 August 1975, 1–3). In October, the Overseas Finance Division presented forecasts that made unclear the extent of Britain's external financing difficulties, suggesting that Britain would have to find between £100 million and £900 million to cover the deficit over the coming six months, and it was in light of its uncertainty that it recommended that it was 'a matter of simple prudence that we should set out now to fill the gap (or the larger part of it) by a drawing of £575 million ... on the IMF oil facility' (TNA T 354/416, Mitchell to Wass, 15 October 1975, 1). The timing of potential action was also advantageous, because the oil facility would only be available for the calendar year, and it was on the basis that should Britain not draw in 1975 resources would be lost, and not a critical external financing need, that the Treasury felt the Fund application should be made (TNA T 354/416, External Finance: Prospects and Policy, 15 October 1975, 9).

© *2009 The Author. Journal compilation* © *2009 Political Studies Association*
BJPIR, 2009, 11(4)

Cabinet was informed of the chancellor's intention to apply for the oil facility loan on 5 November, on the grounds that Britain's external creditworthiness had not improved enough to make market borrowing plausible (TNA CAB 128/57, CC (75) 46th Conclusions, 6 November 1975, annex, 2), despite uncertainty surrounding forecasts about whether or not Britain would face a large external financing gap. The impression of crisis, however, was encouraged at cabinet the following week, when Healey argued:

> It might well prove impossible in the interim to borrow overseas in order to finance the current account deficit, and the Government would then be forced to borrow from international institutions on conditions which would almost certainly include public expenditure cuts even more severe than those now contemplated (TNA CAB 128/57, CC (75) 48th Conclusions, 13 November 1975, annex, 2).

The prospect of an external financing crisis and the prospect of conditionality were therefore used to justify an application to the IMF, which in turn helped to mobilise support for further public expenditure cuts. This is because despite the distinction that the Fund made between 'soft' drawings from the oil facility and low credit tranches, and 'hard' drawings from the higher credit tranches so far as conditionality was concerned (TNA T 354/415, Littler to Fogarty, 24 April 1975, 1–2), it was noted that oil facility drawings would mean that import controls could not be introduced without prior consultation with the Fund, and would lead to any request for borrowings from the higher tranches to be denied (TNA T 385/30, Outstanding Fund Questions, 21 October 1975, 1–2). The December IMF application therefore appeared to limit the government's room for manoeuvre to fiscal policy, which it suggested was effectively beyond its control because it had to foster confidence overseas in order to ensure continued access to international finance while the balance of payments was restored to equilibrium in the medium term. This endeavour was no doubt helped by the fact that Tony Benn had himself cast the debate in terms of a choice between extensive public expenditure cuts and generalised import controls.

As early as February Benn had informed the Ministerial Committee on Economic Strategy that a fast improvement in the balance of payments would require a substantial reduction in the standard of living imposed by a fiscal reduction of about £3 billion, but that a slower adjustment could be made on the basis of selective assistance to industry and price and import controls (TNA CAB 134/3929, MES (75) 4, 11 February 1975, 1–3). Benn's view was that public expenditure cuts represented 'a policy of despair representing an admission of the failure of our economic policy', and that Britain 'must now seriously consider an explicit commitment to a protectionist strategy for industrial reconstruction and a return to full employment' (TNA PREM 16/341, Benn to Wilson, 24 March 1974, 2–3). Presenting the debate in these terms, however, helped to consolidate the Treasury's argument for a multilateral solution underscored by expenditure cuts. Not only would the imposition of import controls run contrary to Britain's commitments under the GATT and the philosophy of Britain's post-war foreign economic policy; it also meant that Britain would be actively taking the decision to isolate itself from Europe and the world, which would mean that the failure of a system of import controls to reverse the decline, or widespread retaliation to the system, had the potential to leave Britain unable to access multilateral credit facilities and facing the prospect of bankruptcy.

Joel Barnett (1982, 80) notes that, in light of Healey's threat of resignation over the issue, 'there was probably never any doubt we would achieve our target', and by 11 December, cuts from the 1976 public expenditure White Paper totalling £3,750 million had been agreed (see TNA CAB 128/57, CC (75) 55th Conclusions, 11 December 1975, annex, 8) on the basis of two arguments. Firstly, it was argued that Britain faced an imminent external financing crisis that required it to borrow from the IMF because confidence was too weak to borrow elsewhere. Secondly, it was argued that if Britain were to avoid even more severe cuts, there would have to be pre-emptive action which occurred within the framework of multilateral co-operation. Both of these arguments suggested that expenditure cuts were inevitable; however, just as was the case with the exchange rate earlier in the year, the crisis was principally one of perception. Neither the Treasury nor the Fund had been convinced throughout the year that the size of the financing gap would be critical, and the decision to draw on the Fund was taken not out of necessity, but out of prudence. This proved politically expedient in so far as it locked Britain into multilateral solutions to adjustment, adding weight to objections to the AES and to the argument that expenditure cuts were required in order to restore British creditworthiness.

Conclusions

At the beginning of this article it was argued that adopting an Open Marxist framework of analysis was beneficial in explaining how governments are able to act in order to help restore conditions for profitable accumulation through the politics of depoliticisation. However, for such a case to be more than simply *plausible*, a number of conditions must be met. Firstly, it must be possible to establish that the preferences of the governing elite stood in contrast to those of organised labour, and would likely exacerbate political tensions were they implemented in a politicised environment. But secondly, it must be possible to demonstrate intention on the part of governing elites to use market forces as the justification for potentially unpopular policy changes as part of an attempt to minimise political dissent. In such a project, the use of primary documents plays a fundamental role, because in a strategy of depoliticisation the preferences of government are not publicly *revealed* preferences. Therefore, a simple comparison of published statements and manifesto commitments taken at face value will tend to amplify the extent to which market forces have appeared to limit policy autonomy.

The article has argued that the politics of depoliticisation was employed in accordance with such a framework in order to introduce incomes policy in July 1975 and to agree public expenditure cuts from the 1976 public expenditure White Paper in December 1975, and the empirical evidence offers strong support. While the return to incomes policy and expenditure cuts was not legitimised through traditional *rule-based* depoliticisation, except in so far as obligations to the IMF, GATT and EEC to remain committed to multilateral solutions to external financing difficulties represented relatively weak and ephemeral rules, by utilising the concept of *preference-shaping* depoliticisation it is possible to see how, during a period often characterised in the literature by indecision and politicised modes of economic management, the government took steps in order to argue that decisions relating to the imposition of incomes policy and the reduction of expenditure were beyond its control because of its dependence on market confidence, despite the fact that its preferences largely concurred with 'market sentiment'.

As early as December 1974 the Treasury made it clear that it should be the aim of government to introduce incomes policy and cut public expenditure, and recognised the potential for this to create political difficulties. However, it had also recognised that these political difficulties could be negotiated in the event of an external crisis, which would change expectations about policy, and while the government did not act to create conditions of crisis, it nevertheless suggested that 1975 was a year of two crises. The first was in the foreign exchange market, as sterling fell in the spring and the summer, which prompted it to argue that it was absolutely necessary to impose an incomes policy. The second was an external financing crisis, which prompted the government to argue that it was absolutely necessary to apply to the IMF, and therefore to cut public expenditure for 1978–79 in order to bolster Britain's creditworthiness among a rapidly shrinking pool of potential lenders.

However, 1975 was actually a year of two 'non-crises'. Firstly, the Treasury had desired the fall in the exchange rate on the grounds that it would help improve the competitive position of British industry, and the Bank of England had been prevented from making a decisive intervention in the market in order that it be allowed to occur. Nevertheless, despite these preferences, the fall in the rate was presented as evidence that confidence in British counter-inflationary credibility was dangerously low and necessitated the introduction of a £6 incomes norm. Secondly, the external financing difficulties at the end of the year were expected and not imminent, and based on forecasts subject to a wide margin of error that reflected the Fund's initial doubts about Britain's need to draw from the oil facility. Furthermore, the drawing was eventually made principally as a matter of prudence because the resources would be lost at the end of the calendar year, but by presenting the application as a response to a further deterioration in confidence, the government was able to argue that large cuts in planned expenditure were necessary in order to restore confidence and help it avoid being forced to take more drastic action in order to secure external finance, while locking policy into multilateral solutions to balance of payments financing through the explicit rejection of import restrictions as an appropriate adjustment tool. The primary documents therefore support the depoliticisation framework in this case. Governing elites clearly had preferences for policy that stood in contrast to those of the labour movement, and acted on more than one occasion to mobilise the logic of market forces in order to argue that decisions in the field of counter-inflation and fiscal policy were, for all intents and purposes, beyond the scope for discretionary control, and it was by shaping preferences in this way that the government was able to move progressively away from the Social Contract.

While this article has argued that Harold Wilson's Labour government used *preference-shaping* depoliticisation, it has made little substantive engagement with the issue of how successful this strategy was. In many respects, this is a difficult question to answer, because while the £6 pay policy held reasonably well, and reaction to the cuts in the 1976 public expenditure White Paper were muted, it did not significantly delay the onset of a political crisis, which emerged during the Winter of Discontent in 1979. The most developed attempt at measuring the effectiveness of depoliticisation is the work of Steve Kettell (2008, 635), which suggests that success should be measured with reference to its material effects— whether the strategy achieves its goals—and its impact on perceptions. But given the immutability of crisis in the Open Marxist framework, it is unclear whether examining the success of strategies of depoliticisation is a meaningful enterprise in the long run: the foundations of the framework, without determining specific outcomes, imply that, ultimately, each attempt will fail. So for the purposes of future research on the success of depoliticisation, the broad strokes must be finessed, with the logical focus of analysis coming to rest on the relative possibilities for the success of rule-based strategies as opposed to the institutional and preference-shaping alternatives.

About the Author

Chris Rogers, Department of Politics and International Studies, University of Warwick, Gibbet Hill Road, Coventry CV4 7AL, UK, email: *christopher.rogers@warwick.ac.uk*

Notes

I am grateful to Wyn Grant and anonymous reviewers for comments on an earlier draft of this article, and to the ESRC for providing the funding to undertake this research (award number PTA-031-2005-00139).

1. Cliff and Gluckstein (1996, 327) coined the term 'Social Contrick'.

2. On Britain's return to the gold standard in 1925, see Kettell (2004). On the ERM, see Bonefeld and Burnham (1996, 1998), Burnham (1999) and Kettell (2008). On New Labour see Burnham (2001a), also Watson and Hay (2003).

3. Sir Douglas Wass succeeded Sir Douglas Allen when Allen took up the post of Head of the Home Civil Service in 1974.

Bibliography

Barnett, J. (1982) *Inside the Treasury* (London: Andre Deutsch).

Benn, T. (1989) *Against the Tide: Diaries 1973–1976* (London: Hutchinson).

Bieler, A. and Morton, A. D. (2003) 'Globalisation, the state and class struggle: A "Critical Economy" engagement with Open Marxism', *British Journal of Politics & International Relations*, 5:4, 467–499.

Bonefeld, W. (1992) 'Social constitution and the form of the capitalist state', in W. Bonefeld, R. Gunn and K. Psychopedis (eds), *Open Marxism Volume I: Dialectics and History* (London: Pluto Books), 93–132.

Bonefeld, W. (2009) 'Society and nature: Some notes on Ian Bruff', *British Journal of Politics & International Relations*, 11:2, 355–359.

Bonefeld, W. and Burnham, P. (1996) 'Britain and the politics of the European Exchange Rate Mechanism', *Capital and Class*, 60, 5–38.

Bonefeld, W. and Burnham, P. (1998) 'The politics of counter inflationary credibility in Britain, 1990–94', *Review of Radical Political Economics*, 30:1, 32–52.

Bruff, I. (2009) 'The totalisation of human social practice: Open Marxists and capitalist social relations, Foucauldians and power relations', *British Journal of Politics & International Relations*, 11:2, 332–351.

Burnham, P. (1994) 'Open Marxism and vulgar international political economy', *Review of International Political Economy*, 1:2, 121–132.

Burnham, P. (1995) 'Capital, crisis and the international state system', in W. Bonefeld and J. Holloway (eds), *Global Capital, National State and the Politics of Money* (Basingstoke: Macmillan), 92–115.

Burnham, P. (1999) 'The politics of economic management in the 1990s', *New Political Economy*, 4:1, 37–54.

Burnham, P. (2001a) 'New Labour and the politics of depoliticisation', *British Journal of Politics & International Relations*, 3:2, 127–149.

Burnham, P. (2001b) 'Marx, international political economy and globalisation', *Capital and Class*, 75, 103–112.

Burnham, P. (2006) 'Marxism, the state and British politics', *British Politics*, 1:1, 67–83.

Butler, D. and Butler, G. (1994) *British Political Facts 1900–1994* (7th edn) (Basingstoke: Macmillan).

Castle, B. (1980) *The Castle Diaries 1974–76* (London: Weidenfeld & Nicholson).

Central Statistical Office (1976) *Economic Trends*, Annual Supplement No. 2 (London: HMSO).

Central Statistical Office (1977) *Economic Trends*, 277 (London: HMSO).

Clarke, S. (1988) *Keynesianism, Monetarism and the Crisis of the State* (Aldershot: Edward Elgar).

Clarke, S. (2001) 'The globalisation of capital, crisis and class struggle', *Capital and Class*, 75, 93–101.

Cliff, T. and Gluckstein, D. (1996) *The Labour Party: A Marxist History* (2nd edn) (London: Bookmarks).

Cmnd 3888 (1969) *In Place of Strife* (London: HMSO).

Cohen, B. J. (1998) *The Geography of Money* (Ithaca, NY: Cornell University Press).

Cox, R. W. (1981) 'Social forces, states and world orders: Beyond international relations theory', *Millennium: Journal of International Studies*, 10:2, 126–155.

Dell, E. (1991) *A Hard Pounding: Politics and Economic Crisis 1974–1976* (Oxford: Oxford University Press).

Dell, E. (1996) *The Chancellors: A History of the Chancellors of the Exchequer 1945–1990* (London: Harper Collins).

Flinders, M. and Buller, J. (2006) 'Depoliticisation: Principles, tactics and tools', *British Politics*, 1:3, 293–318.

Harmon, M. D. (1997) *The British Labour Government and the 1976 IMF Crisis* (Basingstoke: Macmillan).

Healey, D. (2006) *The Time of My Life* (London: Politico's).

Helleiner, E. (1992) 'States and the future of global finance', *Review of International Studies*, 18:1, 31–49.

Holloway, J. (1995) 'Global capital and the national state', in W. Bonefeld and J. Holloway (eds), *Global Capital, National State and the Politics of Money* (Basingstoke: Macmillan), 116–140.

Kettell, S. (2004) *The Political Economy of Exchange Rate Policy Making: From the Gold Standard to the Euro* (Basingstoke: Palgrave Macmillan).

Kettell, S. (2008) 'Does depoliticisation work? Evidence from Britain's membership of the European Exchange Rate Mechanism, 1990–92', *British Journal of Politics & International Relations*, 10:4, 630–648.

Koelble, T. A. (1987) 'Trade unionists, party activists, and politicians: The struggle for power over party rules in the British Labour party and the West German Social Democratic party', *Comparative Politics*, 19:3, 253–266.

Ludlam, S. (1992) 'The gnomes of Washington: Four myths of the 1976 IMF crisis', *Political Studies*, 40:4, 713–727.

Marx, K. (1973) *Grundrisse* (London: Allen Lane).

Offe, C. (1975) 'The theory of the capitalist state and the problem of policy formation', in L. Lindelberg, R. Alford, C. Crouch and C. Offe (eds), *Stress and Contradiction in Modern Capitalism: Public Policy and the Theory of the State* (Lexington, MA: Lexington Books), 125–145.

Pauly, L. W. (1997) *Who Elected the Bankers?* (Ithaca, NY and London: Cornell University Press).

Roberts, J. M. (2002) 'From reflection to refraction: Opening up Open Marxism', *Capital and Class*, 78, 87–116.

Sheldrake, J. (1991) *Industrial Relations Politics in Britain 1880–1989* (London: Pinter).

Strange, S. (1994) *States and Markets* (2nd edn) (London and New York: Continuum).

Tarling, R. and Wilkinson, F. (1977) 'The Social Contract: Post-war income policies and their inflationary impact', *Cambridge Journal of Economics*, 1:4, 395–414.

Taylor, R. (2000) *The TUC: From the General Strike to New Unionism* (Basingstoke: Palgrave).

Tomlinson, J. (1990) *Public Policy and the Economy since 1900* (Oxford: Oxford University Press).

TUC/Labour Party Liaison Committee (1973) 'Economic policy and the cost of living', in TUC, *Report of the 105th Annual Trades Unions Congress* (London: TUC).

Wass, D. (2008) *Decline to Fall: The Making of British Macro-economic Policy and the 1976 IMF Crisis* (Oxford: Oxford University Press).

Watson, M. and Hay, C. (2003) 'The discourse of globalisation and the logic of no alternative: Rendering the contingent necessary in the political economic of New Labour', *Policy & Politics*, 31:3, 289–305.

doi: 10.1111/j.1467-856X.2009.00375.x   *BJPIR: 2009 VOL 11, 652–665*

Laughter and Liability: The Politics of British and Dutch Television Satire

Stephen Coleman, Anke Kuik and Liesbet van Zoonen

Contemporary politicians face immense rhetorical and communicative challenges. Performing on the intertwined stages of politics, media (including Internet) and everyday life, they need to master diverse and contrasting repertoires of talk. Political communication research, at present, has ignored the question of how politicians face and experience these challenges, and how they reflect on the new communicative field. In this article, we begin to redress this situation by analysing and comparing the motives, experiences and reflections of politicians who appeared in the British satirical TV show, Have I Got News for You, and its Dutch adaptation, Dit was het Nieuws. Based on in-depth interviews with seven Dutch and 14 English MPs, we conclude that they draw from three repertoires to legitimise and reflect on their participation: a strategic, indulgent and anti-elitist repertoire. The first repertoire is predictable in the context of current political communication research, whereas the latter two add new dimensions of pleasure and bottom-up representation to it.

Keywords: Satire; political communication; rhetoric; performance

Contemporary politicians face immense rhetorical and communicative challenges. Performing on the intertwined stages of politics, media (including Internet) and everyday life, they need to master diverse and contrasting repertoires of talk. Nowhere is this challenge more pertinent than in the many genres of infotainment that popular television offers. The combination of entertainment and information defining talk shows, satire and comedy requires a much wider range of communicative styles than a public speech, a journalistic interview or an intervention in parliament. Performing a convincing political persona in these contexts requires continuous and effortless shifts from anecdote to analysis, emotion to reason, polemic to moderation, personal to political, serious to humorous and back again.

While a whole industry of spin doctors and media trainers continuously coaches politicians for these sheer insurmountable trials, political communication scholars have been slow to examine systematically if, how and under what circumstances politicians recognise these requirements and manage to meet them. Studies on infotainment have focused on questions about its alleged ubiquity (e.g. Brants 1998) or its possible effects (e.g. Baum 2003); studies on the articulation of politics and popular culture have mostly addressed its democratic potential (e.g. Street 1997; Coleman 2003), and its meaning for citizens (Van Zoonen 2005). Some analyses of political television talk have taken place in the field of linguistic pragmatics, yet at present these do not add up to a coherent body of knowledge (e.g. Lauerbach 2007). As a result of these research agendas, current scholarship has little to offer for what can be considered the most pressing need of politicians today: the ability to communicate effectively in a range of mediated contexts through a diversity of appropriate and effective styles. While one might argue that political communication scholarship does not exist in order to advise politicians how to become more culturally relevant, there are also more pressing academic reasons for analysing the experience of politicians as media performers. Media, and television in particular, currently provide the wider rhetorical environment in which politicians have to operate; a study of media performance therefore relates directly to classic issues in political science concerning rhetoric and theatre. Secondly, the increased convergence of politics and media has been referred to as 'media logic' which, according to many scholars and critics, leads political actors, parties and institutions to neglect structural political and policy issues and focus instead on short-term, individual media success. A study of the performance of politicians in the media therefore directly addresses whether and how such media logic is indeed experienced as an inescapable force which hinders the discussion of politics. Finally, the changing communicative environment raises more general issues about the nature of 'representation', in its meaning as delegation on behalf of citizens and in its meaning as a mimetic reflection of citizens, especially with respect to the question of whether a different kind of representation is enforced by media logic.

We address these issues in this article by analysing and comparing the participation of politicians in the British satirical TV show, *Have I Got News for You*, and its Dutch adaptation, *Dit was het Nieuws*. We examined both the actual appearance of the British and Dutch politicians who participated in the show, and their subsequent reflections on their own performance in the programme. In this article we present the latter part of this research based on interviews with 14 British and Dutch politicians. Before we specify theory and method, we introduce the programme and its political participants in some detail.

Have I Got News for You and *Dit was het Nieuws*

Have I Got News for You (HIGNFY) is a satirical BBC television show which has run twice a year since 1990 and will be entering its 38th season in 2009. The format consists of a presenter and two teams comprising a captain and a different guest each week, all of them sitting behind a news desk. The teams compete in four rounds, ostensibly to test their knowledge of and commentary upon current affairs. In the end a winner is declared, although there is no obvious logic to the way points are acquired. The conversations are informal, confrontational and satirical. The show is recorded live before a studio audience a day before the actual broadcast, which is edited. *HIGNFY* has been the subject of public controversies in the United Kingdom, the most notable of which occurred when its original presenter was 'outed' by the press for visiting prostitutes and using drugs. (Since then there has been a different guest presenter each week.) Other debates occurred over presenters making insulting and allegedly libellous remarks about public figures.

The format has seen a number of international adaptations, for instance in all Scandinavian countries, Germany and the Netherlands. The Dutch version is a direct copy of the original *HIGNFY*, and has run successfully since 1996 under the title *Dit was het Nieuws (DWHN, This was the News)* on one of the public channels.

© 2009 The Authors. Journal compilation © 2009 Political Studies Association
BJPIR, 2009, 11(4)

The presenters and the editorial teams have been mostly recruited from a Dutch stand-up comedian group with its own venue in Amsterdam.

Because of its nature as a satirical current affairs programme, politicians, journalists and artists are the most likely guests in *HIGNFY* and *DWHN*. Famous politicians have appeared on the show, for instance Ken Livingstone, Clare Short and Neil Kinnock in the UK, and Mark Rutte, Geert Wilders and Wouter Bos in the Netherlands.

Existing Research and Theoretical Framework

The present inquiry is located within a wide and somewhat incoherent research field constituted by, among others, studies of infotainment, satire, image building, political personalisation and communicative competence. In this field, political television comedy is increasingly gaining attention, especially due to its growing audience success and alleged political impact on young people. The US-based *The Daily Show* is the main programme that has aroused academic interest, with research divided into analyses of its particular form, content and humour (Baym 2005; Brewer and Marquardt 2007; Feldman 2007; Fox et al. 2007; Gaines 2007; Warner 2007), usage by young people (Jones 2005; Young and Tisinger 2006) and effects on candidate evaluations (Young 2004; Baumgartner and Morris 2006), political knowledge (Hollander 2005), political gratifications (Holbert et al. 2007) and political participation (Cao and Brewer 2008).

Conspicuously absent in these studies is a set of key actors, namely politicians and candidates who appear on *The Daily Show* and similar programmes, either as the objects of jokes or as actively participating guests. While Matthew Baum (2005) discusses various reasons why political candidates might choose to appear in talk and comedy shows, his argument is based on general considerations about campaigning rather than on direct questioning of politicians featured in these programmes. More generally, how politicians reflect on their own performances in the media has hardly been the subject of any research. Some studies have focused on the experience of female politicians with journalists and media, but they have been articulated mainly within the theme of gender and politics, and much less in connection with political communication and performance (e.g. Sreberny and Van Zoonen 2000). Yet, it has been widely recognised that the media performances of politicians are key to their public persona and their political ups and downs (e.g. Corner 2003). In an era typified by personalised and celebrity politics, the question of how politicians fail or succeed to manage their media performance and public persona is of paramount relevance to practitioners and academics alike. Complicating the matter is the fact that politicians need to perform a consistent and coherent public persona on different public stages which require the mastery of widely dissimilar and often contrasting communicative styles. John Corner (2003) identified three spheres of action in which politicians operate, which can also be considered as stages on which they must perform. There is the political stage where performance relates to the development and negotiation of political ideas, and the exercise of administrative power; there is the stage of private life, increasingly a platform for politicians where personal integrity and reliability are at stake; and there is the media and Internet stage with its various possibilities of autonomous (on the Internet mainly) and mediated performance.

As Van Zoonen (2005, 75) notes, the repertoires of talk that the media stage requires are immensely heterogeneous, ranging from online chat, blogging, TV debates, soundbite quotes and rational analysis, to personal anecdotes, emotional sharing and witty participation. Political comedies like *The Daily Show* or the programmes that are the subject of our present analysis—*HIGNFY* and *DWHN*—offer an additional challenge because of their indistinct generic boundaries which thwart a preset definition of appropriate communicative behaviour and produce an unpredictable oscillation within the programme between the serious and the amusing. Appearing on such shows therefore contains definite political risks, as the unfortunate performance of the Dutch Social Democrat leader, Wouter Bos, in *DWHN* demonstrated. Bos could not help laughing when one of the team captains made a profoundly inappropriate joke about the circumcision of one of his fellow members of parliament. The next day, a leading national newspaper scorned him for lacking the guts to stand up to the joke and criticise the team captain. To this day the party leader does not want to be reminded of his participation in *DWHN*.[1] Such risks notwithstanding, politicians have appeared in political comedy shows, some of them eagerly (London mayor Ken Livingstone appeared no less than seven times on *HIGNFY*), others reluctantly, but participating nonetheless. This prompts several questions which will be examined in this article:

(1) Why do politicians and candidates appear in *HIGNFY* and *DWHN* (motives)?
(2) How do they fare in the actual recording and broadcast (experiences)?
(3) How do they look back on their participation and—more generally—on the changing communicative landscape of politics (reflection)?

Method

In the absence of a cumulative body of knowledge about politicians' experiences of and reflections upon participation in political satire shows, our study starts more or less from empirical scratch and is exploratory rather than explanatory. We chose to contrast the experiences of British and Dutch politicians to cast the net of possible motives, experiences and reflections as wide as possible, and to open up some space for addressing both the specificities and the similarities of national political and television cultures. Our first step was to take stock of all the politicians who appeared in the two programmes since their beginning in, respectively, 1990 (UK) and 1996 (NL). Our second step involved inviting the politicians to participate in the research. Assuming that their performance on the programme should be relatively recent to remember their motives and experience, we chose to approach only those participants who appeared on the shows after 2000. In the Netherlands, this produced 19 possible interviewees (13 men, six women) who were all approached by email or phone. Thirteen of them responded to our invitation to participate in the study with seven unwilling to co-operate; illness, moving or lack of time were the reasons given. One of the politicians apparently doubted the relevance of the project given his email response: 'Is this a joke?' As already reported, the leader of the Social Democrats refused because of his negative experience with the programme. A total of seven Dutch MPs were interviewed. In Britain, 14 politicians who had appeared on *HIGNFY* were contacted (10 men, four women) and 10 responded. One refused to participate on the grounds that she did not 'consider the subject worthy of academic research' and two were unable to be interviewed because of illness or other commitments. Seven British MPs were interviewed.

The interviews were semi-structured and focused on politicians' reasons for accepting the invitation to participate in the programme, their assessment of potential risks, the emergence of effects after participating and how they looked back on their performance. All the interviews were recorded and transcribed. Data analysis took place with computer software for the analysis of qualitative data, MaxQda. The initial round of analysis was conducted top-down by imposing the three research questions (motives, experiences and reflections) on the categorisation of the data, and bottom-up by allowing for other, more specific categories to emerge from the data. This resulted in the identification of 10 sub-themes in the overall categories, namely motifs (visibility, political influence, image and pleasure), experience (nerves, preparation and recording, and audience reactions) and reflections (media and political logic, risks and limits). We reconstructed three repertoires which intersect these themes and bind them together in meaningful individual narratives; a strategic repertoire that was somewhat dominant, an indulgent repertoire and an anti-elitist repertoire.

Motives, Experiences and Reflections

We organised the results under the headings motives, experiences and reflections. Most of the categories were relevant for the British and the Dutch interviews. We therefore present in each category one British and one Dutch quote that can be considered typical for the whole corpus. However, as we shall see, the reflections did signal particular British and Dutch concerns.

Motives

Almost all interviewed politicians argued in different wordings that participating in *HIGNFY* and *DWHN* increased their *visibility*:

> You make a great speech in the Commons and you find that no one's bothered about it, no one's heard it and no one's thought about it. You do a thing like *HIGNFY* and everyone seems to have watched it (British MP).

> You bring yourself to attention of a lot of people who usually don't see you, or not very often and with that, one enlarges one's reputation. And reputation, preferably a positive reputation but even a negative reputation is always better than no reputation at all. The worst thing which can happen to you is the fact that you are not mentioned, that you don't belong to it and that nobody knows you (Dutch MP).

A second reason for participating in the shows concerned the possibility of enhancing one's *political impact*:

> The inhibitions and problems which are thrown up by the procedures in parliament make it very difficult to control the executive. So, if you are going to control the executive, it is in the media. That's where they hate it. That's where you do it (British MP).

> I was able to propagate some political things about on another party, and I managed to insert our campaign slogan a couple of times (Dutch MP).

However, not all politicians saw this as a valid argument:

> I don't think you really reach anyone with your appearance, maybe on a very basic level: there are MPs, there are elections ... but nothing further (Dutch MP).

> I don't think I've been able to address any specific issues on the programme itself. All you can do on that programme is project yourself, more than any political philosophy (British MP).

Thirdly, some politicians mentioned the importance of providing the public with a more multi-sided *image* of politicians:

> Voters also want to see what kind of man or woman the politician is. And if you don't know your bird, it becomes a bit difficult to vote for that person (Dutch MP).

> If you want to get politics out to a wider audience, you've got to show politicians as being humorous, presentable, quick-witted and appealing (British MP).

Finally, some MPs basically consider the programme good fun, and claimed to participate mainly for their own *pleasure*:

> Parliament's a rather boring, dull place, but it gives you a chance to go to exciting places. And the one thing about *HIGNFY*, it was exciting (British MP).

> Everybody said, you should not have done that, but it was good fun! (Dutch MP)

Experiences

When asked how they felt when invited to join the programme, a number of politicians expressed serious *nervousness*:

> First you think, this is a huge privilege to be on a programme that I myself watch ... But also you get butterflies in your stomach, thinking, am I going to look like a complete idiot if I go on that? So it's a combination of pride and crapping yourself, basically (British MP).

> You have to trust that they broadcast the good things and that they don't fool you. And when you are in the show, you have to pay attention, you have to be aware that if you make an inappropriate joke, it will be taped and it can be used (Dutch MP).

The actual experience of doing the show must have disappointed some politicians who were surprised by the level of detailed *preparation* for the *recordings*:

> They go through all the pictures. They show you which is the odd one out and blah blah blah. And you say vaguely funny things as they come up.

> And then you go in a room with press cuttings and the comedians make
> up one-liners. And people like me get very bored. And that's my point: it's
> rehearsed. And I think most people don't know that ... It's a bit of a con
> (British MP).

For most of the politicians, the *audience response* after the show was amazing and a
ratification of their initial motive to participate for wider visibility:

> The first time I did it I was absolutely amazed at the number of people
> who came up to me in the street in my constituency. You suddenly
> realised that there are 9 million people out there watching (British MP).

A Dutch MP, however, said he did not believe in such an effect, nor had he
experienced it:

> When nobody knows you, being on *DWHN* will not have an effect. And it
> won't result in suddenly being a celebrated politician the next day (Dutch
> MP).

Reflections

Both the British and the Dutch politicians articulated their presence in *HIGNFY* and
DWHN with the changing political culture in their countries. The *media logic* of
contemporary politics was an obvious part of these considerations:

> It's more important in politics now generally to go on television and to
> look good on television. That demands youth, it demands intellectual
> quickness, it demands a good sense of humour. A personable politician ...
> Most politicians, and I include myself, are fairly dull, old or middle-aged,
> overweight individuals who aren't naturally funny (British MP).

Not coincidentally, given the above quote, it seems, one of the younger female
participants in *DWHN* said she feels more at ease in light-hearted, entertaining
programmes:

> My style is unconventional. I have difficulties with debates in *NOVA*, for
> instance, where it is all about conventional politics and style. And then I
> think: guys, be normal, you know, chill. I am often one of the youngest,
> I am with all these old persons who think it has to be like that. I have
> more difficulty with that, than with funny settings, I do feel more com-
> fortable there (Dutch local MP).

A clear difference between the British and Dutch MPs emerged when talking about
the wider media landscape in which politicians have to perform. One British MP
connected his appearance on *HIGNFY* with the sorry state of British television
journalism:

> The problem is that that's the only kind of programme that's available.
> More straightforward political programmes in which we argue with each
> other, arguably more seriously ... they've been cut back and cut back to
> very little. And interviews, in which we can expound our truth ... these

are now very brief ... you're never allowed to say what you want to say at appropriate length. It might be that we talk for too long (British MP).

That problem was framed differently in the Netherlands. The interviewed politicians did not complain about a lack of news and debate programmes, but rather about the lack of people watching them:

As a politician you can of course go to *Een Vandaag, NOVA* or *Den Haag Vandaag*, but it's only a very small proportion of the Dutch people that watch these programmes (Dutch MP).

Such reflections demonstrate that media logic may take different forms in different countries, and—as the quote of the young politician showed—presents different challenges for politicians. Occasionally, both the British and the Dutch respondents would point at the *political logic* behind their appearance in *HIGNFY* and *DWHN*. Some British participants expressed aversion to developments in British political culture that necessitated their participation in *HIGNFY*. Two of them said that parliamentary mores and language had deteriorated so much that their seeking of another platform was inevitable:

I think politics is broken ... I think this sort of bureaucratic-speak is revolting and puts people off. People in government don't know how to speak English properly because they speak that management-speak. (British MP)

A Dutch MP, on the other hand, argued that appearance in programmes like *DWHN* was necessary because of the disappearance of substantial political differences in Dutch politics:

The political parties resemble each other, and increasingly you have to distinguish on the basis of personalities. And voting is more and more about the feelings you have about a person. If you know that a political programme will be dated after a year you need to be able to trust that the person you voted for will react more or less the same when new issues come up (Dutch MP).

A second area of reflections considered the possible *risks* of participating in *HIGNFY* and *DWHN*, and other infotainment programmes. Here it seemed that clear national differences emerged from the interviews. The Brits discussed risks mainly in terms of potential individual reputational damage, with some identifying possible dangers:

I think you have to be careful. Charlie Kennedy was known as Chat Show Charlie because he was forever on chat shows and on *HIGNFY*. So if you take yourself seriously you need to be careful (British MP).

Your image can be damaged if you end up looking stupid, if you burst into tears, if you don't look funny, but just look boring (British MP).

Other British MPs, however, were less concerned:

I think that even if they take the piss out of MPs, it might not do them any harm. It still humanises people. Get the sympathy vote (British MP).

It can't do any damage, it shows politicians as humans (British MP).

© *2009 The Authors. Journal compilation* © *2009 Political Studies Association*
BJPIR, 2009, 11(4)

While reflections on the (lack of) danger for reputation risk did emerge in the Dutch interviews, their emphasis was a little different. Most of the politicians claimed that risks were as big if not bigger in the serious programmes:

> It can't do any harm, as long as you don't say the wrong things, but that goes for serious programmes as well (Dutch MP).

More pressing than individual reputational damage, in the Dutch interviews, was a notion of political dignity:

> You continuously make an assessment how your participation in these programmes corresponds with the dignity of your particular office or political role. And the dignity of the PM is different than that of a party leader, and that is again different from that of a minister or a vice-PM (Dutch MP).

> It only works if you are capable of meeting the expectations of such a programme, if you can keep your political dignity and if you manage to remain yourself (Dutch MP).

The Dutch interviews abounded with anecdotes of fellow politicians who failed to maintain their dignity (a former minister performing on *Who Wants to be a Pop Star*, for instance), and examples of the *limits* the politicians drew for their and others' participation in entertainment programmes. A first limit mentioned had to do with overexposure:

> I would not advise doing such a programme every week. Then you're continuously performing the bloke next door. That won't work, you'd better do that in the pub. But once every half a year or so would be fine (Dutch local MP).

> As long as they see me for 80 per cent in the serious news and current affairs programmes it's fine, and if then once in a while I do a show, it's fine (Dutch MP).

A second boundary the politicians put around their popular performance related to the question of whether it was possible to address political issues:

> The thing is, get across a theme. There's no point in just going and smiling or laughing ... If, for example, you're worried about the trees in London falling down and not being replaced, *HIGNFY*'s a better way of getting that issue across to people and making them think about it than writing five articles for the *Financial Times* (British MP).

> I wouldn't participate in *Dancing on Ice*, for two reasons: I can't get a political message across and I can't skate at all. I don't want to expose myself to such physical things and I think most of the politicians should not come in their bathing suit either (Dutch MP).

Yet opinions were divided on the latter issue, with politicians also going on *HIGNFY* and *DWHN* and other entertainment shows for fun and their own pleasure (as discussed in the section on motives).

© 2009 The Authors. Journal compilation © 2009 Political Studies Association
BJPIR, 2009, 11(4)

Repertoires

Each individual interview with the politicians who participated in *HIGNFY* and *DWHN* produced a coherent narrative about their motives, experiences and reflections. These narratives were not completely idiosyncratic but appeared to draw from three distinct but overlapping repertoires: a strategic repertoire, an indulgent repertoire and an anti-elitist repertoire.

Strategic Repertoire

It became clear from our interviews that both British and Dutch politicians are well versed in the idea of self-marketing with a view to being a successful politician. Most of our respondents drew from a strategic repertoire to express their ideas on their participation in the two shows. Typical motives that fit in the strategic repertoire are the desire to enhance one's personal visibility for a wider audience—'it probably increased my recognition levels in the country' (British MP)—and thereby to increase one's political effectiveness. For some, it does not really matter whether that results in positive or negative visibility, since visibility in itself is considered necessary: 'a negative reputation is always better than no reputation at all, the worst thing that can happen is that nobody knows you' (Dutch MP). A more controversial strategic motive concerned the desire to put political messages across in popular contexts. Both the necessity and the possibility of such endeavours were contested. In looking back on their performance, politicians using the strategic repertoire discussed whether they had been able to insert some politics in the show, including often an assessment of the editorial team as well: 'you are at the mercy of the editors' (British MP). In the strategic repertoire, the number of viewers and their feedback to the politicians are crucial measures of success. Media logic is accepted as the inevitable cultural context for contemporary politics and it is seen as being better to adjust to its rules than to fight or lament it. Reflections in this repertoire are basically pragmatic, addressing the potential and risk of *HIGNFY* and *DWHN* for personal reputation, and the question of how to devise a strategically wise mix of media appearances.

Indulgent Repertoire

Some of our respondents considered their participation in *HIGNFY* and *DWHN* mainly a matter of *good fun*: a nice change from day-to-day politics. They see their participation as one of the pleasant by-products of being a well-known politician, but do not expect or need any direct political benefits from it. There are some strategic motives of personal visibility involved here, but these are absent for the well-established politicians. The respondents talking about *HIGNFY* and *DWHN* in this way were mainly senior politicians with considerable political track records who could afford to abstain from efforts to include political messages in their performance. Experiences on the recording day are framed basically in terms of having had a nice day or not, and having managed to evoke a laugh from the presenters and the audience ('I was delighted when they asked me back'). As long as there is a relevant political or social context to a programme, much is allowed:

> The *Sound Mix* show was for charity, that is an interesting case ... different
> from simple commercial purposes. Everybody said, you should not have
> done that, but it was nice! (Dutch MP)

Such appearances are the object of criticism as well ('there are some politicians who
try to turn themselves into show people ... well it's better to be noticed than not
noticed'), but the main limits that the politicians involved in this repertoire draw
consider their individual dignity and the dignity of politics, with the latter being
mainly a Dutch frame.

Anti-Elitist Repertoire

In this repertoire, parliamentary politics and the media responsible for covering it
are presented as institutions crowded by elites possessing their own language, style
and in-groups which are more or less alienated from their constituencies and the
public at large. The politicians drawing from this repertoire see it as their responsibility to perform differently and show that politicians are also ordinary human
beings, with their ups and downs, their flaws and imperfections. They participate in
HIGNFY, DHWN and similar programmes to show such a diverse picture of politicians. Typical quotes are therefore: '[the programme] shows politicians as humans',
or '*HIGNFY* shows that you can do politics with a smile'. Almost inevitably their
actual experiences while being in the studio were somewhat disheartening, because
of the lack of spontaneity and the manufacturing of discussions and jokes before-
hand. As a British MP said, 'what is the point of doing *HIGNFY* if it is all a bit of a
fiddle and they sometimes turn on people?' In their reflections, the politicians who
use this repertoire point at supposedly devastating effects of both media logic and
political logic, both of them corrupting the possibility for politicians to converse
directly with the people. In this repertoire, infotainment, comedy and other genres
of popular culture of which *HIGNFY* and *DWHN* are part, offer sincere and appropriate ways to communicate with the people:

> ... people don't realise the extent to which parliamentary government has
> gone down and the extent to which broadcasts like *HIGNFY* keep its good
> name. I'm not being silly about this ... The politicians' standing has gone
> right down. The interest of the public in politics has gone right down.
> Whereas *HIGNFY* has kept up its high standards (British MP).

While traces of this repertoire were found in the interviews with Dutch politicians
(see, for instance, the quote of the young Dutch local MP about her problems with
the traditional style of politics above), and while anti-elitism is not uncommon in
Dutch politics, we found mainly British politicians using this repertoire.

Summary and Exploration

We asked three questions in this article: why do politicians and candidates appear
in *HIGNFY* and *DWHN*, how do they fare in the actual recording and broadcast, how
do they look back on their participation and—more generally—on the changing
communicative landscape of politics? With our answers we hoped to contribute

Table 1: Themes and Repertoires of Politicians Talking about *HIGNFY* and *DWHN*

		Strategic	Indulgent	Anti-Elitist
Motives	Visibility	++		+
	Political influence	+		+
	Different image of politician			++
	Pleasure		++	
Experiences	Nerves		+	
	Recording day		++	
	Audience response	++		++
Reflections	Media logic	++	+	+
	Political logic			++
	Risks—reputation	++		
	Risks—dignity		++	
	Limits	+	+	

to a gap in political communications research where there has been little to no attention given to how politicians perform and communicate in the context of televised satire formats. A secondary aim has been to provide scholarly support for democratic politicians and candidates facing the challenge of communicating effectively in a range of mediated contexts through a diversity of appropriate and effective styles. We reconstructed 11 themes and three repertoires from the interviews, the articulation of which we summarise in Table 1.

In the table, one can see that the visibility motive holds more strongly for politicians using a strategic repertoire than for those referring to an anti-elitist repertoire. For respondents who mainly framed their presence in *HIGNFY* and *DWHN* in terms of pleasure, visibility was not a key motive. The other entries to the cells can be similarly described in terms of (strong) presence and (relative) absence.

The table demonstrates that there is considerable overlap between the politicians in terms of motives, experiences and reflections. It also shows that individual politicians draw from different repertoires to construct a coherent narrative about their participation in *HIGNFY* and *DWHN*. Yet, all repertoires have their distinct key entries: visibility and reputational risk in the strategic repertoire, pleasure and dignity in the indulgent repertoire, and countering the image of politicians and resisting current political logic in the anti-elitist repertoire.

Having thus summarised the results on the level of content and repertoires of talk, we can now tentatively explore the outcomes in terms of individual politicians. The combination of themes and repertoires suggests that three types of political guest appear on *HIGNFY* and *DWHN*. Firstly, there are those who have adjusted to the current rules of the game, so to speak: they accept the present media logic and think mainly in terms of individual and political strategic gains and losses. We find these both among the British and the Dutch respondents. A second group consists of established politicians who legitimate their participation in terms of more-or-less

© 2009 The Authors. Journal compilation © 2009 Political Studies Association
BJPIR, 2009, 11(4)

warranted individual pleasures which serve little political purpose. Having mostly acquired a solid reputation for themselves, the only risk that these politicians take seriously is the loss of dignity of public office. This group too consists of British and Dutch politicians, although the concept of dignity seems to be specifically Dutch. Finally, there is a small group of outspoken anti-elitist politicians who seem to detest current political logic and its formal bureaucratic procedures and styles. They seek ways of presenting politicians as ordinary human beings and want to connect to apolitical, lay citizens. They hardly fear reputation or dignity loss.

Our analysis of the changing and pluralistic landscape of contemporary political communication, with its ubiquitous media logic, suggests that politicians' appreciation of the challenges, benefits and fundamental changes in political culture is only partly in line with what political communication research might predict. While the strategic repertoire resonates clearly with research about political marketing and packaging, the indulgent and the anti-elitist repertoires sit uneasily with the dominant research agenda of political communication. While the strategic repertoire resonates clearly with research that identifies an inescapable need to succumb to media logic, the indulgent and the anti-elitist repertoires sit uneasily with this perspective. The anti-elitist repertoire is clearly cast in the classic terms of representation and the need to represent and communicate with 'ordinary' citizens who are not part of the political elite. Performing in *HIGNFY* and *DWHN* is thus constructed as part of a traditional self-conception as a people's representative. The repertoire of enjoyment, on the other hand, is neither related to perspectives about media logic, nor to ideas of representation. In fact, the finding that politicians also simply derived pleasure from participating in *HIGNFY* and *DWHN* is hard to articulate within common frames of political science and political communication, and seems to be more easily explained in terms of biographical or psychological profiling of political candidates and leaders. While our study was based on the identification of a significant gap in the research literature, the outcomes point towards new and pressing issues. Political communication research at present has little to say about some of the main themes that politicians raise in explaining their decision to participate in *HIGNFY* and *DWHN*: what exactly does visibility achieve for individual politicians? Is it possible to insert an effective political message in an entertainment context? Does one really broaden and soften the image of politicians by appearing on popular programmes? What kind of reputational gains and risks are involved? And how might such appearances endanger the dignity of public office? These are questions of both practical and academic relevance which we propose to pursue in the next stage of this study.

About the Authors

Stephen Coleman, Professor of Political Communication and Director of Research, The Institute of Communications Studies, University of Leeds, Houldsworth Building, Clarendon Road, Leeds LS2 9JT, UK, email: *s.coleman@leeds.ac.uk*

Anke Kuik, c/o Brockington Building, Department of Social Sciences, Loughborough University, Loughborough, Leicestershire LE11 3TU, UK, email: *e.a.van-zoonen@lboro.ac.uk*

Liesbet van Zoonen, Professor in Communication and Media Studies, Brockington Building, Department of Social Sciences, Loughborough University, Loughborough, Leicestershire LE11 3TU, UK, email: *e.a.van-zoonen@lboro.ac.uk*

© 2009 The Authors. Journal compilation © 2009 Political Studies Association
BJPIR, 2009, 11(4)

Note

Thanks to Scott Anthony for his contribution to the UK interviews.

1. Wouter Bos declined our invitation to be interviewed for this research project and said he wanted to talk to us about his media performance in all other news and infotainment programmes, but not about *Dit was het Nieuws*.

Bibliography

Baum, M. (2003) 'Soft news and political knowledge: Evidence of absence, or absence of evidence?', *Political Communication*, 20:2, 173–190.

Baum, M. (2005) 'Talking the vote: Why presidential candidates hit the talk show circuit', *American Journal of Political Science*, 49:2, 213–234.

Baumgartner, J. and Morris, J. (2006) '*The Daily Show* effect: Candidate evaluations, efficacy, and American youth', *American Politics Research*, 34:3, 341–367.

Baym, G. (2005) '*The Daily Show*: Discursive integration and the reinvention of political journalism', *Political Communication*, 22:3, 259–276.

Brants, K. (1998) 'Who's afraid of infotainment', *European Journal of Communication*, 13:3, 315–335.

Brewer, P. and Marquardt, E. (2007) 'Mock news and democracy: Analyzing *The Daily Show*', *Atlantic Journal of Communication*, 15:4, 249–267.

Cao, X. and Brewer, P. (2008) 'Political comedy shows and public participation in politics', *International Journal of Public Opinion Research*, 20:1, 90–99.

Coleman, S. (2003) *A Tale of Two Houses: The House of Commons, the Big Brother House and the People at Home* (London: Hansard Society).

Corner, J. (2003) 'Mediated persona and political culture', in J. Corner and D. Pels (eds), *Media and the Restyling of Politics* (London: Sage), 66–84.

Feldman, L. (2007) 'The news about comedy: Young audiences, *The Daily Show*, and evolving notions of journalism', *Journalism*, 8:4, 406–427.

Fox, J., Koloen, G. and Sahin, V. (2007) 'No joke: A comparison of substance in *The Daily Show* with Jon Stewart and broadcast network television coverage of the 2004 presidential election campaign', *Journal of Broadcasting & Electronic Media*, 51:2, 213–227.

Gaines, E. (2007) 'The narrative semiotics of "*The Daily Show*" ', *Semiotica*, 166:1/4, 81–96.

Holbert, R., Lambe, J., Dudo, A. and Carlton, K. (2007) 'Primacy effects of *The Daily Show* and national TV news viewing: Young viewers, political gratifications, and internal political self-efficacy', *Journal of Broadcasting & Electronic Media*, 51:1, 20–38.

Hollander, B. (2005) 'Late-night learning: Do entertainment programs increase political campaign knowledge for young viewers?', *Journal of Broadcasting & Electronic Media*, 49:4, 402–415.

Jones, J. (2005) *Entertaining Politics* (Boulder, CO: Rowman & Littlefield).

Lauerbach, G. (2007) 'Argumentation in political talk show interviews', *Journal of Pragmatics*, 39:8, 1388–1419.

Sreberny, A. and Van Zoonen, L. (eds) (2000) *Women, Politics and Communication* (Cresskill, NJ: Hampton Press).

Street, J. (1997) *Politics and Popular Culture* (Cambridge: Polity Press).

Van Zoonen, L. (2005) *Entertaining the Citizen: When Politics and Popular Culture Converge* (Boulder, CO: Rowman & Littlefield).

Warner, J. (2007) 'Political culture jamming: The dissident humor of "*The Daily Show with Jon Stewart*" ', *Popular Communication*, 5:1, 17–36.

Young, D. (2004) 'Late-night comedy in election 2000: Its influence on candidate trait ratings and the moderating effects of political knowledge and partisanship', *Journal of Broadcasting & Electronic Media*, 48:1, 1–22.

Young, D. and Tisinger, R. (2006) 'Dispelling late-night myths. News consumption among late-night comedy viewers and the predictors of exposure to various late-night shows', *The Harvard International Journal of Press/Politics*, 11:3, 113–134.

doi: 10.1111/j.1467-856X.2009.00386.x   *BJPIR: 2009 VOL 11, 666–689*

Confounding Conventional Wisdom: Political not Principled Differences in the Transatlantic Regulatory Relationship

Alasdair R. Young

The transatlantic complaints over hormone-treated beef and genetically modified organisms before the World Trade Organisation (WTO) seem to confirm two separate but related conventional wisdoms about the transatlantic economic relationship: that it is highly conflictual and that many of the conflicts are rooted in profoundly different approaches to regulation. This article argues that neither of the two conventional wisdoms is accurate. Rather, it contends that they are products of two, compounding analytical shortcomings: one methodological, one empirical. The methodological shortcoming takes the form of an implicit selection bias. While WTO complaints are high profile they are rare and extreme examples; it is, therefore, unsound to generalise from them to the regulatory relationship as a whole. The empirical shortcoming has to do with neither the beef hormones nor the GMO dispute demonstrating what it is purported to. The article thus serves as a cautionary tale about the dangers of relying on obvious cases and the need to question whether evidence really does support a prevailing popular narrative.

Keywords: precautionary principle; trade disputes; transatlantic relations; World Trade Organisation

In 2008 two long-standing regulatory disputes between the United States and the European Union again hit the news. In January 2008 the deadline for the EU's compliance with the World Trade Organisation's (WTO) ruling on its procedures for approving genetically modified organisms (GMOs) expired with only partial compliance. In October 2008 the WTO ruled that the US and Canada had not violated WTO rules by continuing to apply sanctions against the EU despite it having modified its ban on hormone-treated beef. These WTO complaints seem to confirm two separate but related conventional wisdoms about the transatlantic economic relationship: that it is highly conflictual and that many of the conflicts are rooted in profoundly different approaches to regulation.

This article argues that neither of these conventional wisdoms is accurate. Rather, it contends that they are products of two, compounding analytical shortcomings: one methodological, one empirical. The methodological shortcoming takes the form of an implicit selection bias. WTO complaints overwhelmingly attract media, political and academic attention. They are, however, rare and extreme examples. Generalising from them to the regulatory relationship in general, therefore, is unsound. If one considers the full range of regulatory measures that impede transatlantic trade but that have not become WTO complaints, the relationship appears to be characterised by tolerance rather than conflict.

The empirical shortcoming has to do with neither the beef hormones nor the GMO dispute demonstrating what it is purported to. The tendency is to depict these WTO complaints as reflecting fundamental differences in the two parties' approaches to regulation, with the US advocating 'sound science' and the EU advocating the 'precautionary principle'. While the US and EU are to an extent responsible for fostering the perception of competing principles, detailed analyses of the prime exhibits invoked to support this conventional wisdom reveal sharply different approaches to risk management within the EU and EU policy outcomes that reflect messy political processes. The EU's regulations, therefore, are more political than principled. Moreover, contrary to how the WTO complaints are normally depicted, how the US pursued those complaints actually supports the characterisation of the transatlantic relationship as tolerant.

In developing this argument, this article draws together research conducted for three previous research projects. One is on the early days of the transatlantic dispute over genetically modified crops conducted when I was a BP Transatlantic Jean Monnet Fellow at the Robert Schuman Centre for Advanced Studies at the European University Institute. One is for the European Commission's Directorate General for External Relations on the state of the transatlantic relationship 10 years after the signing of the New Transatlantic Agenda.[1] One is on the EU's use of WTO dispute settlement, which was funded by the British Academy.[2] In all the article draws on 28 not-for-attribution interviews with trade officials, regulators and business groups on both sides of the Atlantic. Regulators and trade officials were asked about their perceptions of sources of regulatory differences. Trade officials were also asked about what influences their decisions to initiate WTO complaints. Business group representatives were asked about their views of the origins of trade barriers, whether and how they sought to address them and what they perceive to influence trade officials' decisions about how to pursue trade barriers. These different perspectives were triangulated with each other and documentary sources.

The article begins by setting out the significance of trade barriers stemming from public health and environmental regulations in the transatlantic relationship and the particular challenges of resolving them. It then describes the established conventional wisdoms about the transatlantic relationship. It then exposes in turn the methodological and empirical shortcomings that underpin those conventional wisdoms. It concludes by drawing out the implications of the analysis and reassessing the transatlantic regulatory relationship.

The Distinctive Politics of Regulatory Trade Barriers

Excluding the European Union itself the transatlantic economic relationship is the largest, broadest and most intensive international economic relationship in the world. As tariffs have been reduced through successive rounds of multilateral trade negotiations, regulatory differences have become increasingly significant obstacles to transatlantic trade in goods (Commission 2008c, 9; USTR 2008, 213). Because regulations are statutory requirements governing products' characteristics or how they are produced, products that do not meet those requirements cannot be sold where the regulations apply. If regulations governing the same product are different in two markets, a product that complies with the rules of its home market may well be excluded from the other market; thus the regulatory difference impedes trade. Although there are a wide variety of regulatory barriers that affect transatlantic trade in goods, most of the most problematic concern public health and environmental rules (Brittan 2000; Atlantic Council 2002; Pollack 2003b, 596; Ahearn et al. 2008, 34).[3]

Trade barriers stemming from public health and environmental rules are particularly difficult to resolve because they are politically distinctive. As with other regulatory trade barriers, the adverse trade consequences of public health and environmental rules are usually unintended side-effects of policies intended to realise other, domestic policy objectives. Because public health and environmental rules are seen as having direct relevance for all citizens of a polity, however, they are widely regarded as being more politically salient than other types of regulation or traditional trade measures (Kahler 1995, 56; Scharpf 1999; Damro and Sbragia 2003; Pollack 2003a, 71; Ahearn et al. 2008, 34).

Consequently, the political calculus of liberalising trade by removing such barriers is distinctive (Evans 2003; Young 2007b). Traditional trade liberalisation through removing tariffs entails concentrated costs for protected firms and their workers and diffuse benefits for consumers. Where public health and environmental regulations impede trade, however, liberalisation also entails diffuse costs for citizens in the form of potentially reduced safety or environmental protection, thereby undermining political support for liberalisation.[4] The difficulty of resolving such disputes is evident in the very few transatlantic public health and environmental regulatory disputes resolved through negotiations despite over a decade of effort within the framework of the New Transatlantic Agenda (see Commission 2005a and 2005b).

Conventional Wisdom or Conventional Folly?

Two reinforcing conventional wisdoms have emerged that characterise the transatlantic regulatory relationship:

(1) that the US is hostile to regulation while the EU favours stringent (precautionary) public health and environmental regulation; and
(2) that the relationship, in part as a consequence, is highly conflictual.

I shall develop each of these conventional wisdoms in turn before turning to their flaws.

CW1: The 'Precautionary Principle' versus 'Sound Science'

There is widespread acceptance that regulatory differences between the EU and US reflect fundamental differences in how the two polities approach risk. *The Economist* (1 March 2008, 69) noted: 'Anybody who dabbles in transatlantic affairs has come across one giant stereotype: Americans admire risk takers, whereas Europeans (at least in the rich, stable parts of the continent) are instinctively risk-averse, expecting the state to shield them from all sorts of dangers'. The Atlantic Council (2002, 2) identified the 'myth' that 'Europe is inherently more prone to precaution in adopting new technologies, while the United States is less likely to respond to innovation with restrictions'. David Levy and Peter Newell (2000, 10) and Jonathan Wiener and Michael Rogers (2002, 318) have also identified the 'conventional wisdom' that transatlantic regulatory differences are due to fundamental cultural differences concerning risk and regulation.

This fundamental difference in risk aversion has been cited to explain transatlantic regulatory differences in newspapers (see, for example, *The Wall Street Journal*, 23 April 2002; *Financial Times*, 22 July 2003, 16; *The Economist*, 22 September 2007) and opinion-shaping magazines, such as *Foreign Policy* (Tama 2004) and *The National Interest* (Kogan 2004). It has also been invoked by US business interests keen to challenge EU regulations (see, for example, NFTC 2003; NAM 2004) and environmental groups seeking to defend them (see, for example, Greenpeace 2003 and 2006; Amicus Coalition 2004). This conventional wisdom is also echoed by European Commission officials. In 1999 then Trade Commissioner Pascal Lamy was quoted as saying: 'In the US they believe that if no risks have been proven about a product, it should be allowed. In the EU we believe something should not be authorized if there is a chance of risk' (cited in Charnovitz 2000, 185, fn. 180). Other Commission officials have echoed similar views in academic texts (see, for example Abbott 2003, 564–565; Christoforou 2004). In interviews a few US government officials also pointed to such fundamental differences contributing to transatlantic regulatory disputes.[5] The view that transatlantic regulatory disputes are rooted in fundamentally different approaches to risk is also found in some academic work (see, for example, Newell 2003, 61–62; Devereaux et al. 2006, 81; Laïdi 2008, 3; Tehrani 2008, 137).

Central to this conventional wisdom is the tension between the 'precautionary principle', which is enshrined in EU law[6] and actively promoted by the EU (European Council 2000) and 'sound science', arguably defended by the US. While 'sound science' is supposed to be more objective and based closely on scientific risk assessment, the 'precautionary principle' suggests action even 'where scientific information is insufficient, inconclusive, or uncertain and where there are indications that the possible effects on the environment, or human, animal or plant health may be potentially dangerous and inconsistent with the chosen level of protection' (Commission 2000, 7). The precautionary principle, thus, suggests an easing of the burden of proof on those seeking to restrict new products or technologies (Woolcock 2002, 9). As caricatured in the conventional wisdom above, this difference boils down to the EU rejecting all risks and the US being unconcerned about them. The implication of this conventional wisdom is that regulatory differences between the US and EU are fundamental, and thus enduring and universal.

CW2: The Prevalence of Trade Wars

As a former senior European Commission trade official (Abbott 2003, 563) noted, there is a 'general perception' of 'one [transatlantic] trade war after another'. WTO complaints figure prominently in academic texts on the transatlantic economic relationship (see, for example, Woolcock 1991; Kahler 1995; Cowles 1997; Vogel 1997; Petersmann and Pollack 2003; Peterson 2004; Steffenson 2005, ch. 7; Pollack and Shaffer 2006; McGuire and Smith 2008, ch. 3). To be fair most of these authors acknowledge that trade disputes should be expected in an economic relationship as large and complex as the one between the EU and the US. Moreover, regulatory disputes are not the only WTO complaints that attract scholarly attention, with those over the EU's banana trade regime, US steel safeguards and the US' Foreign Sales Corporation (FSC) tax break featuring particularly prominently (see, for example, Peterson 2004; Steffenson 2005; McGuire and Smith 2008). In addition, many authors also spend considerable time discussing the myriad efforts at regulatory co-operation since the launch of the New Transatlantic Agenda in 1995 (Cowles 1997; Bermann et al. 2000; Peterson 2004; Andrews et al. 2005; Pollack 2005; Steffenson 2005; Peterson and Young 2007).

Nonetheless, with respect to regulatory differences the EU and US have been depicted as 'trading blows' (Woolcock 1991), being 'über-competitors' (Carlarne 2007, 303), engaging in regulatory 'competition' (Kupchan 2003, 212–213), 'conflict' (Cowles 1997, 8) and 'rivalry' (Ahearn et al. 2008, 35), and experiencing 'system friction' (Pollack 2003b, 595). The Atlantic Council (2002, 8), therefore, identified as its second 'myth' about the transatlantic regulatory relationship that trade disputes pit the 'pro-environment' EU against the 'anti-environment' US; a view articulated by the Amicus Coalition (2004), Carlarne (2007) and Greenpeace (2003 and 2006).

Mutually Reinforcing Conventional Wisdoms

These two conventional wisdoms are mutually reinforcing in two ways. First, regulatory WTO complaints—those concerning the EU's ban on hormone-treated meat and the EU's procedures for approving GMOs—figure prominently in accounts depicting the EU as risk-averse and the US as hostile to regulation (Atlantic Council 2002; and see, for example, NFTC 2003; Thompson 2003; NAM 2004; Ahearn 2007; Carlarne 2007). The Bush administration's hostility to addressing climate change and resistance to the EU's efforts to promote adoption of the 'precautionary principle' in international agreements also played a role (Atlantic Council 2002).[7]

Second, the perception that regulatory differences are persistent and universal is seen by some as encouraging the US to be more aggressive in challenging EU measures that may not have great economic significance before the WTO in order to discourage it from adopting more precautionary regulations (Ten Eyck et al. 2004, 266; Murphy and Levidow 2006, 7). Thus transatlantic regulatory WTO complaints serve as evidence supporting the conventional wisdom that that the US and EU have fundamentally different approaches to public health and environmental regulations and that their differences are so fundamental arguably encourages WTO complaints.

Two Conventional Follies

Because WTO complaints are central to both conventional wisdoms, both are rooted in the same methodological and empirical problems. The methodological

© 2009 The Author. Journal compilation © 2009 Political Studies Association
BJPIR, 2009, 11(4)

problem is one of selection bias, considering only those disputes that achieve the prominence of WTO complaints. To an extent this is a manifestation of the 'availability heuristic', a psychological phenomenon in which people tend to evaluate the frequency or the probability of events by the ease with which relevant instances come to mind (Tversky and Kahneman 1973 and 1974). This means that more easily recalled events tend to be thought to be more common or likely than less easily recalled ones, even if this is not the case.

CW1—that the precautionary approach that the EU supposedly adopted in measures challenged in the high-profile WTO complaints and the US' apparent antipathy to it holds for all regulatory decisions—is informed by the 'availability heuristic'. CW1 goes beyond a focus on the probability of events to generalise from the readily available examples (WTO complaints) to the many, lower-profile regulatory differences (Wiener 2004, 75). In the vast majority of cases the act of generalisation is implicit.[8] CW2—about the conflictual nature of the transatlantic regulatory relationship—is a more straightforward manifestation of the 'availability heuristic', in which the overwhelming focus on the WTO complaints that there have been rather than considering those issues that have not become WTO complaints creates the impression of extensive conflict. Generalisations based on this type of selection bias, however, are methodologically unsound (King et al. 1994, 129; Moses and Knutsen 2007, 114).

The beef hormone and GMO disputes are highly atypical as they represent the only two transatlantic public health and environmental regulatory disputes to have been pursued through adjudication before the WTO.[9] In contrast, examination of the Commission's and United States Trade Representative's (USTR) annual reports on the other's trade barriers reveals a great many environmental and public health rules that have provoked concern, but that have not escalated, despite being long-standing sources of irritation (see Table 1).

An even smaller number of measures has been raised by each side in the WTO committees that oversee the Technical Barriers to Trade (TBT) and Sanitary and Phytosanitary (SPS) Agreements, which govern the adoption of environmental and public health regulations, respectively (see Figure 1). It is worth noting that other countries, particularly China, have expressed many more concerns about EU and US regulations than they have about each other's. For example, 56 EU SPS measures were raised as being of 'specific concern' between 1995 and 2007, but the US was involved in only 17 of those; 24 US SPS measures were raised, with the EU involved in only nine (WTO 2008b).[10]

Moreover, there are a great many regulatory measures adopted by both sides that have not prompted even this level of concern. Both parties have notified large numbers of potentially trade-impeding regulations (and conformity assessment procedures) to the WTO's TBT and SPS Committees. During 1995–2007 the US notified 530 measures to the WTO's TBT Committee and 1,745 measures to the SPS Committee, while the EU (excluding notifications by individual member states) notified 356 TBT measures and 320 SPS measures (WTO 2008a; SPS Information Management System). Moreover, this understates the number of potential

Table 1: Transatlantic Regulatory Barriers

Type of measure	EU concerns about the US	US concerns about the EU
Environment	Shrimp/turtle legislation (EU third party)	AGRICULTURAL BIOTECHNOLOGY PRODUCTS*
	Reformulated gasoline (EU third party)	Hushkits Regulation (challenged before ICAO)
	Marine Mammal Protection Act (challenged under GATT)	rBST†
	Corporate Average Fuel Economy (CAFÉ) (challenged under GATT)	Ban on fur from animals caught in leg-hold traps
	Ban on harp-seal fur coats	Triple superphosphate fertiliser standard
	Magnuson-Stevens Fishery Conservation and Management Act (drift-net fishing)	Restrictions on wood packaging material
	Certification on Fisheries (yellow fin tuna)	Registration, Evaluation, and Authorization of Chemicals (REACH)
	Recreational marine	Restriction of the Use of certain Hazardous Substances (RoHS)
	Pre-clearance inspection programme (apples and pears)	Waste Electrical and Electronic Equipment (WEEE)
	Pathogen Free Regions: restrictions on the import of fresh fruit and vegetables	Battery Directive
	Standards and certification of plants established in growing media	Draft Directive on Electrical and Electronic Equipment (EEE)
	Hardy nursery stock	Accelerated phase-out of ozone-depleting substances and greenhouse gases
	Restrictions on Spanish clementines	
Public health	BAN ON IMPORTS OF POULTRY AND POULTRY PRODUCTS	EU HORMONE DIRECTIVE
	Public Health Security and Bioterrorism Preparedness and Response Act	POULTRY MEAT RESTRICTION: ANTI-MICROBIAL TREATMENT
	Electrical and electronic equipment barriers	Gas connector hoses
	Pharmaceutical and herbal products (FDA Approval)	Pressure Equipment Directive (PED)
	Pasteurized Milk Products (Grade A)/ Import Milk Act	Roofing shingles
	Refrigeration and labelling of shell eggs	Anchor bolts
		Aflatoxin limits
		Draft Directive on Aircraft Certification
		Directive on gelatine for human consumption

Table 1: Continued

Type of measure	EU concerns about the US	US concerns about the EU
	Restrictions foie gras (state and municipal level)	EU Directives 2002/46/EC and 2006/37/EC (vitamins and
	Pressure equipment regulation	health food products)
	Sanitary measures on live oysters	Animal by-products legislation Transmissible Spongiform
	Rules on the import of bovine animals	Encephalopathies (TSE) Regulations
	Mature meat products	
	Non-cominglement requirements	
Other	Section 232 of 1962 Trade Expansion Act	Care labelling standard Electromagnetic Compatibility
	Cumbersome inspection and approval procedures	(EMC) Restriction affecting US wine
	National organic products	exports
	Non-use of international standards	Framework Directive Promoting Eco-Design for Energy Using
	Digital terrestrial television	Products
	Fastener Quality Act (FQA)	
	Nutrition Labelling and Education Act	
	Non-recognition of regionalisation	

Sources: Commission, 'United States Barriers to Trade and Investment: Reports' 1997–2008 (available online at: http://trade.ec.europa.eu/doclib/cfm/doclib_search.cfm?action=search); USTR *National Trade Estimate Reports* 1996–2007 (available online at: http://www.ustr.gov/Document_Library/Section_Index.html).
Note: Issues in small caps have been the subject of a WTO complaint.
* There are also public health issues associated with the dispute over GMOs, but the main area of difference has to do with cultivation and protecting the environment.
† rBST does not appear in the USTR's reports, but it is commonly recognised as one of the emblematic transatlantic disputes (Vogel 1997; Wiener and Rogers 2002). Although there were consumer health concerns, animal welfare was a more important motivation.

regulatory barriers as the individual EU member states are also active regulators. Between 1999 and 2007 EU member states notified 61 SPS measures (Commission 2008a), and between 1995 and 2007 the 15 states that were members of the EU for that whole period notified 1,592 TBT measures (WTO 2008a).

This reveals that only a tiny proportion of EU and US regulations prompt concern by the other party, let alone WTO complaints. Like an iceberg, therefore, the vast majority of the regulatory relationship is below the 'waterline'. Unlike an iceberg, where the danger is what you do not see, the danger here is assuming that what you do not see is the same as what you do see.

© 2009 The Author. Journal compilation © 2009 Political Studies Association
BJPIR, 2009, 11(4)

Figure 1: Transatlantic Regulatory 'Icebergs'

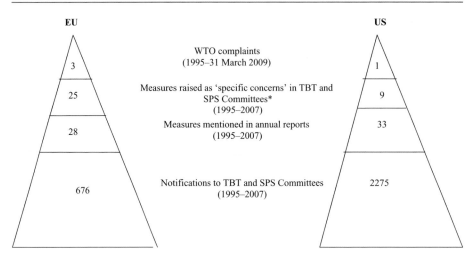

Sources: WTO complaints are from the WTO's dispute settlement gateway. Concerns raised in the TBT Committee are from the Committee's annual reports covering 2005–08 (see note) and for the SPS Committee annual reports covering 1995–2007. The concerns raised in the Commission's and the USTR's annual reports are listed in Table 1. The notifications to the TBT and SPS Committees are from WTO (2008a and 2008b), respectively.

Notes: The figures for the EU exclude member state measures.
* Figures for concerns raised in the TBT Committee are incomplete because they were not provided prior to the 2006 report (covering 2005). I included 'previously raised' concerns listed in the 2006–09 reports. In addition, the US raised WEEE and RoHS at the same time. They counted separately here.

The shortcoming of generalising from the most visible cases is compounded by an empirical one. The WTO complaints that are normally taken as confirming the conventional wisdoms do not demonstrate what they are purported to, either as examples of the EU's risk aversion or the US' aggression in challenging regulatory barriers. Strikingly, most of the academic literature that analyses these transatlantic disputes in detail does not make these mistakes. The empirical shortcoming, however, appears in pieces that seek to generalise about the state of the transatlantic relationship and are the product of focusing on differences in regulatory outcomes (in CW1) and on the existence of a WTO complaint (in CW2). As discussed below, analyses of the political processes leading to those regulatory outcomes and WTO complaints actually confound the conventional wisdoms.

The next two sections of the article take each conventional wisdom in turn. In each case the article examines both how consideration of the full range of regulatory activity in the EU and US paints a different picture of the regulatory relationship than that painted by a focus on only WTO complaints and how detailed analysis of the prime exhibits for the conventional wisdoms do not actually support their claims.

© 2009 The Author. Journal compilation © 2009 Political Studies Association
BJPIR, 2009, 11(4)

Countering CW1: Not Sound Science versus the Precautionary Principle

The conventional wisdom suggested by a focus on only the high-profile transatlantic WTO disputes implies that the US should not have any public health or environmental regulations that impede trade. Looking beyond the transatlantic disputes, however, yields a different picture. The US too has stringent public health and environmental rules, as the EU's litany of US rules that impede trade (see Table 1), the 'specific trade concerns' regarding US rules raised in the TBT and SPS Committees and the number of notifications by the US to those committees suggest (see also Kahler 1995; Vogel 1997; Wiener and Rogers 2002; Vig and Faure 2004; Wiener 2004; Hammitt et al. 2005). This suggests that the transatlantic regulatory relationship is not nearly as lopsided as the conventional wisdom depicts.

Rather than the US simply being less risk-averse than the EU, as CW1 suggests, there are three distinct qualifications regarding their respective attitudes towards risk. One concerns differences in priorities. Another concerns change over time. The third concerns differences within each of the polities. Although these qualifications are often depicted as alternatives, they essentially reinforce each other. The first two qualifications are based primarily on assessments of regulations and the outputs of political processes, while the third emphasises that regulatory decisions are contested. It is, therefore, not surprising that the stringency of regulations varies across issues or over time.

The first qualification to the conventional wisdom that the US is less risk-averse than the EU is that they actually differ with regard to which risks they prioritise (Wiener and Rogers 2002, 319; Wiener 2004, 74). James K. Hammitt et al. (2005, 1223), for instance, found that US regulations tend to be more precautionary than the EU's with respect to pollution and medication/medical treatment, while EU rules are more precautionary with regard to food/agriculture, human disease/health, toxic substances and ecological risks. The two polities' rules were equally precautionary with respect to consumer protection. Even within these broad categories there are marked differences with respect to which risks are regulated stringently. With regard to food safety, for example, the US rules tend to be more precautionary than the EU's with regard to potential carcinogens and traditional foods, such as raw milk cheeses and cured meats (Vogel 2003, 562).[11] One Commission regulator described the US approach to many aspects of food safety as 'very precautionary and distortive'.[12] The EU, by contrast, tends to be more precautionary with regard to new food technologies, including the use of hormones, genetic modification and irradiation (Vogel 2003, 562). Thus the two high-profile WTO complaints that inform CW1 both happen to concern issues about which the EU is more precautionary than the US.

The second qualification to CW1 is that the relative stringency of US and EU regulation has changed over time. US regulations tended to be more precautionary than the EU's into the 1980s, but the EU has adopted more precautionary rules than the US since 1990 (Mavroidis 2003; Vogel 2003, 561–562, 579; Christoforou 2004, 18; Vig and Faure 2004, 1). The volume of US notifications to the TBT and SPS Committees, discussed above, however, testifies to continued regulatory activism (see also Wiener 2004). Nonetheless, almost all of the US federal measures that the EU has raised as trade barriers—including the poultry ban, CAFE payment, Marine Mammal Protection Act, shrimp/turtle, BSE-related restrictions and restrictions on drift-net fishing—were adopted prior to 1990. Meanwhile, most of the EU's measures about which the US objects—including the bans on rBST and hormone-treated beef, GMO approvals and the Registration, Evaluation and Authorization of Chemicals (REACH) regulation—have been adopted since the late 1980s.

The comparative literature on transatlantic regulation suggests that contingent factors have shaped differences in regulatory approaches since 1990. In particular, a number of regulatory failures in Europe in the 1980s and 1990s—including the Chernobyl nuclear disaster, the Sandoz river fire, BSE, dioxin and AIDS-tainted blood—contributed to public distrust of regulation and gave European policy-makers strong incentives to err on the side of caution (Vogel 2003, 572–573; Christoforou 2004, 31; Ahearn 2007, 26).[13] The variance in the relative stringency of US and EU regulations over time and across issues is inconsistent with a deep-rooted cultural difference with respect to risk aversion (Wiener and Rogers 2002, 339; Vogel 2003, 580; Wiener 2004, 91).

The third qualification to CW1—that attitudes towards risk vary within the two polities—helps to explain variation across issues and over time. Joseph Murphy and Les Levidow (2006, 1, 8) explicitly criticise many of the existing accounts of the transatlantic dispute over GMOs for treating the EU and the US as the units of analysis, which, they argue, leads to 'a tendency to stereotype the EU and the US and to imply that a consensus has emerged in each one'. By contrast, studies of regulatory policy-making within each polity emphasise how contested regulations are (see below).

With regard to EU policy-making much of the focus tends to be on the different policy preferences of the member states, which are usually assumed to be informed by the preferences of the parties in government and the strength of environmental and consumer groups and business interests (for a review see Young (2010)). Significantly, Sheila Jasanoff (2005 and 2008) has identified significant differences in the preference for precaution within and between EU member states. Because the EU's treaties permit member states to maintain stringent national environmental and public health regulations, subject to certain conditions and judicial review, the drive to create the single European market by eliminating regulatory barriers to trade from the mid-1980s created a dynamic of 'trading up' through which the product regulations of the more risk-averse states have tended to be adopted at the EU level (Vogel 1995; Young and Wallace 2000; Young 2004).[14] Thus it is not surprising that Noelle Eckley and Henrik Selin (2004, 98) found that the 'precautionary principle' has affected debates within and international pronouncements by the EU, but has had little impact on policy outcomes.

Political contestation has also shaped the contours and evolution of environmental and public safety regulation in the US, although the political dynamics have been very different. While interest group competition and institutional changes were crucial to explaining the contours of US environmental and public health regulation through the 1980s (Vogel 1989), subsequently the relative power of the political parties has been seen as the crucial factor. In particular, the Republican party, which has become resistant to public health and environmental regulation, used its control of at least one house of Congress (1995–2007) and/or the presidency (2001–09), to impede and in some cases roll back US regulatory legislation (Vogel 2003, 578; Lazarus, cited in Hammitt et al. 2005; Vig and Faure 2004, 7). The Democratic party, by contrast, is seen as much more favourably disposed towards public health and environmental regulation. In part reflecting different balances of political power at the sub-federal level, there are profound differences among the US states in their approaches to particularly environmental legislation (see *The Economist*, 25 January 2007). State-level initiatives and the marked shift in US policy on climate change in the wake of the success of the Democratic party in the 2008 elections (see *The Economist*, 14 March 2009) lend credence to the thesis that US environmental and public health regulation is shaped more by politics than by a fundamental attitude towards risk.

Empirical Shortcomings: Politics rather than Principle

Although there are exceptions (see, for example, Krenzler and MacGregor 2000, 314–315), the vast majority of detailed analyses of the EU decision-making processes leading to the ban on hormone-treated beef and the adoption and application of GMO approval procedures do not explain the outcomes in terms of fundamental risk aversion. Rather, they provide additional support for the view that transatlantic regulatory differences reflect political rather than principled differences. CW1's focus on regulatory outcomes, therefore, tends to exaggerate the underlying differences.

The beef hormone dispute was due to the EU banning the use of growth-promoting hormones permitted in the US because of concerns that their residues could adversely affect human health. The ban had its origins in highly publicised health scares stemming from prohibited hormones used in raising livestock. At the time the EU's member states had very different assessments of the safety of five other hormones used in raising beef; the Italian and Luxembourg governments banned all five, the British and Irish governments permitted all five and the Danish, French and German governments permitted the use of some (*Agence Europe*, 29/30 September 1989, 9; Vogel 1997). These differences impeded the free circulation of beef within the EU, which was particularly problematic given the objective of eliminating regulatory barriers to trade (creating a single European market) by 1992 (Vogel 1997).

The European Commission, the EU's supranational executive, initially proposed banning only the two synthetic hormones but permitting the controlled use of the three natural hormones. In the face of stiff opposition from consumer groups, the European Parliament and most of the member states, however, the Commission revised its proposal to ban the three natural hormones as well (WTO 1997, para II.29; Princen 2002). Some governments opposed the ban, but were outvoted. Moreover, the Parliament 'regret[ted]' that the Commission had proposed banning the two synthetic hormones without waiting for scientific committee reports, but still welcomed the ban because their safety had not been conclusively proven.[15] The

© 2009 The Author. Journal compilation © 2009 Political Studies Association
BJPIR, 2009, 11(4)

adoption of the beef hormone ban, while perhaps reflecting a precautionary approach on the part of the European Parliament and some member states, reveals significant differences with regard to precaution within the EU. It was the EU's institutional framework—both the drive to create the single European market and the EU's decision rules—which resolved the internal political contest in the form of a precautionary regulatory outcome.

The adoption, development and application of the EU's GMO approval procedures were also characterized by the need to reconcile different approaches to regulation within the Commission and among the member states. The resulting procedures were also markedly different from those in the US, with the US treating GM crops and foods as 'substantially equivalent' to non-GM varieties and, therefore, not requiring special regulatory procedures, and the EU regarding them as inherently different and requiring a distinctive approval process (see Young 2001; Pollack and Shaffer 2009). The EU's approach is thus more precautionary than that adopted by the US.

This outcome, however, was the product of political competition between those in the Commission and among the member states who advocated a pro-biotechnology approach and those in the Commission and among the member states who favoured a more precautionary approach (Patterson 2000; Pollack and Shaffer 2009). Although the EU's approval process was slow, it worked at first, but in 1998 the member states stopped considering approvals. Although the Commission had the authority to approve GM varieties, it did not do so because it was concerned about antagonising the member states and public opinion.[16] In addition, during 1997–98 several member states prohibited the sale or cultivation of even EU-approved varieties of GM crops. In 1999 several member states declared that they would not approve any new GM crops until more stringent procedures were adopted (Council 1999). In order to get the approval process going again, the Commission initiated a series of reforms, which, because they had to placate the most reluctant member states, meant that the EU further tightened its regulation of genetically modified crops (Young 2004; Pollack and Shaffer 2009). The reforms extended the regulatory framework to include GM animal feed; placed greater emphasis on precaution and on environmental risk assessment based on common principles; limited approvals to 10 years (which may be extended upon review); eliminated the assumption that foods derived from GM crops but no longer containing genetic modification are 'substantively equivalent' to existing foods; required traceability, monitoring and labelling throughout the production process; and (from April 2007) prohibited any residues of non-EU approved GMOs in food or feed. The reforms also require that decisions be based on a scientific risk assessment,[17] but broaden the factors that can be considered in approving GMOs to include the 'consumer interest' and 'other legitimate factors' (Pollack and Shaffer 2009, 241).

In 2004 the EU resumed approving GM crop varieties for sale (not cultivation), but these approvals have been on the Commission's initiative as there have not been enough member states in favour. The splits among the member states over the approval for sale of genetically modified soybean A2704-12 are typical. On 12 February 2008 in the Standing Committee on the Food Chain and Animal Health

13 member states' representatives voted in favour of approving the GM soybean, eight voted against, five abstained and one was not represented (Commission 2008b). As with the ban on hormone-treated beef, therefore, the EU's GMO approval process reflects the outcome of political competition among actors within the EU with different views of the relative desirability and riskiness of agricultural biotechnology.[18]

The preceding discussion underlines that attitudes towards risk regulation are not monolithic within either the US or the EU. Moreover, the differences between the US' and EU's approaches to regulation are much less stark than CW1 suggests. Both the US and the EU acknowledge the need for precaution, particularly when regulating new technologies that might affect human health or the environment (Atlantic Council 2002, 5).[19] This is not to say that there are no differences in regulation between the EU and the US; there clearly are, and not only with respect to the level of risk aversion.[20] These differences, however, are not the product of profoundly different attitudes towards risk, but reflect the outcomes of different political processes. Transatlantic regulatory differences, therefore, are more of scale than of type.

Countering CW2: Tolerance, not Trade Wars

The tendency to depict the transatlantic regulatory relationship as highly conflictual (CW2) in some respects reflects a more straightforward example of the 'availability heuristic' than CW1. Here the high-profile disputes are not taken to reflect underlying regulatory differences, but to characterize the nature of the relationship; the perception of the frequency of conflict is distorted by the few high-profile disputes. Strikingly, WTO complaints regarding regulatory barriers are more likely to escalate to formal adjudication than are other types of complaint (Guzman and Simmons 2002; Busch and Reinhardt 2003, 475). This finding, however, has to be treated with caution as the analysis is based on only those trade disputes that become formal WTO complaints; a significant selection bias, again based on the most readily available cases (Busch and Reinhardt 2002). The vast number of regulatory barriers, including many that have been long-standing irritants, that have not become transatlantic WTO complaints suggests that the transatlantic relationship is characterised by tolerance more than by conflict.

Although a comprehensive analysis of why only a few regulatory barriers have been the subject of transatlantic WTO complaints is beyond the scope of this article, the literature on WTO complaints suggests several possible, reinforcing explanations. Four particularly important considerations seem to inform the decision to initiate (or not) a WTO complaint: the value of the impeding measure (Sherman 2002; Allee 2004; Shaffer 2003; Bown 2005a and 2005b); the likelihood of winning the complaint and securing compliance (Allee 2004; Bown 2005a and 2005b); the potential political repercussions of initiating a complaint (Bown 2005b; Guzman and Simmons 2005); and the danger of setting a precedent that constrains one's own regulatory autonomy (Busch and Reinhardt 2002; Shaffer 2003; Bown 2005a).

Whether it is worth pursuing a regulatory measure depends in large part on how much trade it prevents. Strikingly, only a very small proportion of the regulations notified by the two polities to the WTO's TBT and SPS Committees appear to be raised as matters of concern by firms, as reflected in the Commission's and USTR's annual reports on trade barriers. This may be because the regulations do not present a particular problem for them; the regulations may be sufficiently similar to domestic rules or the firm's own standards so as not to hinder trade or they may be accommodated by an easy and relatively inexpensive change in design or production.[21] Moreover, according to both industry[22] and government[23] sources firms often do not recognise trade barriers as such, or at least do not recognise that they are actionable under multilateral trade rules (see also Commission 2007). Further, firms often prefer to try to resolve matters directly with the foreign government in question.[24] Such considerations are likely to be particularly pronounced in the transatlantic relationship given the extremely high degree of interpenetration between the EU and US economies, reflected in very high levels of mutual foreign direct investment and, associated, intra-firm trade (Hamilton and Quinlan 2005). Thus it would seem that the vast majority of environmental and public health regulations adopted by both the EU and the US cause only minimal trade friction.

If a regulation does impose significant economic costs, there is the crucial question of whether it is permitted under WTO rules. Subject to procedural requirements, the WTO's rules give governments a considerable degree of regulatory autonomy, including with regard to the level of risk they are willing to accept (PIU 2000; Hoberg 2001; DeSombre and Barkin 2002; Marceau and Trachtman 2002; Esserman and Howse 2003; Neumann and Türk 2003; Young 2005; Young and Holmes 2006; Pollack and Shaffer 2009). As a result, it is perfectly possible for a regulation to impede trade, but to still be compatible with WTO rules. As government officials do not want to lose complaints they bring, they bring them very selectively, targeting only the most clear-cut violations of WTO rules (Allee 2004).[25]

If trade officials think a complaint is winnable, they also weigh the political implications of initiating and winning it. Because initiating a WTO complaint is seen as an aggressive act, the WTO dispute literature notes that states are, *ceteris paribus*, less likely to initiate a complaint against a country with which they have close relations (Bown 2005b; Guzman and Simmons 2005). As noted earlier, public health and environmental regulations are particularly politically salient and so challenging them might be especially disruptive to good relations. As a consequence, trade officials may think twice before initiating a WTO complaint against a regulatory measure that has strong domestic support. Trade officials also consider whether by successfully challenging a foreign government's rule they might establish a precedent that applies to their own policies (Shaffer 2003; Young 2009a).[26] These considerations can affect whether a measure is challenged at all, but also the legal grounds on which it is challenged (Shaffer 2003, 104–105).[27]

There are thus a series of layered considerations that may explain why so few public health and environmental regulations are challenged in the context of the transatlantic relationship. First, they may not impose sufficient costs on the other's firms to make action worthwhile. Even if they do, the regulations may be consistent with WTO rules and so not be actionable. Even if the costs are significant and the case seems winnable it might still not be worth initiating because doing so might damage the wider relationship or winning the complaint might have adverse implications for one's own regulatory activity. That CW1 is incorrect is crucial to the likelihood of winning and concern about avoiding precedents being relevant in transatlantic WTO complaints. If the US were as hostile to environmental and public health regulation as CW1 suggests, it would have resisted, rather than supported, ensuring that governments' regulatory autonomy was safeguarded in WTO rules. Moreover, it would be unconcerned about setting precedents that constrain its own regulatory activity.

Empirical Shortcoming: Surgical Strikes, Not All-Out Assaults

Contrary to many depictions (see, for example, Bernauer 2003, 167; Greenpeace 2003 and 2006; Amicus Coalition 2004; Guzman 2004–05, 32; Ramjoué 2007, 420), the US's WTO complaints against the EU's ban on hormone-treated beef and moratorium on approvals of genetically modified crops were not all-out assaults on the precautionary principle, but were actually fairly narrow challenges to the EU's measures.[28] Moreover, how the US pursued these complaints reflects the considerations discussed above; what is permissible under WTO rules, seeking to avoid setting awkward precedents and, to a limited extent, by consideration of political repercussions.

In its challenge to the EU's ban on hormone-treated beef,[29] the US accepted that the EU had the right under the SPS Agreement to set the level of protection it considered appropriate, although it argued that the ban was 'arbitrary and unjustified', because the EU permitted the use of other additives that posed similar risks (WTO 1997, 37).[30] Another key argument was that there was no scientific evidence that the hormones were unsafe when used appropriately. This was relevant to the principle of precaution as the EU justified its action on there being reason to doubt that the hormones were safe because evidence of their safety was incomplete. The Commission's (subsequent) guidance on the precautionary principle, however, states that recourse to it 'presupposes that potentially dangerous effects deriving from a phenomenon, product or process have been identified, and that scientific evaluation does not allow the risk to be determined with sufficient certainty' (Commission 2000, 3). The US also argued that the ban was really motivated by the EU not wanting to increase beef production given existing costly surpluses generated by the Common Agricultural Policy. The WTO's Appellate Body ruled that the EU's bans were incompatible with WTO rules because they were not based on a risk assessment, but in this and subsequent judgments it has allowed a significant degree of discretion with the management of identified potential risks—what level of risk is acceptable and how that level is realized—even when there is uncertainty about the scientific evidence of the risk involved (PIU 2000, 94; Skogstad 2001, 494–495).

These clarifications of WTO disciplines shaped the substance of the US' subsequent WTO complaint against the EU's GMO approval procedures (USTR 2004, 1),[31] as did concerns about establishing awkward precedents.[32] The timing of the complaint was shaped by concern about adverse political repercussions, with the complaint being delayed until after the conclusion of conventional fighting in the 2003 Iraq War so as not to put off European allies (Baucus 2003, 4; Pollack and Shaffer 2009, 179). The complaint did not challenge the basis on which the EU approves GM crops nor, despite considerable political pressure, did it challenge the EU's traceability and labelling requirements (see Young 2009b). Rather it focused on the EU's 'moratorium' on approvals and the refusal of some member governments to accept GM crops that have been approved by the EU (USTR 2004, 1).[33] It argued that the 'moratorium' constituted an 'undue delay' and that it and the individual member state bans had not been based on risk assessments. Thus the challenge was to the EU's failure to apply its own procedures and to enforce its own rules rather than to the substance of or principles underpinning those procedures. The WTO panel found that the moratorium violated WTO rules, but only because it led to undue delays, and that the member states' bans violated WTO rules because they were not based on risk assessments. Notably, neither the EU nor the US appealed the ruling. The details of the two high-profile WTO complaints, in addition to being rare exceptions, therefore, suggest a much more constrained contestation than is commonly depicted.

Conclusion

This article has argued that the two prominent conventional wisdoms about the transatlantic regulatory relationship—that it is highly conflictual and that the conflicts are rooted in profoundly different approaches to regulation—are ill-founded. First, they are based on implicit selection bias, a manifestation of the 'availability heuristic', and generalise from the extreme and rare cases of full-blown WTO complaints about regulatory trade barriers to the whole of the transatlantic regulatory relationship. Looking beyond the regulation of hormone-treated beef and the approval of genetically modified crops reveals a more varied and less asymmetrical transatlantic regulatory relationship. Second, the cases that inform the conventional wisdoms do not actually support the claims made. The disputes are not clear-cut contests between 'sound science' and the 'precautionary principle'. The adoptions of the EU's ban on hormone-treated beef and its approach to the approval of genetically modified crops were the products of political competition among actors with very different approaches to the regulation of risk. The regulatory outcomes therefore reflect the hurly-burly of politics rather than the neat application of a regulatory principle. Moreover, the US' WTO complaints against the hormone-treated beef ban and the EU's moratorium on approvals of genetically modified crops did not challenge the precautionary principle.

Although the EU and the US do adopt different regulations and these differences can and do impede trade and create trade tensions, this article argues that these differences are not rooted in profoundly different approaches to regulation between the two polities. Different approaches to the regulation of risk exist within each polity and the ensuing political competition within each polity produces regulatory outcomes of different stringency across issues and over time. While this distinction may not seem great, it has great consequence. Because both polities sometimes regulate stringently each is more tolerant of the other doing so. Rather than being characterised by conflict or co-operation, therefore, the transatlantic regulatory relationship is really one of tolerance, in which the vast majority of regulatory differences are not resolved, either amicably or through litigation.

More broadly, this article should serve as a cautionary tale about the dangers of relying on obvious cases when describing and explaining political phenomena.

WTO complaints are both the most visible disputes and the most atypical. Generalising from them gives both a distorted picture of the transatlantic relationship and suggests misleading explanations for regulatory differences. These misperceptions can then influence policy by making accommodation seem harder and confrontation more necessary.

About the Author

Alasdair R. Young, Department of Politics, Adam Smith Building, University of Glasgow, Glasgow G12 8RT, UK, email: *a.young@lbss.gla.ac.uk*

Notes

A very rudimentary version of this article was presented to the University of Edinburgh's Transatlantic Seminar (4 March 2005). An intermediate version was presented to the 'Domestic Sources of Transatlantic Regulation' Workshop, Freie Universität, Berlin (27–28 June 2008). I am grateful to the participants in both workshops and to two anonymous referees for their comments. I would also like to thank all of those who took time out of their busy schedules to discuss these issues with me. I am grateful to Poppy Winanti for research assistance in developing the database of transatlantic disputes and to Glasgow's Department of Politics for funding her assistance.

1. 'Review of the Framework for Relations between the European Union and the United States' (Contract SI2.391098).

2. Grant SG-35702.

3. Author's interview with a US trade official (6 January 2005).

4. Although trade liberalisation within the EU has been achieved by agreeing stringent common rules ('positive integration') (for a survey of the literature see Young 2007a, 383–385), the common expectation in the international setting is that regulatory barriers will simply be removed ('negative integration').

5. Author's interviews with US government officials (11 and 12 January 2005).

6. The 1992 (Maastricht) Treaty on the European Union incorporated the precautionary principle as one of the principles to be taken into account in EU environmental policy (Art. 174(2)).

7. The US government's position is not complete hostility to the idea of precaution; rather it argues that existing international rules, including those of the WTO, adequately acknowledge the right of governments to exercise precaution and that the balance between scientific uncertainty and the potential for benefit or harm be evaluated on a case-by-case basis (Atlantic Council 2002, 5). The leaders of the EU (European Council 2000, point 4) also think that WTO rules allow sufficient scope for members to exercise precaution.

8. Greg Shaffer and Mark Pollack (2005, 172) are rare in that they explicitly 'resist extrapolating' from their study of GMOs to the relative importance of precaution in the EU and US.

9. Another WTO complaint was the EU's challenge to a US ban on poultry imports, which was resolved at the consultation phase (USTR 2009). The US filed a WTO complaint in January 2009, in the final days of the Bush administration, against the EU's ban on antimicrobial treatment of poultry. At the time of writing (April 2009) it is too soon to tell whether and how it will be pursued, particularly given the subsequent change in the US administration. In any event, this dispute is too recent to have shaped the conventional wisdoms. Another dispute involved a US challenge to EU restrictions on aircraft retrofitted with 'hushkits' to comply with noise limits, which was addressed through mediation by the International Civil Aviation Organisation (ICAO) and resolved as part of an overall agreement on new ICAO standards and policies (Abbott 2003).

10. The TBT Committee does not systematically report issues of concern raised prior to 2005.

11. For an overview of precaution in US food safety see FDA and DoA (2000).

12. Author's interview, 15 March 2005.

13. Author's interview with a Commission regulator, 16 September 2003.

14. For a review of the literature on how the single European market process tends to lead to more stringent public health and environmental regulation, see Young (2007a, 383–385).

15. *EC Official Journal,* C288/158 11 November 1985, Point E.

16. Author's interviews with a Commission regulator (4 December 2000) and trade official (10 January 2001).

17. The Commission had systematically sought scientific risk assessment since at least 1997 when responsibility for approvals passed to the Directorate General for Health and Consumer Protection (Author's interview with a Commission trade official, 10 January 2001).

18. It is worth noting that this is how many US regulators and interest groups came to see the origins of the EU's GMO rules. Author's interviews with US government regulators (9 and 11 January 2001; 13 January 2005) and trade officials (11 and 12 January 2005), and representatives of a transatlantic business association (8 January 2001) and US trade associations (9 and 11 January 2001).

19. The US government's intervention on discussions within the UN's Codex Alimentarius, which sets international food safety standards, on Working Principles for Risk Analysis, 'endorse[d]' that 'precaution has been and should remain an essential element of risk analysis in the formulation of national and international standards', and went on to state: 'The United States believes that precaution is essential throughout risk analysis, including risk assessment, risk management and risk communication' (FSIS 2000, 3).

20. The US, for example, tends to make greater use of market incentives, while the EU relies more heavily on command and control measures. US regulations are usually adopted as administrative decisions while in the EU they take the form of legislation. In the US there is greater faith in *ex post* monitoring and producer liability, while the EU emphasises *ex ante* regulation. Both sides adopt rules with extraterritorial implications, albeit on different issues. See also Woolcock (1991); Wiener (2004).

21. Author's interviews with a British trade association representative (11 September 2003) and a senior Commission trade official (18 September 2003).

22. Author's interview with a British business association representative (21 May 2003).

23. Author's interview with a British trade official (21 May 2003).

24. Author's interviews with a British trade official (21 May 2003), a European trade association representative (16 September 2003) and a senior Commission trade official (18 September 2003).

25. Author's interview with a Commission trade official (17 September 2003).

26. Author's interview with a Commission trade official (17 September 2003) and European trade association representatives (16 and 17 September 2003).

27. Author's interview with a Commission regulator (16 September 2003).

28. With respect to beef hormones, author's interview with a Commission trade official (24 March 2004).

29. For a summary of the arguments, see Roberts (1998, 388–392).

30. In its response to the EU's challenge to it not lifting its sanctions in the wake of the EU's revised rules, the US again did not challenge the precautionary principle, but complained that the EU's bans were still not based on adequate risk assessment (USTR 2005).

31. Author's interviews with US trade officials (11 and 14 January 2005).

32. One US trade official noted that while one could 'find fault' with the EU's approval procedures, one could also find fault with US rules (Author's interview, 14 January 2005).

33. Author's interviews with US trade officials (11 and 14 January 2005) and agricultural officials (11 January 2005).

Bibliography

Abbott, K. W. (2003) 'EU–US disputes over technical barriers to trade and the "Hushkits" dispute', in E.-U. Petersmann and M. A. Pollack (eds), *Transatlantic Economic Disputes: The EU, the US and the WTO* (Oxford: Oxford University Press), 247–280.

Ahearn, R. J. (2007) 'Trade conflict and the US–European Union economic relationship', CRS Report for Congress, RL30732, updated 11 April.

Ahearn, R. J., Fischer, J. W., Goldfarb, C. B., Hanrahan, C. E., Eubanks, W. W., and Rubin, J. E. (2008) 'European Union—US trade and investment relations: Key issues', CRS Report for Congress, RL34381, updated 8 April.

Allee, T. (2004) 'Legal incentives and domestic rewards: The selection of trade disputes for GATT/WTO dispute resolution', University of Illinois, October. Available online at: http://www.law.northwestern.edu/colloquium/international/Allee.pdf

Amicus Coalition (2004) 'Information submitted to the panel by non-parties', European Communities—Measures Affecting the Approval and Marketing of Biotech Products, DS291, DS292, DS293), 27 May. Available online at: http://www.genewatch.org/uploads/f03c6d66a9b354535738483c1c3d49e4/PublicInterestAmicus_2.pdf (accessed 7 July 2008).

Andrews, D. M., Pollack, M. A., Shaffer, G. C. and Wallace, H. (2005) *The Future of Transatlantic Economic Relations: Continuity amid Discord* (San Domenico di Fiesole: Robert Schuman Centre for Advanced Studies).

Atlantic Council (2002) 'Risk and reward: US–EU regulatory co-operation on food safety and the environment', Atlantic Council Policy Paper, November.

Baucus, M. (2003) 'Opening statement', Senate Finance Committee Hearing on the Administration's Trade Agenda', S. Hrg., 108–139, 5 March.

Bermann, G. A., Herdegen M. and Lindseth, P. L. (eds) (2000) *Transatlantic Regulatory Co-operation* (Oxford: Oxford University Press).

Bernauer, T. (2003) *Genes, Trade and Regulation: The Seeds of Conflict in Food Biotechnology* (Princeton, NJ: Princeton University Press).

Bown, C. P. (2005a) 'Trade remedies and World Trade Organization dispute settlement: Why are so few challenged?', *Journal of Legal Studies*, 34:June, 515–555.

Bown, C. P. (2005b) 'Participation in WTO dispute settlement: Complainants, interested parties and free riders', *The World Bank Economic Review*, 19:2, 287–310.

Brittan, L. (2000) 'Transatlantic economic partnership: Breaking down the hidden barriers', in G. A. Berman, M. Herdegen and P. L. Lindseth (eds), *Transatlantic Regulatory Co-operation* (Oxford: Oxford University Press), 17–23.

Busch, M. L. and Reinhardt, E. (2002) 'Testing international trade law: Empirical studies of GATT/WTO dispute settlement', in D. L. M. Kennedy and J. D. Southwick (eds), *The Political Economy of International Trade Law* (Cambridge: Cambridge University Press), 457–481.

Busch, M. L. and Reinhardt, E. (2003) 'Transatlantic trade conflict and GATT/WTO dispute settlement', in E.-U. Petersmann and M. A. Pollack (eds), *Transatlantic Economic Disputes: The EU, the US and the WTO* (Oxford: Oxford University Press), 465–485.

Carlarne, C. (2007) 'From the USA with love: Sharing home-grown hormones, GMOs and clones with a reluctant Europe', *Environmental Law*, 37:2, 301–337.

Charnovitz, S. (2000) 'The supervision of health and biosafety regulation by world trade rules', *Tulane Environmental Law Journal*, 13:2, 271.

Christoforou, T. (2004) 'The precautionary principle, risk assessment and the comparative role of science in the European Community and US legal systems', in N. J. Vig and M. G. Faure (eds), *Green Giants: Environmental Policies of the United States and European Union* (Cambridge, MA: MIT Press), 17–51.

Commission (2000) 'Communication ... on the precautionary principle', COM (2000), 1 Final, 2 February.

Commission (2005a) 'Joint RELEX–TRADE paper on EU–US relations', January. On file with the author.

Commission (2005b) 'Review of the framework for relations between the European Union and the United States: An independent study'. Available online at: http://www.isg-london.org/fileadmin/user_upload/GPI/Research/TEIP/Key_Documents/TER_Reader_part2.pdf, 693–784.

Commission (2008a) 'EC SPS notification authority and enquiry point activity report year 2007: Synopsis', Health and Consumer Protection Directorate General, Unit D3.

Commission (2008b) 'Proposal for a Council decision authorising the placing on the market of products containing, consisting of, or produced from genetically modified soybean A2704-12 (ACS-GH005-3) pursuant to Regulation (EC) 1829/2003 ...', COM (2008), 218 final, 28 April.

Commission (2008c) *United States Barriers to Trade and Investment: Report for 2007* (Brussels: European Commission).

Council (1999) '2194th Council Meeting—Environment—Luxembourg, 24/25 June 1999', Press 203—Nr 9406/99.

Cowles, M. G. (1997) *The Limits of Liberalization: Regulatory Co-operation and the New Transatlantic Agenda* (Washington, DC: American Institute for Contemporary German Studies: The Johns Hopkins University).

Damro, C. and Sbragia, A. M. (2003) 'The new framework of transatlantic economic governance: Strategic trade management and regulatory conflict in a multilateral global economy', in M. L. Campanella and S. C. W. Eijffinger (eds), *EU Economic Governance and Globalization* (Cheltenham: Edward Elgar), 105–141.

DeSombre, E. R. and Barkin, J. S. (2002) 'Turtles and trade: The WTO's acceptance of environmental trade restrictions', *Global Environmental Politics*, 2:1, 12–18.

Devereaux, C., Lawrence, R. Z. and Watkins, M. D. (2006) *Case Studies in US Trade Negotiation: (Vol. 2) Resolving Disputes* (Washington, DC: Institute for International Economics).

Eckley, N. and Selin, H. (2004) 'All talk, little action: Precaution and European chemicals regulation', *Journal of European Public Policy*, 11:1, 78–105.

Esserman, S. and Howse, R. (2003) 'The WTO on trial', *Foreign Affairs*, 82:1, 130–140.

Commission (2007) 'Report on the Public Consultation on the EU Market Access Strategy', Directorate General for Trade, Directorate G, 5 February.

European Council (2000) 'Council resolution on the precautionary principle', Annex III, Annexes to the European Council Conclusions, Bulletin EU 12-2000.

Evans, P. (2003) 'Is trade policy democratic? And should it be?', in N. Bayne and S. Woolcock (eds), *The New Economic Diplomacy: Decision-Making and Negotiations in International Economic Relations* (Farnham: Ashgate), 147–159.

FDA and DoA (2000) 'Precaution in US food safety decision making: Annex II to the United States' National Food Safety System Paper', 3 March (Food and Drug Administration and Department of Agriculture). Available online at: http://www.foodsafety.gov/~fsg/fssyst4.html (accessed 10 July 2008).

FSIS (2000) *Draft US Response to CL 2000/12-GP* (Washington, DC: Food Safety and Inspection Service, US Department of Agriculture).

Greenpeace (2003) 'The US assault on biosafety—Renewed aggression by a rogue state'. Available online at: http://www.greenpeace.org/raw/content/international/press/reports/the-us-war-on-biosafety-rene.pdf (accessed 8 July 2008).

Greenpeace (2006) 'The US assault on biosafety—The WTO dispute on GMOs', February. Available online at: www.saveourseeds.org/downloads/GP_WTObriefing0602.pdf (accessed 7 July 2008).

Guzman, A. T. (2004–05) 'Food fears: Health and safety at the WTO', *Virginia Journal of International Law*, 45, 1–39.

Guzman, A. T. and Simmons, B. A. (2002) 'To settle or empanel? An empirical analysis of litigation and settlement at the World Trade Organization', *Journal of Legal Studies*, 31:1, S205–S235.

Guzman, A. T. and Simmons, B. A. (2005) 'Power plays and capacity constraints: The selection of defendants in World Trade Organization disputes', *Journal of Legal Studies*, 34:2, 557–598.

Hamilton, D. S. and Quinlan, J. P. (2005) 'Partners in prosperity: The changing geography of the transatlantic economy', in D. M. Andrews, M. A. Pollack, G. C. Shaffer and H. Wallace (eds), *The Future of Transatlantic Economic Relations: Continuity Amid Discord* (San Domenico di Fiesole: Robert Schuman Centre for Advanced Studies), 9–34.

Hammitt, J. K., Wiener, J. B., Swedlow, B., Kall, D. and Zhou, Z. (2005) 'Precautionary regulation in Europe and the United States: A quantitative comparison', *Risk Analysis*, 25:5, 1215–1228.

Hoberg, G. (2001) 'Trade, harmonization and domestic autonomy in environmental policy', *Journal of Comparative Policy Analysis Research and Practice*, 3:2, 191–217.

Jasanoff, S. (2005) *Designs on Nature* (Princeton, NJ: Princeton University Press).

Jasanoff, S. (2008) 'Trading uncertainties: The transatlantic divide in regulatory biotechnology', CESifo DICE Report, 2/2008, 36–43.

Kahler, M. (1995) *Regional Futures and Transatlantic Economic Relations* (New York, NY: Council on Foreign Relations Press).

King, G., Keohane, R. O. and Verba, S. (1994) *Designing Social Enquiry: Scientific Inference in Qualitative Research* (Princeton, NJ: Princeton University Press).

Kogan, L. A. (2004) 'Exporting Europe's protectionism', *The National Interest*, 77:Fall, 91–99.

Krenzler, H. G. and MacGregor, A. (2000) 'GM food: The next major transatlantic trade war?', *European Foreign Affairs Review*, 5, 287–316.

Kupchan, C. A. (2003) 'The rise of Europe, America's changing internationalism and the end of US primacy', *Political Science Quarterly*, 118:2, 205–231.

Laïdi, Z. (2008) 'The normative empire: The unintended consequences of European power', Garnet Policy Brief 6. Available online at: http://www.garnet-eu.org/fileadmin/documents/policy_briefs/Garnet_Policy_Brief_No_6.pdf

Levy, D. L. and Newell, P. (2000) 'Oceans apart: Business responses to global environmental issues in Europe and the United States', *Environment*, November, 8–20.

Marceau, G. and Trachtman, J. P. (2002) 'The technical barriers to trade agreement, the sanitary and phytosanitary agreement, and the general agreement on tariffs and trade: A map of the World Trade Organization Law of Domestic Regulation of Goods', *Journal of World Trade*, 36:5, 811–881.

Mavroidis, P. C. (2003) 'The trade disputes concerning health policy between the EC and the US', in E.-U. Petersmann and M. A. Pollack (eds), *Transatlantic Economic Disputes: The EU, the US and the WTO* (Oxford: Oxford University Press), 233–245.

McGuire, S. and Smith, M. (2008) *The European Union and the United States: Competition and Convergence in the Global Arena* (Basingstoke: Palgrave Macmillan).

Moses, J. W. and Knutsen, T. L. (2007) *Ways of Knowing: Competing Methodologies in Social and Political Research* (Basingstoke: Palgrave Macmillan).

Murphy, J. and Levidow, L. (2006) *Governing the Transatlantic Conflict over Agricultural Biotechnology: Contending Coalitions, Trade Liberalisation and Standard Setting* (London: Routledge).

NAM (2004) *Improving Regulatory Co-operation to Create a Seamless Economic Partnership: NAM Submission on Enhancing the Transatlantic Economic Relationship* (Washington, DC: National Association of Manufacturers).

Neumann, J. and Türk, E. (2003) 'Necessity revisited: Proportionality in World Trade Organization law after Korea—beef, EC—asbestos and EC—sardines', *Journal of World Trade*, 37:1, 199–233.

Newell, P. (2003) 'Globalization and the governance of biotechnology', *Global Environmental Politics*, 3:2, 56–71.

NFTC (2003) *Looking Behind the Curtain: The Growth of Trade Barriers that Ignore Sound Science* (Washington, DC: National Foreign Trade Council).

Patterson, L. A. (2000) 'Biotechnology policy: Regulating risks and risking regulation', in H. Wallace and W. Wallace (eds), *Policy-Making in the European Union* (3rd edn) (Oxford: Oxford University Press), 317–343.

Petersmann, U.-E. and Pollack, M. A. (2003) *Transatlantic Economic Disputes: The EU, the US and the WTO* (Oxford: Oxford University Press).

Peterson, J. (2004) 'The politics of transatlantic trade relations', in B. Hocking and S. McGuire (eds), *Trade Politics* (2nd edn) (London: Routledge), 36–50.

Peterson, J. and Young, A. R. (2007) 'Trade and transatlantic relations', in S. Meunier and K. McNamarra (eds), *Making History: European Integration and Institutional Change at Fifty: The State of the European Union* (vol. 8) (Oxford: Oxford University Press), 283–298.

PIU (2000) *Rights of Exchange: Social, Health, Environmental and Trade Objectives on the Global Stage* (London: Cabinet Office Performance and Innovation Unit).

Pollack, M. A. (2003a) 'The political economy of transatlantic trade disptutes', in E.-U. Petersmann and M. A. Pollack (eds), *Transatlantic Economic Disputes: The EU, the US and the WTO* (Oxford: Oxford University Press), 65–118.

Pollack, M. A. (2003b) 'Managing system friction: Regulatory conflicts in transatlantic relations and the WTO', in E.-U. Petersmann and M. A. Pollack (eds), *Transatlantic Economic Disputes: The EU, the US and the WTO* (Oxford: Oxford University Press), 595–602.

Pollack, M. A. (2005) 'The new transatlantic agenda at ten: Reflections on an experiment in international governance', *Journal of Common Market Studies*, 43:5, 899–919.

Pollack, M. A. and Shaffer, G. (2009) *When Co-operation Fails: The International Law and Politics of Genetically Modified Foods* (Oxford: Oxford University Press).

Pollack, M. A. and Shaffer, G. C. (2006) 'Transatlantic economic relations: Continuity amid discord', *European Political Science*, 5:1, 62–68.

Princen, S. B. M. (2002) *The California Effect in the Transatlantic Relationship* (University of Utrecht, Ph.D. thesis, unpublished).

Ramjoué, C. (2007) 'The transatlantic rift in genetically modified food policy', *Journal of Agricultural and Environmental Ethics*, 20:5, 419–446.

Roberts, D. (1998) 'Preliminary assessment of the effects of the WTO agreement on sanitary and phytosanitary trade regulations', *Journal of International Economic Law*, 1:3, 377–405.

Scharpf, F. (1999) *Governing in Europe: Effective and Democratic* (Oxford: Oxford University Press).

Shaffer, G. C. (2003) *Defending Interests: Public–Private Partnerships in WTO Litigation* (Washington, DC: Brookings Institution Press).

Shaffer, G. C. and Pollack, M. A. (2005) 'Reconciling (or failing to reconcile) regulatory differences: The ongoing transatlantic dispute over the regulation of biotechnology', in D. M. Andrews, M. A. Pollack,

G. C. Shaffer and H. Wallace (eds), *The Future of Transatlantic Economic Relations: Continuity amid Discord* (San Domenico di Fiesole: Robert Schuman Centre for Advanced Studies), 167–229.

Sherman, R. (2002) 'Targeting democracies: Regime type and America's "aggressively unilateral" trade policy', *Social Science Quarterly*, 83:4, 1063–1078.

Skogstad, G. (2001) 'The WTO and food safety regulatory policy innovation in the European Union', *Journal of Common Market Studies*, 39:3, 485–505.

Steffenson, R. (2005) *Managing EU–US Relations: Actors, Institutions and the New Transatlantic Agenda* (Manchester: Manchester University Press).

Tama, J. (2004) 'Is Europe too cautious?', *Foreign Policy*, 140, 88–90.

Tehrani, M. (2008) 'European Union and the US trade disputes: The role of the WTO', *Organizational Management Journal*, 5:3, 135–148.

Ten Eyck, T. A., Gaskell, G. and Jackson, J. (2004) 'Seeds, food and trade wars: Public opinion and policy responses in the USA and Europe', *Journal of Commercial Biotechnology*, 10:3, 258–267.

Thompson, R. (2003) 'Transatlantic Business in an Era of Crisis and Change', *The Transatlantic Index*, June, 6–7.

Tversky, A. and Kahneman, D. (1973) 'Availability: A heuristic for judging frequency and probability', *Cognitive Psychology*, 5:2, 207–232.

Tversky, A. and Kahneman, D. (1974) 'Judgement under uncertainty: Heuristics and biases', *Science*, 185:4157, 1124–1131.

USTR (2004) 'European Communities—Measures affecting the approval and marketing of biotech products (WT/DS291, 292, and 293): Executive Summary of the First Submission of the United States', 30 April.

USTR (2005) 'United States—Continued suspension of obligations in the EC-hormones dispute (WT/DS320): First Written Submission of the United States of America', 8 August.

USTR (2008) *2008 National Trade Estimate Report on Foreign Trade Barriers* (Washington, DC: United States Trade Representative).

USTR (2009) 'Snapshot of WTO cases involving the United States', Update 17 January. Available online at: http://www.ustr.gov/sites/default/files/Snapshot%20of%20WTO%20Cases%20Involving%20the%20United%20States.pdf (accessed 24 July 2009).

Vig, N. J. and Faure, M. G. (2004) 'Introduction', in N. J. Vig and M. G. Faure (eds), *Green Giants: Environmental Policies of the United States and the European Union* (Cambridge, MA: The MIT Press), 1–14.

Vogel, D. (1989) *Fluctuating Fortunes: The Political Power of Business in America* (New York, NY: Basic Books).

Vogel, D. (1995) *Trading Up: Consumer and Environmental Regulation in a Global Economy* (Cambridge, MA: Harvard University Press).

Vogel, D. (1997) *Barriers or Benefits? Regulation in Transatlantic Trade* (Washington, DC: Brookings Institution Press).

Vogel, D. (2003) 'The hare and the tortoise revisited: The new politics of consumer and environmental regulation in Europe', *British Journal of Political Science*, 33:4, 557–580.

Wiener, J. B. (2004) 'Convergence, divergence and complexity in US and European risk regulation', in N. J. Vig and M. G. Faure (eds), *Green Giants: Environmental Policies of the United States and European Union* (Cambridge, MA: MIT Press), 73–109.

Wiener, J. B. and Rogers, M. D. (2002) 'Comparing precaution in the United States and Europe', *Journal of Risk Research*, 5:4, 317–349.

Woolcock, S. (1991) *Market Access in EC–US Relations: Trading Partners or Trading Blows?* (London: Pinter for Royal Institute of International Affairs).

Woolcock, S. B. (2002) *The Precautionary Principle in the European Union and Its Impact on International Trade Relations* (CEPS Working Document 186) (Brussels: Centre for European Policy Studies).

WTO (1997) 'EC measures concerning meat and meat products', hormones)—Complaint of the United States: Report of the Panel', WT/DS26/R/USA, 18 August.

WTO (2008a) 'Thirteenth Annual Review of the implementation and operation of the TBT Agreement', G/TBT/23, Committee on Technical Barriers to Trade, 20 February.

WTO (2008b) 'Specific trade concerns: Note by the secretariat: Revision', SPS/GEN/204/Rev.8, 27 March.

Young, A. R. (2001) *Trading Up or Trading Blows? US Politics and Transatlantic Trade in Genetically Modified Food* (EUI Working Paper RSC 2001/20) (San Domenico: European University Institute).

Young, A. R. (2004) 'The incidental fortress: The single European market and world trade', *Journal of Common Market Studies*, 42:2, 393–414.

Young, A. R. (2005) 'Picking the wrong fight: Why attacks on the World Trade Organization pose the real threat to environmental and public health protection', *Global Environmental Politics*, 5:4, 47–72.

Young, A. R. (2007a) 'The politics of regulation and the internal market', in K. E. Jørgensen, M. A. Pollack and B. Rosamond (eds), *The Handbook of European Union Politics* (London: Sage), 373–394.

Young, A. R. (2007b) 'Trade politics ain't what it used to be: The European Union in the Doha Round', *Journal of Common Market Studies*, 45:4, 789–811.

Young, A. R. (2009a) 'Prosecuting trade disputes: The European Union's initiation of WTO complaints', unpublished manuscript, University of Glasgow.

Young, A. R. (2009b) 'International law and executive autonomy: The domestic politics of the transatlantic GMO dispute', unpublished manuscript, University of Glasgow.

Young, A. R. (2010) 'The European policy process in comparative perspective', in H. Wallace, M. A. Pollack and A. R. Young (eds), *Policy-Making in the European Union* (6th edn) (Oxford: Oxford University Press).

Young, A. R. and Holmes, P. (2006) 'Protection or protectionism? EU food safety rules and the WTO', in C. Ansell and D. Vogel (eds), *What's the Beef? The Contested Governance of European Food Safety* (Cambridge, MA: MIT Press), 281–305.

Young, A. R. and Wallace, H. (2000) *Regulatory Politics in the Enlarging European Union: Weighing Civic and Producer Interests* (Manchester: Manchester University Press).

doi: 10.1111/j.1467-856X.2009.00385.x   *BJPIR: 2009 VOL 11, 690–708*

The Liberal Peace at Home and Abroad: Northern Ireland and Liberal Internationalism

Roger Mac Ginty

Northern Ireland, we are told, holds positive lessons for other societies emerging from violent conflict. As Britain is one of the leading proponents of liberal internationalism, this article considers whether the liberal internationalism pushed with so much enthusiasm abroad through British foreign policy has been applied with diligence at home—in the Northern Ireland peace process. The findings suggest that Northern Ireland is by no means a poster child for liberal internationalism. Instead, British government handling of the Northern Ireland peace process shows serious deviations from the liberal internationalist canon. This article argues that liberal peace-lite has been tolerated and facilitated at home, while a stricter variant is often expected in overseas contexts.

Keywords: liberal peace; peacemaking; Northern Ireland

Introduction

One of Tony Blair's last acts as prime minister was to help engineer the resumption of a devolved power-sharing administration in Northern Ireland. This seemed fitting for a prime minister who had invested so much energy in the peace process. Many commentators noted how Blair's Northern Ireland experience would prove a useful grounding for his subsequent work as a Middle East envoy (Wintour and Black 2007). The notion that the Northern Ireland peace process holds positive lessons for other societies emerging from protracted conflict has been seized upon enthusiastically by British and Irish political leaders, politicians from Northern Ireland, media commentators and academics (Guelke 2008). While most, like former Irish prime minister Bertie Ahern, are realistic enough to note that 'no two conflicts are exactly the same and no two solutions will ever be alike', the essential message is that we 'can share our past experience and newfound hope with others who are caught up in conflict' (Ahern 2007). The theme that Northern Ireland 'holds a lesson for conflict everywhere' was made repeatedly by Blair (Blair 2006 and 2007). This article seeks to analyse critically the notion of the transferability of lessons from Northern Ireland by placing British government handling of the Northern Ireland peace process in the context of wider British foreign policy. Much of British foreign policy from the mid-1990s onwards (a time coterminous with the Northern Ireland peace process) could be characterised as liberal internationalism. This article seeks to address the following question: was the liberal internationalism in British foreign policy reflected in the British government's peace process strategy 'at home'?

There can be no doubting the successes of the Northern Ireland peace process. The mechanism has allowed the protagonists to bring to an end a violent conflict (approximately 3,500 deaths over 25 years) and has spared governments, communities, businesses and individuals further years of missed opportunities and the attendant human indignities. But the peace process was by no means an unalloyed success. Not only did it involve many setbacks, but it was marked by a series of uncomfortable moral and practical compromises: the early release of paramilitary prisoners, the inclusion of political parties with armed wings in negotiations and then the Assembly, and the quiet dropping of judicial scrutiny of British government sponsorship of loyalist paramilitaries, etc. In one sense all peacemaking processes in complex ethno-national disputes must involve compromise and we would be naïve to expect some sort of stain-free process. Yet, in another sense, the British government has established itself as one of the leading states in the international promotion of conflict resolution and peace-building. It has adopted an interventionist foreign policy and, through its liberal internationalism, has been involved in peace promotion in multiple contexts during the Blair era and beyond. As a result, British government conflict management strategy in Northern Ireland deserves critical scrutiny, particularly in relation to the similarities and divergences between the promotion of the liberal peace at home and abroad.

Most studies of liberal internationalism look outwards from the global north to the sites of civil war. This article seeks to invert the usual approach. It uses liberal internationalism as an analytical device to present a critical appraisal of a peace process close to the centre. Since Britain has been, and still is, a leading proponent of liberal internationalism it is legitimate to ask if the principles of the liberal internationalism preached so enthusiastically abroad were adhered to at home. The article is in part inspired by a polemical essay by M. L. R. Smith (1999, 77–97) which admonished the academic community for its failure to make connections between the Northern Ireland conflict and wider academic debates. Decrying the 'intellectual internment' of the conflict, Smith noted that 'international relations scholars and analysts of the Northern Ireland crisis have passed each other like ships in the night: wending their respective ways, one barely cognisant of the other, with no, or at least very minimal, cross-fertilization of ideas' (Smith 1999, 81).

This article can be read as a modest attempt to redress Northern Ireland's intellectual insularity. It deliberately connects with a wider academic (and policy) debate—that on liberal internationalism—and seeks to provide a critique of British government handling of its peace process at home in order to assess the utility of the 'Northern Ireland model' abroad. It begins with a critical overview of liberal internationalism or 'the liberal peace', and then makes the case that Britain can be seen as a leading exponent of the liberal peace. By identifying five key themes in liberal internationalism (security and stability, reinforcing statehood, democratic governance, sustainability of a peace settlement and the promotion of free markets) it is possible to reflect on the extent to which liberal internationalist best practice can be found in British government conflict management strategy in contemporary Northern Ireland and overseas. It is argued that British government peace promotion efforts in Northern Ireland can be described as 'liberal peace-lite' or a compromised version of the liberal peace. This finding prompts questions on Britain's role as proselytiser-in-chief for liberal internationalism.

© 2009 The Author. Journal compilation © 2009 Political Studies Association
BJPIR, 2009, 11(4)

Any work of this kind requires caveats. One objection to the approach taken in this article may be that the liberal internationalism lens is inappropriate for matters of domestic policy. Yet, Northern Ireland's conflict and its complex identity constructions mean that it is not simply just another region of the United Kingdom. The conflict was internationalised through the unique intergovernmental British–Irish relationship, as well as the involvement of the United States and the European Union (Arthur 2000). Moreover, the explicit adoption of Northern Ireland by the British government as a conflict resolution exemplar means that it is appropriate to hold Northern Ireland to scrutiny in an international context. A further objection to the approach taken in this article may be to point to the vast contextual gulf between Northern Ireland and the sites of most other civil wars and international peace support interventions. Northern Ireland has an advanced economy, long experience of electoral democracy, benefits from a supportive regional context and has not involved United Nations intervention. It has been spared the complex social emergencies, public health catastrophes and large-scale population displacements of many civil wars. Its civil war was largely contained and was simply not of the order of many other civil conflagrations. As a result, it did not require the extensive state-building and development programmes that accompany many international interventions. Yet, despite these differences, many of the core elements of liberal internationalism have been used both in Northern Ireland and in international contexts and so it is legitimate to apply the liberal internationalism lens to Northern Ireland. The primary time focus of this article is from 1997 onwards as the Northern Ireland peace process stepped up a gear and moved to serious inter-party negotiations leading to the 1998 Good Friday Agreement, the establishment of the devolved institutions and further negotiations that eventually led to the 2007 Sinn Féin–Democratic Unionist Party accommodation.

Liberal Internationalism

The historian Michael Howard (1976, 5–19) reminds us how peace is a social construction. Rather than a utopian state of nature to which we revert in the absence of warfare, peace is invented and reinvented by power-holders to suit each context (Howard 2000). Thus peace must not be regarded as a neutral concept or blindly accepted as normatively good. Moreover, rather than a universal concept in which peace has the same qualities regardless of context, we should be alert to varieties of peace, with some varieties having more dominance than others (Richmond 2005; Richmond and Franks 2007, 27–48). In line with critical scholars of peace and conflict, this article holds that the currently dominant version of peace (as promoted by leading states, international organisations and international financial institutions) is the 'liberal peace' or the liberal internationalist peace (Chandler 2004; Jacoby 2007).

Liberal internationalism may be regarded as the dominant normative and operational framework for peace support interventions (Mac Ginty and Richmond 2007, 491–497). It is manifest in the complex multilateralism behind contemporary internationalised peace-building and post-war reconstruction (Shaw et al. 2006, 3–18). Its intellectual foundations lie in liberal optimism and associated beliefs that people, institutions, states and relationships can be reformed (Mandelbaum 2002).

The nature of this reform, according to its critics, is often prescriptive and reflects western and highly specialised notions of liberalism, democracy and governance (Mac Ginty 2006). These underpinnings of liberal internationalism often run counter to indigenous or traditional norms, but champions of the liberal peace are convinced of its superiority over alternatives. Thus, for example, the preferred notion of liberalism prioritises the individual (rather than the group) through the promotion of human and gender rights and the extension of the franchise. The preferred notion of democracy prioritises western-styled political parties, electoral contests and civil society (Salih 2001). The much-abused 'democratic peace thesis' has been repeatedly invoked on the questionable assumption that the democrati-sation of the post-civil war society will prevent conflict recidivism. The preferred notion of governance prioritises building, shoring up and reforming states so that they conform to western good practice. Francis Fukuyama and others referred to this 'good' governance and institutional reform agenda as 'getting to Denmark', thus reflecting a core element of the liberal internationalism model: the transfer of western ideas, institutions and practices as part of peace-building after civil war (Woolmark and Pritchett, 2002; Fukuyama 2004, 30). In this view, liberal interna-tionalism is much more than the mere extension of conflict resolution assistance and technocratic aid in the form of state-building or development activities. Instead, it must be regarded as part of a wider package with a distinct normative agenda that will have implications for the culture and value system of the society targeted by liberal international intervention (Sriram 2008).

The promotion of open markets is a fundamental canon of liberal internationalism. Historical and contemporary advocates of the liberal peace have pointed to the pivotal role played by the market. Free markets, they argue, make free men (Mandelbaum 2002, 265). And free men are more likely to be immune to the provocations of ethnic entrepreneurs and others who seek to exploit inter-group tensions. As President George W. Bush (2007) put it, 'prosperous nations are less likely to breed violence' and so the United States saw its role to 'advance peace and prosperity across the world'. With the market regarded as a route out of conflict, the World Bank, International Monetary Fund and international businesses have—in a number of cases—played significant roles in shaping peacemaking processes and post-conflict reconstruction programmes (Woodward 2002, 185).

The post-cold war period has provided a propitious environment for the promotion of liberal internationalism, or of a dominant, western-inspired form of peacemaking and peace-building. Certainly, the period has seen a significant number of conflict de-escalations in which liberal internationalism could be deployed. An end to superpower rivalry, an—at times—interventionist United States, an extension of UN and EU ambition and capability and the explosion in the number of NGOs and INGOs all benefited the promotion of the liberal peace and the notion that there were few alternatives to it. Until the onset of the global credit crisis in mid-2008 it seemed as though neo-liberal prescriptions had universal application to the needs of developing and post-conflict societies. Interventions in Bosnia, Kosovo, Sierra Leone, Bougainville, Timor Leste, the Solomon Islands, Darfur, Afghanistan, Iraq, Lebanon and many other locations have seen the extension and further refinement of the liberal internationalist model.

© 2009 The Author. Journal compilation © 2009 Political Studies Association
BJPIR, 2009, 11(4)

The regularity with which some elements of the international community have participated in peace support operations means that many such operations have adopted an increasingly formulaic character (Mac Ginty 2006, 5–16). Thus, a 'typical' internationally supported peace intervention will involve a security and stabilisation programme, democratisation and civil society capacity building, institutional reform to promote good governance and the marketisation and formalisation of the economy so that it is harmonious with international trading regimes. While the primary agents of the liberal internationalism are leading states, leading international organisations and the international financial institutions, they can only promote this version of peace through the co-option of INGOs, NGOs and national elites in war-affected societies. These transmission agents play an important role not only in transfer of resources but also in the diffusion of culture and values. The immense resources associated with liberal internationalism (finances, political power, international legitimacy, etc.), and its ability to squeeze the space available for alternative forms of peacemaking, mean that many actors in war-torn societies regard the liberal peace, or elements of it, as an attractive prospect.

Although many elements of the liberal peace are formulaic in their application, it is important to note that there are varieties of this form of peacemaking. Oliver Richmond (2005, 217–218) has identified hyper-conservative, conservative, orthodox and emancipatory models of the liberal peace, with the intensity of application depending—among other factors—on the strategic importance accorded to the post-civil war society by leading states. Moreover, there have been changes in the nature of liberal internationalism over time, with the early 1990s seeing the growing complexity and ambition of liberal peace projects, the mid-to-late 1990s witnessing a softening and broadening of the liberal peace through the human security agenda and the post-9/11 period seeing a renewed emphasis on security and stabilisation (Duffield 2007). The post-cold war period also saw the proponents of liberal internationalism take on board two lessons that had consequences for the character of their interventions and conflict resolution activities. The first was a growing realisation of the complexity of armed conflict, its causes and management which resulted in more complex international interventions that attempted to address economic, social and cultural issues as well as political and security ones (International Development Committee 2006). The second was a growing recognition of the regional and international implications of civil wars and the necessity to contain conflict overspill such as refugee flows to the developed world (Blair 1999). It is also important not to characterise citizens and groups as mere passive recipients of liberal internationalism. It is becoming clear that communities in post-civil war societies have been adept at bending, subverting and even resisting the ministrations of leading elements of the international community (Franks and Richmond 2006).

There is a burgeoning literature on the failings of liberal internationalism. Edward Said (2002), Roland Paris (2001), Oliver Richmond (2005) and David Chandler (1999 and 2004, 59–81), among others, have illustrated how the liberal peace has often resulted in a poor-quality peace in which a peace agreement between political elites masks continuing insecurity, chronic inter-group mistrust and the failure of any peace dividend to be shared evenly. Thus the peace in Bosnia, Timor Leste or El Salvador may be popular in western diplomatic capitals, but it may fail to deliver appreciable quality-of-life benefits beyond an end to direct violence. Critics have also noted that while the liberal peace can have success with regard to specified technocratic tasks such as rebuilding housing units or repatriating displaced persons, it is less well suited to dealing with the affective dimension of conflict societies in which perceptions of security, inter-group equity and grievances can spark a resumption of violence (Mac Ginty 2006, 180–189). International relations scholars have also condemned the liberal peace for its 'top-down grand designs' which reinforce existing international power structures that privilege the interventionist rights of western states (Pugh 2006, 1).

The essential aim of this article is to examine the extent to which elements of liberal internationalism found in British foreign policy from the mid-1990s onwards can be found in British government handling of the Northern Ireland peace process. A five-part analytical framework is used to demonstrate firstly that Britain is a leading proponent of the liberal peace, and secondly to assess the extent to which the liberal peace so actively promoted abroad is applied 'at home'. The analytical framework comprises five essential criteria of liberal internationalism: security and stability, reinforcing statehood, democratic governance, sustainability of a peace settlement and the promotion of free markets. The elements of this framework are overlapping and mutually facilitating. The next section will explain that British governments developed and maintained the institutional apparatus and policy stances to promote the liberal peace.

Britain as a Leading Proponent of Liberal Internationalism

Any analysis of contemporary British foreign policy requires a word of caution. As Paul Williams (2004, 910) notes, it is perhaps more accurate to refer to British 'foreign policies' whereby 'the government simultaneously pursues multiple foreign policies involving different combinations of institutions, actors and external pressures depending on the issue in question'. These foreign policies are based on at times contradictory and at times complementary commitments to multilateralism, Atlanticism and neo-liberalism. Despite the cross-currents, it is possible to make the case that the various policy strains are compatible with the liberal internationalist rubric. It is important to note that while Britain has retained significant foreign policy autonomy, much of its foreign policy activity is conducted bilaterally (primarily in concert with the United States in the cases of Kosovo, Afghanistan and Iraq) or mediated through the complex multilateralism of the UN, EU, NATO or the international financial institutions. As a result, it is not always possible to identify a policy stance as peculiarly British. While much of British policy in relation to peace and conflict interventions is indistinguishable from that of other democracies, Britain can be identified as a leader of liberal internationalism and not just a follower or fellow traveller in a multilateral convoy.

Tony Blair's (1999) 'Doctrine of the international community' speech can be regarded as the benchmark statement of contemporary liberal internationalism. It called for 'new rules for international co-operation and new ways of organising our international institutions' and made clear that the new rules and reformed institutions must prioritise liberal values (Blair 1999). The speech placed emphasis on open markets, democratisation, the need for a re-examination of the principle of non-interference and the importance of an internationally engaged United States. By the end of Blair's tenure, liberal internationalist themes were firmly embedded in foreign policy rhetoric and strategy, and were enthusiastically endorsed by Gordon Brown's administration (Brown 2007). The strategic priorities set out in the 2006 foreign policy White Paper, *Active Diplomacy for a Changing World* were replete with the language of the liberal peace (Foreign and Commonwealth Office 2006, 26). Priorities included: 'Preventing and resolving conflict through a strong international system'; 'Building an effective and globally competitive EU in a secure neighbourhood'; 'Supporting the UK economy and business through an open and expanding global economy'; and 'Promoting sustainable development and poverty reduction underpinned by human rights, democracy [and] good governance': all tenets of liberal internationalism. The normative ambitions of the foreign policy strategy were made clear by the preface to the White Paper from then foreign secretary Jack Straw:

> At the heart of any foreign policy must lie a set of fundamental values. For this Government, the values that we promote abroad are those that guide our actions at home. We seek a world in which freedom, justice and opportunity thrive, in which governments are accountable to the people, protect their rights and guarantee their security and basic needs. We do so because these are the values we believe to be right (Foreign and Commonwealth Office 2006, 4).

The statement reveals both a certainty in the superiority of liberal values and a commitment to promote them overseas.

This was not a state hunkered down, attempting to achieve anonymity and damage limitation in a context dominated by predatory global forces. Instead, it was a state with an enhanced sense of global responsibility, and willing to adopt foreign policy activism on certain issues. Institutional structures were set in place to help facilitate this post-realist foreign policy. The Department for International Development (DFID) was created in 1997 as a separate entity from the Foreign and Commonwealth Office (FCO), and was instrumental in promoting the view that issues such as poverty reduction, conflict resolution and HIV/AIDS were legitimate foreign policy concerns. Traditional concerns (such as the importance of open markets) remained, with the result that a more complex and holistic (if not always coherent) foreign policy emerged (Wheeler and Dunne 1998, 851).

Significant tangible state resources were invested in foreign policy-making. In 2006, the Foreign and Commonwealth Office had a staff of 16,000 and maintained 200 offices. Its budget had increased in real terms from £1.5 billion in 2001–02 to almost £1.9 billion in 2006–07 (HM Treasury 2007, 15). The Department for International Development had 2,500 staff and 66 offices, with a real-terms budget increase from £3.1 billion in 2001–02 to just under £4.2 billion in 2006–07 (Treasury 2007, 15). In addition, the British Council maintained a staff of 7,500 and 234 offices. The prosecution of liberal internationalism was joined by the Ministry of Defence and the Department for Trade and Investment. The location of the interdepartmental

'Post-Conflict Reconstruction Unit' (later renamed the 'Stabilisation Unit') in Number 10 itself illustrated the prime ministerial importance devoted to foreign policy issues.

The institutions, resources and rhetoric described above enabled an activist liberal internationalist foreign policy. The first essential criterion of liberal internationalism (security and stability) can be illustrated by the hard-power interventions in Iraq and Afghanistan. Commitments to the second and third criteria, reinforcing state-hood and democratic governance, are evidenced by the enormous investments of energy in 'stabilisation', state-building and governance programming in Afghani-stan, Iraq, Nepal, Sierra Leone and elsewhere. The extent and implications of governance programming award external powers the potential to shape a series of relationships in the target state: between citizens, between the citizen and the state and between the citizen and the market. Through their bilateral relations, DFID and the FCO have invested massive energy in civil society and public sector capacity building, anti-corruption drives, women's inclusion programmes and technical assistance in support of Poverty Reduction Strategy Papers. In some cases, a plu-ralist agenda was promoted through illiberal means. New constitutions and political dispensations in Afghanistan, Iraq, Bosnia-Herzegovina and Nepal—all of which received active support from the United Kingdom—were prescriptively liberal. In many cases, host societies were expected (even compelled) to adopt fundamental changes; for example electoral processes based on universal suffrage, and the extension of human rights legislation.

In terms of the fourth criterion of liberal internationalism, the sustainability of peace settlements, British foreign policy shows an understanding of the long-term nature of peacemaking. There have been repeated references in foreign policy statements to 'lasting peace', 'lasting settlements' and to peace processes. There was also a recognition that inhabitants in post-war societies—with support from the international community—must take responsibility for peace (Blair 2002). Despite domestic political pressure, Britain did not 'cut and run' from commitments in Afghanistan and Iraq. Indeed, in a message to Afghans in the wake of 9/11, Foreign Secretary Jack Straw said: 'In the past we have let you down. We will not turn our backs on you again' (Straw, cited in Hain 2001). Long-standing partnership agree-ments with a number of societies emerging from civil war, as well as conflict prevention and early warning activities in societies that have had civil wars, reflected an internalisation of the need to make peace a sustained endeavour.

The fifth criterion, the promotion of free markets, is evidenced by the commitment to the private sector and international trading regimes. Blair's (1999) Chicago speech championed the free market as the route to prosperity and poverty reduc-tion (though it is worth noting from the hindsight of the global credit crisis that he also called for tougher international regulation of financial markets). British foreign and development policy placed enormous emphasis on privatisation in post-civil war societies. One observer noted:

> Despite its avowed commitment to poverty reduction and realisation of the Millennium Development Goals, the UK Department for International Development (DFID) has invested heavily in ... creating a host of new bodies and financing mechanisms to advance the cause of privatization

© *2009 The Author. Journal compilation* © *2009 Political Studies Association*
BJPIR, 2009, 11(4)

across the developing world ... DFID channels large sums of the UK aid budget every year to privatization consultants such as Pricewaterhouse-Coopers, KPMG and Deloitte Touche in order to drive forward the privatization of public services in developing countries (Hilary 2005, 134).

The FCO Country Strategy Papers on virtually all societies emerging from violent conflict stressed the importance of 'developing a viable and sustainable private sector' (FCO 2004). As further evidence of the UK's vanguard role in the promotion of a privatisation agenda as part of a wider development strategy, over half the total funding for the World Bank's Public Private Infrastructure Facility, which promoted the privatisation of infrastructure projects in developing states, came from the UK (IRC 2007).

It would be wrong to caricature British foreign policy as some sort of unthinking liberal internationalist behemoth. Instead, it was a much more nuanced foreign policy, with strong elements of Keynesianism in its development assistance and an interest in poverty reduction and human rights. Moreover, the liberal peace was not promoted uniformly across all locations. Nor was it uniformly accepted. Host states and communities were adept at resisting, subverting and modifying liberal internationalism to the extent that western liberal goals were often imposed in a hybridised fashion (Mac Ginty 2008, 139–163). Despite these caveats, it is important to note that the United Kingdom has done more than just maintain a rhetoric of liberal internationalism; instead, it actively shaped and promoted it.

Liberal Internationalism as Applied to Northern Ireland

The task now is to reflect on the extent to which the liberal internationalism expounded in British foreign policy can be found in British government stewardship of the Northern Ireland peace process. This section is organised according to the five criteria of liberal internationalist interventions in war-torn societies: security and stability, reinforcing statehood, democratic governance, sustainability of a peace settlement and the promotion of free markets.

Security and Stabilisation

The first criterion, security and stability, has been met in Northern Ireland via a long-term project combining hard security measures with incentives for militants to investigate political routes. Northern Ireland no longer threatens the security of the United Kingdom (nor for that matter the Republic of Ireland). If one of the strategic aims of the British government towards Northern Ireland was the taming of the militant groups, then that strategy has been a resounding success (McIntyre 1995, 97–122). Although convoluted and highly politicised, significant advances were made in the Security Sector Reform and disarmament agendas. August 2007 marked the conclusion of 'Operation Banner' or the British Army's support to the civil power. This followed a programme of military base closures, the downsizing of troop deployments and police reform. After many false starts, the Irish Republican Army declared an end to its 'war' and disarmed. The Independent Monitoring Commission has subsequently satisfied itself that most paramilitary activity is at an end. Its Eighteenth Report, in May 2008, reaffirmed that the IRA's 'leadership remained firmly committed to the political path'. Reflecting the sea change in Northern Ireland's politics, the Report notes that 'the organisation continues to work with the policing institutions and encourages interaction with PSNI [Police Service of Northern Ireland]' (IMC 2008, 9). The main loyalist groups remain on long-term ceasefire and spoiler activity is largely contained. While there have been many setbacks and controversies associated with security and stabilisation (for example, political wrangling over the devolution of policing powers, or the ambitions of MI5 following the building of their new headquarters outside Belfast), the general trend has been towards the pacification of Northern Ireland and this element of the liberal peace can be deemed to have been achieved.

Reinforcing Statehood

British government strategy has also had significant success in maintaining a functioning state during the Troubles and peace process. A mixture of direct rule, oversight from Westminster and containment of the security situation has allowed the maintenance of a functioning bureaucracy replete with multi-level governance, extensive social provision and state revenue collection. This is not to underestimate the very real difficulties faced in the past by the Northern Ireland state: its very existence was contested, it was capable of being deeply partisan, its activities were often interrupted, but, by and large, the state was able to function. One South African acquaintance characterised Northern Ireland's apparent normalcy thus: 'Northern Ireland is the only civil war context in which the rubbish is collected each Tuesday'. The safety net of direct rule from Westminster meant that complete state collapse, and thus the necessity to rebuild the state, was never an option. As a result, Northern Ireland has been spared many of the state-building activities that comprise liberal internationalist interventions.

The maintenance of the state (albeit a state that underwent extensive reform) had important cultural implications. One of the key aspects of liberal internationalism in post-civil war contexts is the cultural baggage it brings with it (Fanthorpe 2005, 27–49). Often these cultural implications are subtle (for example, the necessity to use the English language to fill out a grant application or the formalisation of transactions previously based on informality), but they can have a significant impact in changing the organisation of society and power relations within it. The maintenance of a functioning state during the Troubles and peace process meant that British social policy, administrative norms, business practices and cultural patterns were operable in Northern Ireland (Porter 1996). This was important in allowing Northern Ireland's citizens to feel part of the wider United Kingdom (if they wished), but also meant that many aspects of liberal internationalism (for example, those associated with 'good' governance) were not regarded as alien impositions that ran contrary to indigenous or traditional norms.

Democratic Governance

The third criterion of liberal internationalism, democratic governance, was only partially met during the 1997–2007 period. On some issues, Northern Ireland is a poster child for the good governance agenda. Northern Ireland has regular elections, a multi-party (if stubbornly bi-ethnic) political system, a free media, a burgeoning civil society and extensive human rights and equality legislation. While many of these good governance elements were introduced in a tardy and begrudging fashion, or were introduced in the face of opposition from one bloc or the other, the sum total of these elements is a polity with significant built-in pluralism. At the macro-political level, Northern Ireland has achieved—with much stumbling along the way—a complex power-sharing arrangement designed to prevent majoritarian rule. The devolved institutions constitute probably the world's most sophisticated example of consociational engineering (O'Leary 1999, 1–22). In this respect Northern Ireland has achieved one of the central aims of many internationally supported peace interventions in deeply divided societies: a political system in which centripetal institutions are structured to outweigh or balance natural centrifugal forces. Yet, significant aspects of the Northern Ireland polity fall short of the liberal peace ideal. Many of these aspects have been facilitated or at least tolerated by British governments, and point to a possible divergence between the promotion and implementation of liberal peace values at home and abroad.

Four examples of Northern Ireland's democratic governance deficit during the peace process and after the 1998 Agreement will illustrate the wider point. Firstly, and typically of many experiences of liberal internationalism in overseas contexts, the emphasis on technocratic and institutional 'solutions' to the conflict and its manifestations risks overlooking the affective dimension of the conflict in terms of grievances and inter-group perceptions (Watson 2008, 35–42). While Northern Ireland is equipped with a complex array of institutions and bodies to ensure the integrity of its democratic governance, the extent to which these bodies can help moderate attitudes and behaviour is unclear. The primary purpose of bodies such as the Parades Commission is to adjudicate between opposing groups rather than address the antagonistic attitudes that support such groups. While Northern Ireland's extremes have tempered much of their behaviour during the peace process, the democratic governance institutions have created new political spaces for inter-group contestation. On some issues, there has been a sense that the emphasis has been on mechanisms, institutions and legislation rather than engaging with the belief systems that underpin the conflict.

A second, and related point has been the shoring up of single-identity groups by the British government in order to facilitate an inclusive and durable peace accord. This was perhaps most evident in attempts to include militant loyalism in the peace process. The pragmatic logic ran along the lines of: only groups confident in themselves can reach an accord with opposing groups. The reinforcement of ethno-sectarian blocs and the legitimacy extended to exclusive positions have obvious consequences for pluralist positions that seek to build on the centre-ground. The peace process has helped maintain the position of the main unionist and nationalist political parties and has left cross-community parties floundering on single-digit percentage electoral returns. In order to reach and implement the peace accord, the British government has helped legitimise exclusive (nationalist and unionist) positions, perhaps storing up the danger of conflict recidivism for a later date (O'Leary and McGarry 2006, 249–277).

© 2009 The Author. Journal compilation © 2009 Political Studies Association
BJPIR, 2009, 11(4)

A third example of the democratic governance deficit comes in the form of a lack of transparency in British government decision-making in relation to demands from particular factions. The appointment of a Victims Commissioner, the establishment of inquiries into state killings and the payment of £1 million 'transition money' to loyalist paramilitaries were all highly political decisions designed to oil the wheels of the peace process at particular moments (NIO 2005; BBC 2007; Erwin and Henderson 2007; McDonald 2007). In a deeply divided society, each of these decisions was seen as a sop to a particular group. It can be argued that the British government needed to be able to act with expediency in its role of peace process guardian, and that the good governance toolkit is of little use when attempting a delicate political choreography involving militant groups and communities with acute grievances. Yet the arbitrary nature of this decision-making transmitted wider messages on transparency and contrasted with the bureaucratic reform assistance given to other states emerging from civil war. The emphasis on administrative due process and the non-partisan disbursement of resources evident in DFID and FCO assistance overseas was, at times, absent from Northern Ireland Office ministrations closer to home. Yet, and in one of the many contradictions found in the peace process, it is clear that the British government regarded administrative due process and a non-discriminatory bureaucracy as key elements of good governance. For example, Section 75 of the 1998 Northern Ireland Act has compelled all government departments to ensure equality of opportunity. The annual progress reports on the implementation of Section 75 stress how diversity is to be mainstreamed, that working environments are to be plural, and constant training on 'good relations' available to state employees (NIO 2006). Section 75 should be seen as just one of a suite of measures (for example, the establishment of the Equality and Human Rights Commissions) designed to curb discriminatory practices in the public and private sectors.

A final example of the democratic governance deficit comes in the form of Northern Ireland's political over-representation in comparison with other devolved regions of the United Kingdom. In 2007 Wales had a ratio of 34,658 eligible electors per Assembly member while Scotland had 23,172 electors per member of the Scottish Parliament. In Northern Ireland the ratio was 10,258 electors per Assembly member. The reason for Northern Ireland being 'blessed' with so many representatives is again linked to political expediency during the peace process when efficient government was sacrificed for the inclusion of potential veto holders in the peace process. An enlarged Assembly was essentially a political bribe offering the possibility of seats in the Assembly in return for compliance during the peace process.

A quick review of post-peace accord liberal internationalist interventions in overseas contexts reveals cases of intolerance for some of the political practices seemingly tolerated in Northern Ireland. One of the most vivid examples of overseas liberal engineering was what some dubbed the 'European Raj' run by the EU in Bosnia-Herzegovina (Knaus and Martin 2003, 60). Nationalist politicians were regularly disbarred from office by the Office of the High Representative (a very different scenario from post-Belfast Agreement Northern Ireland). The British government has made it very clear (for example via Afghanistan's National Solidarity Programme which it has supported to the tune of $75 million) that it equates democratic governance with administrative due process and the non-sectarian distribution of public resources (Miliband 2008). Northern Ireland, however, was far from being the poster child for democratic governance.

Sustainability

The fourth criterion of liberal internationalist interventions in post-war societies is sustainability. The ultimate aim of international peace support interventions is to create a self-sustaining polity which facilitates the withdrawal of international support (Caspersen 2004, 570). International interventions are often time-limited, and leading states in the international community have a well-rehearsed public rhetoric of the dangers of open-ended nation-building commitments. The Northern Ireland peace process has certainly been sustained (despite many setbacks), a power-sharing Assembly is in place and there is little anticipation of a return to large-scale violence. Yet the peace process and 1998 peace accord were not *self*-sustaining. Both required substantial intervention from the British and Irish governments and others. Prime ministerial attention to Northern Ireland has been enormous. The devolved Assembly repeatedly collapsed as a result of chronic mistrust between the Northern Ireland parties, with each resumption of devolution requiring intensive peace summits. The default mechanism of Direct Rule from Westminster helped engender a political culture of learned helplessness or a non-hurting stalemate whereby the Northern Ireland state functioned as normal despite the inability of local parties to reach an accord. In short, Tony Blair's willingness to 'go the extra mile' on Northern Ireland encouraged the Northern Ireland parties to adopt high-maintenance stances and thus helped undercut the notion that the local political parties could reach an accommodation unaided. This pattern continued post-Blair. On Peter Robinson's first full day as first minister (June 2008), along with the deputy first minister he traipsed to Downing Street in the hope that prime ministerial intervention could smooth difficulties concerning policing and the Irish Language Act.

Open Markets

The fifth criterion of liberal internationalism is a commitment to open markets. Advocates of the liberal peace are certain of the mutually reinforcing nature of free trade and peace. A strong argument can be made that Northern Ireland fell short of the free market as envisioned by champions of the liberal peace. This deviation is all the more startling given the strictness with which neo-liberal economic mores are implemented (indeed imposed) in other societies emerging from civil war. International peace and reconstruction support is often predicated on World Bank and IMF conditionality, austerity programmes, agreement to settle past external debts, the formalisation of the economy and conformity to international trading regimes (Mac Ginty 2006, 136–154; Pugh and Cooper 2006). While Northern Ireland, as part of the United Kingdom and the European Union, did not have to renegotiate its external economic relations, its economy fell short of the neo-liberal goals set for many economies experiencing liberal internationalist interventions.

The Northern Ireland economy can be described as semi-protected, or a hybrid economy whereby an open and prospering free economy in most sectors of private enterprise (for example, banking and the construction industry) coexists with a Keynesian public sector. In contrast to the public sector 'right-sizing' and austerity programmes that are often central to economic reforms in many internationally supported post-civil war economies, Northern Ireland has a bloated public sector. Massive subventions from the British Exchequer have insulated the Northern Ireland economy from the streamlining that has affected the public sector in other parts of the UK. Take, for example, this 2006 account of the Northern Ireland economy:

> Inward investment is sluggish and indigenous entrepreneurialism low-key; employment is now concentrated around a service sector that is an extension of mainland Britain's. The result is an economy that has more in common with the old communist regimes in eastern Europe than with the dynamism just across the border in the Republic of Ireland.

> Public spending by the British government is responsible for 63 per cent of Northern Ireland's gross domestic product, and the state directly employs about a third of all those in work, double the rates south of the border and substantially more than in the rest of the UK. The effect is economic sclerosis, with statistics that point to steady economic growth masking Northern Ireland's suckling dependency on government spending.

> Last year, Northern Ireland received £5 billion more from the British government than it contributed, a subvention that has been rising steadily each year despite a decade of 'peace', yet the province remains one of the poorest regions in the UK, with GDP per head of population almost 20 per cent below the UK average.

> Low unemployment figures of 4 per cent conceal the fact that the levels of economic inactivity are far higher than the rest of the UK, with the number of people on incapacity benefit 74 per cent higher than average (Ruddock 2006).

Treasury spending estimates for 2007–08 revealed that citizens in Northern Ireland were expected to receive over two thousand pounds per capita more than fellow citizens in England. This was despite any 'peace dividend' the Treasury may have expected in terms of a lessening security budget. In Northern Ireland, public spending per head was estimated at £9,485, with Scottish citizens receiving £8,894, Welsh citizens £8,311 and English citizens £7,302 (HM Treasury 2008, 116).

While much of the development assistance offered to post-civil war societies is in the form of loans, Northern Ireland's assistance has been in the form of grants. Nor does Northern Ireland start from the base of underdevelopment afflicting many post-civil war societies. Northern Ireland was also able to benefit from the European Union's multi-billion pound Peace I and Peace II Programmes.

Concluding Discussion

Inverting the liberal internationalist lens, or applying it to part of the United Kingdom rather than to overseas sites of conflict, has been a revealing exercise. The

© 2009 The Author. Journal compilation © 2009 Political Studies Association
BJPIR, 2009, 11(4)

British government has been unwilling or unable to introduce key elements of the liberal internationalist creed in Northern Ireland. There are deficiencies in democratic governance, the economy is less than open and the peace process has required constant ministration from its guardians (the British and Irish governments). Yet some of the less-than-liberal aspects of British government conflict resolution strategy can be viewed as time-limited expediencies necessary in making peace. Peace pragmatists might argue that the wider goal of securing the peace process and peace accord justified the constructive ambiguities and deviations from accountability that characterised some British government actions. Slippage from the liberal peace ideal may be portrayed as short-term slippage that was necessary to bear long-term fruit.

Three points are worth making by way of a conclusion. The first point is methodological. The liberal internationalist lens, and particularly the identification of criteria of liberal internationalism with respect to peace processes and post-peace accord reconstruction, has allowed the construction of a useful analytical framework with which to scrutinise critically British conflict resolution strategy in Northern Ireland. Moreover, this approach has used the very criteria that the champions of liberal internationalism use themselves in their overseas peacemaking and reconstruction activities.

The second point is a reminder that liberal internationalism is not applied uniformly in all locations. Despite its formulaic elements, especially in the implementation of post-peace accord peace-building programmes, liberal internationalism is contested, adapted and executed in different ways in different locations. Internationally, there is a variable geometry of the liberal peace, with different elements implemented with different degrees of enthusiasm, encouragement and compulsion in different contexts. It would be erroneous to contrast Northern Ireland's 'liberal peace-lite' with a picture of the zealous implementation of the liberal peace by the British government and its partners elsewhere. Instead, we see shades of grey and hybridity. It is remarkable, however, to see the derogation from the liberal peace model on the doorstep of one of the champions of the liberal peace.

A third concluding point is that Northern Ireland—in comparison with many other post-peace accord societies—represents a favourable implementation environment. It lacks the hostile neighbours, lootable natural resources and the multiplicity of armed groups that contribute to the vastly more complex peace implementation environments in other locations (Stedman 2001; Ball, 2001, 19–36). Yet, despite this comparatively favourable implementation environment, Northern Ireland falls short on a number of the essential criteria of the liberal peace. This suggests that the implementation of the liberal peace—especially an emancipatory version of it—is an extremely ambitious target in many societies emerging from civil war (Richmond 2005, 217). It requires time, resources and sustained political will. The incomplete introduction of the liberal peace in the 'near abroad' of Northern Ireland reveals the difficulty of the task facing liberal internationalists in more hostile and less proximate environments. The implications of such a realisation may be a redoubling of efforts to promote liberal internationalism, or a hard-headed realisation of the limits of liberal internationalism and the need to be more selective in the targeting, type and ambitions of liberal interventions.

Given the compromised version of the liberal peace in operation in Northern Ireland, it is worth considering whether the British government chose to diverge from the liberal peace model, or if it was forced to do so by circumstances. One way of approaching the question is through an 'ends justify the means' lens. The Northern Ireland peace process, for all its flaws, has delivered significant quality-of-life benefits, addressed grievances and provided a mechanism for the sharing of power. It has also largely removed a major irritant from the British political agenda. As a result, many observers and participants are likely to conclude that the result (the ending of 'the Troubles') justified either a deliberate or enforced deviation from the liberal peace model. Moreover, the complexity of the peace process (a long drawn-out process involving multiple actors and multiple issues) means that it is impossible to reach a definitive answer to the question. The British government shared responsibility for the management of the peace process with the Irish government, so many decisions were intergovernmental, and thus the British government cannot be regarded as a discrete unit with complete agency on all issues.

On balance though, it is possible to argue that the British government found that it *had* to compromise on core elements of the liberal peace in Northern Ireland in order to keep the peace process going. Partly this was a function of the micro-management of the process by the Prime Minister's Office and the path dependency that this encouraged among Northern Ireland's political parties. Why agree something with the Northern Ireland Office minister when you can have direct access to the prime minister and the resources he could promise? Certainly on the democratic governance and free market agendas, there were significant retractions from liberal peace ideals (less so on the security agenda). The need to intervene to keep the peace process going, and to make exceptions that would not be accepted in other parts of the UK, or in some other peace-building locations abroad, calls into question the extent to which elements of the liberal internationalist agenda had universal applicability. If liberal peace ideals were found to be impracticable at home, then their promotion abroad suggests a degree of hypocrisy.

The final concluding point is to ponder Britain's holding of highly normative and prescriptive positions in relation to the nature and organisation of societies emerging from civil war when it has a mixed record of liberal peace implementation at home. Of course all foreign policies hold contradictions, but the approach taken in this article suggests that caution is required before identifying the transferable lessons from Northern Ireland (or indeed any other peace process). This is not to say that politicians and policy-makers in civil war contexts should not look overseas for conflict resolution best practice. Instead it is to caution that modesty might be the best strategy when recommending to foreign guests the 'successes' at home. Hopefully the Blair memoirs will reflect such modesty.

About the Author

Roger Mac Ginty, School of International Relations, University of St Andrews, The Scores, St Andrews, Fife KY16 9AX, UK, email: hrm21@st-andrews.ac.uk

© 2009 The Author. Journal compilation © 2009 Political Studies Association
BJPIR, 2009, 11(4)

Note

The author is grateful to the anonymous referees for their comments on this piece.

Bibliography

Ahern, B. (2007) 'Address by the Taoiseach, Mr Bertie Ahern, to the joint Houses of Parliament, 15 May 2007'. Available online at: http://www.taoiseach.gov.ie/index.asp?IocID=5588docID=3427 (accessed 20 May 2008).

Arthur, P. (2000) *Special Relationships: Britain, Ireland and the Northern Ireland Problem* (Belfast: Blackstaff).

Ball, N. (2001) 'The challenge of rebuilding war torn societies', in C. Crocker, F. Hampson and P. Aall (eds), *Turbulent Peace* (Washington, DC: United States Institute of Peace Press), 719–736.

BBC (2007) '£1m is confirmed for UDA project', *BBC News Online*, 22 February.

Blair, T. (1999) 'Speech by Tony Blair on "The doctrine of the international community" to the Economic Club, Chicago, 24 April'. Available online at: http://www.number-10.gov.uk/output/Page 1297.asp (accessed 21 May 2008).

Blair, T. (2002) 'Sierra Leone: A message from the British prime minister', 19 February. Available online at: http://www.fco.gov.uk/en/newsroom/latest-news/?=view=new&id=2242843 (accessed 21 May 2009).

Blair, T. (2006) 'Speech to the Los Angeles World Affairs Council, 1 August 2006'. Available online at: http://www.number10.gov.uk/output/Page9948.asp (accessed 20 May 2008).

Blair, T. (2007) 'Transcript of address by Tony Blair to the Northern Ireland Assembly', 8 May. Available online at: http://www.number-10.gov.uk/output/Page11643.asp (accessed 20 May 2008).

Brown, G. (2007) 'Lord Mayor's Banquet Speech, 12 November'. Available online at: http://www.number10.gov.uk/Page13736 (accessed 2 December 2008).

Bush, G. (2007) 'US takes new steps for peace, prosperity, president says', statement from United States Embassy, London. Available online at: http://london.usembassy.gov/bush730.html (accessed 20 May 2008).

Caspersen, N. (2004) 'Good fences make good neighbours? A comparison of conflict-resolution strategies in postwar Bosnia', *Journal of Peace Research*, 41:5, 569–588.

Chandler, D. (1999) *Bosnia: Faking Democracy after Dayton* (London: Pluto).

Chandler, D. (2004) 'The responsibility to protect? Imposing the "liberal peace"', *International Peacekeeping*, 11:1, 59–81.

Duffield, M. (2007) *Development, Security and Unending War: Governing the World of Peoples* (Cambridge: Polity).

Erwin, A. and Henderson, D. (2007) 'Government accused of "cover-up" over Finucane inquiry', *Independent*, 6 August.

Fanthorpe, R. (2005) 'On the limits of the liberal peace: Chiefs and democratic decentralization in post-war Sierra Leone', *African Affairs*, 105, 27–49.

Foreign and Commonwealth Office (2004) 'History of DFID engagement in BiH'. Available online at: http://www.ukinbih.fco.gov.uk/en/working-with-bosnia/dfid-in-bih/about-dfid/past-projects (accessed 21 May 2009).

Foreign and Commonwealth Office (2006) *Active Diplomacy for a Changing World: The UK's International Priorities*, UK Government White Paper. 23 March.

Franks, J. and Richmond, O. (2006) 'A square peg for a round hole? Cambodia and the liberal peace', Centre for Peace and Conflict Studies working paper.

Fukuyama, F. (2004) 'The imperative of state-building', *Journal of Democracy*, 15:2, 17–31.

Guelke, A. (2008) 'Israeli flags flying alongside Belfast's apartheid walls: A new era of comparisons and connections', in G. Ben-Porat (ed.), *The Failure of the Middle East Peace Process* (Basingstoke: Palgrave Macmillan), 19–38.

Hain, P. (2001) 'A global approach to peace', *The Guardian*, 30 October.

Hilary, J. (2005) 'DFID, UK and public services privatization', *Global Social Policy*, 5:2, 134–136.

HM Treasury (2007) *Public Expenditure Statistical Analyses 2007* (London: The Stationery Office).

HM Treasury (2008) 'PESA 2008 public spending by country and region'. Available online at: http://www.hm-treasury.gov.uk/d/11(1).pdf (accessed 12 January 2009).

Howard, M. (1976) *War in European History* (Oxford: Oxford University Press), 5–19.

Howard, M. (2000) *The Invention of Peace: Reflections on War and International Order* (New Haven, CT: Yale University Press).

International Development Committee (2006) *Conflict and Development: Peacebuilding and Post-Conflict Reconstruction*. Sixth Report of the Session 2005–06 (vol. 1) (London: The Stationery Office).

International Monitoring Commission (2008) *Eighteenth Report of the International Monitoring Commission* (London: Stationery Office).

IRC (2007) 'Privatization: UK government should stop funding World Bank body, says World Development Movement', 27 January. Available online at: http://www.irc.ni/page/32451

Jacoby, T. (2007) 'Hegemony, modernization and post-war reconstruction', *Global Society*, 21:4, 521–538.

Knaus, G. and Martin, F. (2003) 'Lessons from Bosnia and Herzegovina: Travails of the European Raj', *Journal of Democracy*, 14:3, 60–74.

Mac Ginty, R. (2006) *No War, No Peace: The Rejuvenation of Stalled Peace Processes and Peace Accords* (Basingstoke: Palgrave).

Mac Ginty, R. (2008) 'Indigenous peace-making versus the liberal peace', *Co-operation and Conflict*, 43:2, 139–163.

Mac Ginty, R. and Richmond, O. (2007) 'Myth or reality: Opposing views on the liberal peace and post-war reconstruction', *Global Society*, 21:4, 491–497.

Mandelbaum, M. (2002) *The Ideas that Conquered the World: Peace, Democracy and Free Markets in the Twenty-First Century* (New York: Public Affairs).

McDonald, H. (2007) 'Why are we funding violent UDA?', *The Observer*, 29 July.

McIntyre, A. (1995) 'Modern Irish republicanism: The product of British state strategies', *Irish Political Studies*, 10:1, 97–122.

Miliband, D. (2008) 'Dilemmas of democracy: Pakistan and Afghanistan', Speech at the Center for Strategic and International Studies, Washington, DC, 21 May. Available online at: http://www.fco.gov.uk/en/newsroom/latest-news/?view=Speech&id=3816688 (accessed 4 December 2008).

Northern Ireland Office (NIO) (2005) 'Peter Hain announces interim commissioner for victims'. Available online at: http://www.nio.gov.uk (20 May 2008).

Northern Ireland Office (NIO) (2006) 'Equality scheme Progress Report 1 April 2005—31 March 2006'. Available online at: http://www.nio.gov.uk/nio_annual_progress_report_on_its_section_75_equality_scheme_1_april_2005_-_31_march_2006.pdf (accessed 18 December 2008).

O'Leary, B. (1999) 'The 1998 British–Irish Agreement: Consociation plus', *Scottish Affairs*, 26, 1–22.

O'Leary, B. and McGarry, J. (2006) 'Consociational theory; Northern Ireland's conflict and its agreement: 2. What critics of consociation can learn from Northern Ireland', *Government and Opposition*, 41:2, 249–277.

Paris, R. (2001) 'Wilson's ghost: The faulty assumptions of postconflict peacebuilding', in C. Crocker, F. Hampson and P. Aall (eds), *Turbulent Peace: The Challenges of Managing International Conflict* (Washington, DC: USIP Press), 765–784.

Porter, N. (1996) *Rethinking Unionism: An Alternative Vision for Northern Ireland* (Belfast: Blackstaff Press).

Pugh, M. (2006) 'Peacekeeping as constant gardening by other means', Paper for the British International Studies Association Conference, Cork, Republic of Ireland, 18–21 December.

Pugh, M. and Cooper, N. (2006) *War Economies in a Regional Context: Challenges of Transformation* (New York: International Peace Academy).

Richmond, O. (2005) *The Transformation of Peace* (Basingstoke: Palgrave).

Richmond, O. and Franks, J. (2007) 'Liberal hubris? Virtual peace in Cambodia', *Security Dialogue*, 38:1, 27–48.

Ruddock, A. (2006) 'Northern Ireland—Where is the bright new future?', *Management Today*, 23 March. Available online at: http://www.managementtoday.co.uk/article/542849/ (accessed 26 May 2008).

Said, E. (2002) *The End of the Peace Process: Oslo and After* (2nd edn) (London: Granta).

Salih, M. (2001) *African Democracies and African Politics* (London: Pluto).

Shaw, T., MacLean, S. and Black, D. (2006) 'Introduction: A decade of human security: What prospects for global governance and new multilateralisms?', in T. Shaw, S. MacLean and D. Black (eds), *A Decade of Human Security: Global Governance and New Multilateralisms* (Aldershot: Ashgate), 3–18.

Smith, M. L. R. (1999) 'The intellectual internment of a conflict: The forgotten war in Northern Ireland', *International Affairs*, 75:1, 77–97.

Sriram, C. L. (2008) *Peace as Governance: Power-Sharing, Armed Groups and Contemporary Negotiations* (Basingstoke: Palgrave).

Stedman, S. (2001) 'Implementing peace agreements in civil wars: Lessons and recommendations for policymakers', IPA Policy Paper on Peace Implementation (New York: International Peace Academy), May.

Watson, A. (2008) 'Can there be a "kindered" peace?', *Ethics and International Affairs*, 21:1, 35–42.

Wheeler, N. J. and Dunne, T. (1998) 'Good international citizenship: A third way for British foreign policy', *International Affairs*, 74:4, 847–870.

Williams, P. (2004) 'Who's making UK foreign policy?' *International Affairs*, 80:5, 909–929.

Wintour, P. and Black, I. (2007) 'From No. 10 to the Middle East: Blair gets a new job', *The Guardian*, 26 June.

Woodward, S. L. (2002) 'Economic priorities for successful peace implementation', in S. Stedman, D. Rothchild and E. Cousens (eds), *Ending Civil Wars: The Implementation of Peace Agreements* (Boulder, CO: Lynne Rienner), 183–214.

Woolmark, M. and Pritchett, L. (2002) *Solutions When the Solution is the Problem: Arraying the Disarray in Development* (Washington, DC: Center for Global Development).

Political Studies Association Specialist Groups

The Political Studies Association supports a diverse range of Specialist Groups covering all major fields of political research. The groups act as networks through which individuals can make contact with colleagues with similar research and teaching interests. Groups disseminate information of interest to their members via newsletters and dedicated websites and hold seminars and conferences to supplement the Annual PSA Conference. They receive financial support for their activities from the Political Studies Association.

To find out more about the Specialist Groups online visit: **www.psa.ac.uk/spgrp**

American Politics

Anarchist Studies

Art and Politics

British and Comparative Territorial Politics

British Idealism

British Liberal Political Studies

Britishness

Caribbean Politics

Citizenship and Democracy

Communist and Post Communist Politics

Comparative European Politics

Conservatives and Conservatism

Development Politics

Disability and Politics

Elections, Public Opinions and Parties

Ethnopolitics

French Politics and Policy

German Politics

Global Justice and Human Rights

Greek Politics

Interpretive Political Science

Irish Politics

Italian Politics

Labour Movements

Local Politics

Marxism

Media and Politics

Pacific Asia

Parliaments and Legislatures

Participatory and Deliberative Democracy

Political Activism

Political Economy

Political Leadership

Political Marketing

Political Thought

Politics of Health

Politics of Property

Politics of South Asia

Public Administration

Scandinavian Politics

Security and Intelligence

Sport and Politics

State Theory

Teaching and Learning

Urban Politics

Women and Politics

www.psa.ac.uk/spgrp

Political Studies Association

Political Studies Association

1950 – 2010

60 years of political studies

60th Annual International Conference

SIXTY YEARS OF POLITICAL STUDIES:
ACHIEVEMENTS AND FUTURES

29 March – 1 April 2010
The George Hotel, George Street, Edinburgh, UK

About the Conference

The Political Studies Association is one of the world's longest established political studies associations. Its 60th anniversary in 2010 is an opportunity to reflect on the achievements of political studies over the last 60 years, in the UK and internationally, on the issues and ideas that are now at the cutting edge of political analysis, and on the new directions we need to pursue in the future.

The 2010 Political Studies Association Annual Conference will be a unique opportunity for debate about the state of the discipline. Already the largest UK gathering of researchers in politics and international relations, in 2010 it will:

• as ever showcase research from across all aspects of political analysis
• build deeper links with politics scholars in other associations, like BISA, UACES and the Britain and Ireland Association for Political Thought
• develop stronger links with political scientists internationally, working with associations like ECPR, APSA and IPSA
• explore the opportunities and problems of engaging politics scholarship with political practice
• debate how we best teach politics in universities and schools

CONTACTS

Academic Convenor
Professor Charlie Jeffery
Email: convenor@psa.ac.uk

Conference Organisers
Sue Forster
Email: sue.forster@ncl.ac.uk

Dr Lisa Harrison
Email: lisa.harrison@uwe.ac.uk

Webmaster
Professor Richard Topf
Email: papers2010@psa.ac.uk

FURTHER INFORMATION

For more information visit
the conference website at
www.psa.ac.uk/2010

www.psa.ac.uk/2010